W9-BUE-036

Praise for *Igniting the Fire*

"Is another book about Billy Graham really needed? Yes, because the author, Jake Hanson, has unearthed valuable yet largely unknown facts about the early life of this man, who was indisputably the most influential evangelist of the twentieth century. He was given access to much information which does not appear in many of the writings about Graham.

The author emphasizes three great facts about Graham's early years: first, the small inner core of men who deeply influenced him by their life and personal friendship; second, the work of God through the Holy Spirit in Billy's life during the formative years; third, his development as a great evangelist.

Although I have known Billy personally for well over fifty years, I found exciting and new perspectives here. I heartily recommend this book as a valuable addition to all that has been written about Billy Graham."

—David M. Howard, Sr., International Director,
World Evangelical Alliance (1982-1992)

"Billy Graham rose from the humblest of beginnings to become during the second half of the twentieth century one of the world's most recognized and respected figures. His evangelistic messages reached a larger audience than any in history. How could it happen? Jake Hanson's *Igniting the Fire* offers an intimate look at the unlikely origins of this extraordinary man, and the still more extraordinary ministry God granted him."

—Dr. Duane Litfin, President Emeritus Wheaton College

"[In *Igniting the Fire* readers will see how God built] His man through the landscape of details, interweaving circumstances, heart wrenching decisions, and human drama. The extra bonus for all who will travel with author Jake Hanson is recognizing the principles of God's care and guidance for Billy. They soon discover that these principles are available to them! This is a must read for all who are walking the Christian life."

—Dr. Mark O'Farrell, President, Trinity College of Florida
(formerly The Florida Bible Institute)

"Reading biographies of persons who have maximized their lives for Christ always inspire me. Given that reality, Jake Hanson has done us all a favor by giving us glimpses not only into Dr. Graham's college years but into the early influences that empowered Dr. Graham's future ministry. This unique perspective on Billy's ministry should make us all aware of the potential of our impact on others and the debt we owe to those who have formatively empowered our journey. *Igniting the Fire* is particularly motivational to me as a college president. This book will stand tall among the many others that have sought to find the key as to why the Graham story is so amazing. I give it five stars!"

—Joseph M. Stowell, President, Cornerstone University, Grand Rapids, Michigan

Igniting *the* Fire

The Movements and Mentors That Shaped Billy Graham

JAKE HANSON

SHILOH RUN PRESS

An Imprint of Barbour Publishing, Inc.

© 2015 by Jake Hanson

Print ISBN 978-1-63058-448-1

eBook Editions:
Adobe Digital Edition (.epub) 978-1-63409-150-3
Kindle and MobiPocket Edition (.prc) 978-1-63409-151-0

The author is represented by Gary D. Foster, Gary D. Foster Consulting, Van Wert, Ohio; www.garydfoster.com

Published by Shiloh Run Press, an imprint of Barbour Publishing, Inc., P.O. Box 719, Uhrichsville, Ohio 44683, www.shilohrunpress.com

Our mission is to publish and distribute inspirational products offering exceptional value and biblical encouragement to the masses.

Member of the Evangelical Christian Publishers Association

DEDICATION

To
Charissa Joy Hanson
and
Lyle Wesley Dorsett
for your unwavering support from beginning to end.

Matthew 9:38

CONTENTS

PREFACE

When I stepped onto the Wheaton College campus nearly sixty years after Billy Graham had begun his studies there, I was consumed with questions: Where had Billy lived? What had he done? Who were his mentors and teachers? Was he unusual? Perhaps most important of all: How had Billy Graham become *Billy Graham*, the most successful evangelist of the twenty-first century?

This book is my answer to those questions.

I began by reading every available biography of Billy Graham, and spent countless hours in the Billy Graham Center Archives at Wheaton College. I quickly realized that my research had to expand beyond Wheaton to include Bob Jones College and the Florida Bible Institute, where Billy had also studied. So I multiplied my research to other towns, archives, and libraries.

But the most fruitful experience of all was interviewing and corresponding with many people who knew or observed Billy in those early days. They shared treasures with me—artifacts and nuggets of information. And several became friends of mine in the process.

Naturally, after more than sixty years, memories had faded or been distorted, but some memories were so clear in detail, because of the profound impact of the events, that astonishing vignettes could often be confirmed by a seemingly obscure detail from another source.

I have been moved by the life of Billy Graham in the early days of his training and ministry, and I'm sure you will be, too. But more than that, I am stirred by how God orchestrated these events, using so many committed people in ways that would profoundly influence our nation—and indeed the world—for Christ. This is more than just a story about the man Billy Graham. This is a story about God's work in the life of one of His servants.

Soli Deo gloria!

INTRODUCTION

IGNITING THE FIRE

How great a forest is set aflame by such a small fire!
JAMES 3:5

On November 20, 1949, anticipation filled the air as throngs of people descended on the final meeting of Billy Graham's Los Angeles Campaign at the corner of Washington and Hill Streets, where a "canvas cathedral" had stood for the past eight weeks—five weeks longer than initially planned. The Canvas Cathedral was a tent originally built to hold six thousand, but it had been extended to accommodate the growing crowds and was now filled to its new, ten-thousand-person capacity, with standing room only and thousands still being turned away. It was a sight unseen since the peak of the Billy Sunday revival meetings four decades earlier.

Boosted by the conversion of famous Hollywood stars and infamous felons at the Los Angeles Campaign—and also by the efforts of newspaper mogul William Randolph Hearst, who had seized on a good story for his nationwide newspaper network—the evangelistic ministry of Billy Graham was becoming a blazing fire that eventually would reach the ends of the earth.

But if you had met the young Billy Graham fifteen years earlier, you would not have found any indication of this blazing fire—or even sparks of hope—but only a high-strung, spiritually indifferent, fifteen-year-old son of a dairy farmer from the as yet inconsequential city of Charlotte, North Carolina.

So what happened during those fifteen intervening years in Billy

Graham's life that would have such an impact on the kingdom of God?

The key to answering this question hinges on what occurred between 1934 and 1943, nine years that laid the foundation for Billy Graham's ministry. As the following pages will show, God was orchestrating His vision to reach the lost through the life and ministry of this young evangelist in three key ways: through an evangelistic environment, through mentors and friends, and through Billy's own growing passions and commitment to the Gospel.

During those formative years, Billy was immersed in an environment of evangelistic vision and fervor that simply does not exist today. It was an environment with flaws, to be sure, but one in which burdens and prayers for the lost were real, evangelistic meetings of all sizes were held regularly, and the evangelistic office was both encouraged and taught.

Billy's life was also invested in by college leaders, teachers, and preachers. Perhaps his unusual charisma brought him more than his fair share of attention from these mentors, but the torch of the Gospel they held as they walked beside him, prayed with him, and counseled him would be a key factor in setting his ministry ablaze.

Finally, Billy was not content to live by the light of the mentors, leaders, and preachers with whom he rubbed elbows. He was determined to see his own flame ignited by the very Source of all holy fire, the Lord Jesus Christ. Billy's earnest pursuit of this fire, after his conversion and surrender, was an undeniable force that thrust him into an effective evangelistic ministry. We'll see this clearly as the story unfolds.

God brought all these factors together—the evangelistic environment, the mentors, and Billy's own energetic pursuit and earnestness—to enact His sovereign plan to reach the world for His glory.

What follows is the story of how Billy Graham's heart was kindled into a flaming passion for reaching the lost with the Gospel of Jesus Christ.

PART 1

KINDLING THE FIRE:

HAM-RAMSEY AND BOB JONES
(1934–1936)

CHAPTER 1

KINDLING PRAYER

*"Lord, we pray that You would raise up somebody
to preach the Gospel around the world!"*
VERNON PATTERSON

As the Lord looked over the dairy farm of William Frank Graham Sr., just five miles from the heart of Charlotte, North Carolina, in May 1934, he saw two contrasting sights. On one side of the farm, a group of men and women had gathered to pray for the rapidly decaying spiritual condition of the city of Charlotte. On the other side, fifteen-year-old Billy Frank Graham was returning from Sharon High School to begin working on his father's farm.

Hearing singing from the gathering across the way, hired hand and friend Albert McMakin asked Billy, "Who are those people on the farm today?"

"I guess they're some fanatics that have talked Daddy into using the place."[1]

＋

The prayer meeting on the Graham farm in the spring of 1934 was the culmination of a series of daylong gatherings between 1932 and

1934. Here, at the lowest point of the Great Depression, with banks across the country failing and leaving millions of Americans without their savings, these laymen came together to pray because they believed the spiritual condition of Charlotte was even more bankrupt than the failed banks.

The roots of these prayer meetings went back a decade, to 1924, when baseball-player-turned-fiery-evangelist Billy Sunday had held meetings in Charlotte and had left behind Billy Sunday Clubs, organized by local laymen who were stirred by Sunday's preaching.

As the memory of the Billy Sunday meetings began to fade, the names of the clubs morphed—first becoming Christian Men's Clubs, and then Christian Business Men's Clubs (CBMC), a movement of laymen that swept across major American metropolises in the 1930s.

Not only were these men concerned for Charlotte's downward spiraling moral condition, but they also were becoming frustrated with the seeming indifference of the local ministers. This concern led to a spiritual war fought on two fronts.

First, in late 1932, the men held the first of four all-day prayer meetings. Then, as an outflow of these prayer gatherings, they decided to hold revival meetings in Charlotte, reminiscent of the Billy Sunday meetings a decade earlier.

In January 1933, the Reverend Marshall Mott of Winston-Salem offered the group a sixty-by-ninety-foot canvas tent in which to hold services, which they promptly accepted. Services were held that year by evangelist George T. Stephens and pastor Archie Dillard of Tenth Avenue Presbyterian Church. The services were beneficial but left the men with a continued hunger for a more widespread movement of the Spirit of God.

The local businessmen were most disheartened by the city's ministerial association, whose indifference tempered the vision for citywide revival. The men continued to gather annually, in 1933 and 1934, for all-day prayer meetings. The first was held on the farm of W. H. Parr, and the second on the farm of William Franklin Graham Sr.

At first, they met for the singular purpose of praying for Charlotte, but soon their prayers grew bolder as something stirred within them—something of a vision that would prove prophetic. They began to see with the eyes of the Lord—eyes that looked deeply into the heart of Charlotte and into the heart of the entire world.

On that day at the Graham dairy farm in May 1934, as many as thirty women prayed in the farmhouse while the men gathered outside in a clearing of pine trees, sometimes standing, sometimes kneeling, and sometimes sitting on blankets, all the while singing and praying. The peak of the prayer time came when Vernon Patterson, leader of the CBMC and successful local businessman, prayed the boldest prayer yet: "Lord, we pray that You would raise up somebody to preach the Gospel around the world!"

The religious atmosphere in which Billy Graham grew up was complex. The faith of his immediate family teetered between pious devotion and rigorous, if not dead, morality and tradition. By 1934, the Christian faith had not yet captured young Billy's heart.

Billy's father, William Franklin, called Frank by his friends, was awakened to his own spiritual need in the early 1930s, though he'd had some previous religious bearing and commitment in his life. In 1908, after a night of dancing had left him feeling guilty, eighteen-year-old Frank entered into an evening evangelistic meeting at Dilworth Methodist Church and stayed behind for prayer after the service ended. Though he made no decision for Christ that evening, he remained ill at ease for several days before committing himself to the Lord while riding alone on the outskirts of Charlotte.[2]

After making his decision for Christ, he returned to the Methodist church. When the preacher saw him enter, he called Frank to the front, put his arm around him, and declared to the congregation, "Here is a young man whom God has called to preach."[3]

Despite the Methodist preacher's exuberance, the spiritual embers grew cold in Frank's heart over the next two decades, even as he continued in rigorous morality and regular church attendance. By his own admission, his shifting membership over the years was an indication of a spiritual lack in his life.

Likewise, Billy's mother, Morrow Coffey Graham, retained a form of godliness by holding family altar gatherings and teaching Billy the Shorter Westminster Catechism. From her own recollection years later, these activities were devoid of the power of God.

This all began to change in 1932, when Frank was nearly killed in a farm accident that shook him out of his spiritual indifference. After being struck in the face by a piece of wood propelled by a mechanical saw, Frank was rushed to the hospital with a crushed jaw and other injuries, and his condition remained uncertain for several days. In response, Morrow called her friends to intensive prayer. What began as a dangerously uncertain prognosis turned hopeful as healing began and the surgeons were able to reconstruct Frank's face. This answer to prayer and the seriousness of the accident rekindled the faith of both Frank and Morrow, who saw evidence of God at work.[4]

While God was at work in the hearts of Frank and Morrow, Billy's faith journey needed to take its own path. Even two years after his father's accident, he had not yet taken the faith as his own—which was made evident by his response to Albert McMakin's inquiry about the prayer meeting, when Billy referred to the participants as fanatics.

During those years, Billy was a hardworking, fun-loving soul, whose heroes were athletes rather than preachers. Though his father had taken him to hear Billy Sunday in Charlotte in 1924 (at the tender age of four), the most significant impression that a preacher had had on Billy during his childhood was that his pastor reminded him of a mortician.[5] In contrast, when he shook the hand of famed baseball star Babe Ruth, Billy did not wash his hands for days.

In short, Billy was a very natural, earthy youth. He was not groomed by his parents to be an evangelist; he was chosen by God. God was superintending something far beyond the hopes and expectations of the Graham family and something especially different from what Billy had hoped for in his youth. Though Billy's young heart wasn't completely committed to the Lord at that time, the Lord had chosen him as His man, and He would pursue him in the coming years until Billy finally surrendered.[6]

The daylong prayer gatherings of the CBMC had local, national, and worldwide concerns, with the prayer that God would raise up an evangelist who would fill the void left by the waning ministry of Billy Sunday.[7]

Within a year, God began to answer their prayer, though the ultimate answer would unfold over the next half century. Early in 1934, when six members of the Christian Business Men's Club gathered together with two pastors in an office building in Charlotte, the Reverend Archie Dillard informed the group that he had heard reports of successful meetings held in Augusta, Georgia, by a fiery Oklahoman evangelist named Mordecai Ham.

Excited about the possibility of having Ham preach in Charlotte, they invited him and his song leader, Walter T. Ramsey, to come at their earliest convenience. The evangelistic duo accepted the invitation, and meetings began in the late summer. These meetings would prove to be an answer to the men's prayers, fanning the spiritual flames in Charlotte and stirring the heart of the young Billy Graham.

CHAPTER 2

FIRE ON THE SAWDUST TRAIL

"We are not fighting men, but for men."
MORDECAI HAM

Billy Graham was spiritually dead. He chafed at the religious requirements of his family and found church less than exciting. So when the revival meetings came to Charlotte in the late summer and early fall of 1934, he took little interest in the meetings. He was not alone.

Many in the city of Charlotte were not exactly eager to have Mordecai Ham hold a campaign in town. Itinerate evangelists had a reputation as surly, money-grubbing hypocrites, helped in part by the 1927 publication of Sinclair Lewis's bestselling novel *Elmer Gantry*, a satirical, but sometimes accurate, look at evangelists of the 1920s and '30s. But Mordecai Ham was notorious in other ways, leading to significant opposition to his ministry.

Mordecai Fowler Ham was a fifty-seven-year-old preacher who had held revival services for the past thirty-three years. He had served as pastor of First Baptist Church of Oklahoma City for a few years but since 1929 had called Louisville, Kentucky, home. His revival campaigns throughout the South had led to thousands of decisions for Christ. But his methods often left rifts that wouldn't heal, and towns were left divided over his legacy.

The fiery evangelist believed that a minister of the Gospel ought to be hated.[1] Some were left to wonder whether Ham was hated for the Gospel or because of the ways in which he pressed his views of sin and vice. Moreover, Ham pointed out not only sin in the city, but also particular sinners, calling on them to repent or face divine wrath.

This method stirred up a hornet's nest wherever he went, and Ham's troubles only increased when he picked a fight with an adversary who bought ink by the barrel—W. O. Saunders, editor of the Elizabeth City *Independent*.

In 1924, while holding a revival in that northeast North Carolina town, Ham singled out an easy prey for his attacks—Sears and Roebuck president Julius Rosenwald, a practicing Jew, whom Ham accused of being connected to the Chicago mob scene. Saunders knew that Rosenwald "was too big to notice" Ham, but he took it upon himself to defend Rosenwald, writing an editorial questioning Ham's spurious accusations and raising questions about Ham's anti-Semitism.[2] Ham responded to the editorial in his services, calling Saunders "a companion of the devil and an enemy of God."[3] With that, according to Saunders, "the fight was on."[4] And the fight would continue long after the Elizabeth City Campaign of 1924.

Determined to continue the battle in every city where Ham intended to hold a campaign, Saunders distributed a pamphlet called *The Book of Ham*, which was a compilation of Saunders's editorials in the *Independent*, along with his commentary about the feud with Mordecai Ham.[5]

This pamphlet, the accusations of anti-Semitism, and the resulting hysteria followed Ham to Charlotte even ten years later—though it didn't seem to bother him. He reveled in controversy. With Ham, there was a sense that all publicity was good publicity and that controversy added intrigue, interest, and—above all—crowds to his campaigns.

In 1934, the Ministerial Association of Charlotte was not exactly opposed to having evangelistic meetings, but they were less than enthusiastic about bringing Mordecai Ham to town.

Vernon Patterson, president of the CBMC, had learned from experience that it was better to invite an evangelist first and ask the ministerial association to support it later, rather than allow the association to stall the scheduling of meetings through endless debate among ministers who were more concerned with protecting their own churches.[6] Patterson successfully used this method to get the Ham meetings approved, but it caused ill will among the ministers, leading to a lack of support from some of the churches in Charlotte and outright opposition from others.

The ministerial association had two valid reasons for opposing the meetings. First, Ham was a firebrand, whose controversial methods could do more harm than good. And second, the churches had been reeling from a lack of funds due to the Great Depression. How could they justify financially supporting an outside "high pressure salesman"[7] like Ham when they were unable to pay their own debts?

The city council also got involved in the controversy, holding several meetings to discuss whether they would grant permits to allow Ham and his music leader, William J. Ramsey, to build a tabernacle structure within the city limits. In a meeting on August 16, one councilman in particular strongly opposed the meetings. He mentioned all the reasons why the ministers opposed the meetings, but also argued that the tabernacle would cause an unwanted and unneeded civil disturbance wherever it was built. One suggested location for the temporary structure was immediately shot down because it was across the street from the city manager's house.[8]

More than that, the councilmen were skeptical when organizers could not answer basic questions, such as how much space the tabernacle would take up, or how much it would cost. "It seems to me," one councilman said, "that if Mr. Ramsey has constructed so many tabernacles over the country, he could give us a definite estimate."[9]

Despite the objections, and with four hundred supporters of the measure in attendance, the council voted to allow the meetings to go forward. The construction of a five-thousand-seat tabernacle could begin, with sawdust covering the uneven ground below. After the measure passed, the large crowd began singing "Old Time Religion," which the city mayor called the beginning of the much-needed revival.[10]

The Ham-Ramsey meetings began on the night of August 30, 1934, and ran throughout the fall, stirring the city of Charlotte with a movement of the Spirit of God that would eventually extend into the heart of fifteen-year-old Billy Graham.

In his opening sermon, based on Ephesians 6, about the cosmic clash between Satan and Christ, Ham declared: "Our foes are unseen, and our great helpers are unseen. Satan and his demons with the help of wicked men, and Christ with angels and spiritual men are arrayed in this battle. . . . We are not fighting men, but *for* men."[11]

Even though Ham saw the conflict in cosmic terms, the "wicked men" he attacked were living, breathing people. Even the local newspapers were in on the conflict—one writing friendly articles in support of Ham while another wrote critically of the meetings.

The conflicts that had begun months before Ham ever arrived in Charlotte continued throughout the campaign, leading Billy Graham to write off the evangelistic meetings as a "religious circus" to stay away from.[12] Ham viewed the controversy as a microcosmic view of the war being waged between heaven and hell.

Vernon Patterson, who was integral in arranging the meetings, later summed up the progression of Ham's messages during the eleven-week campaign: *sin*, *salvation*, and *separation*. Ham started by preaching against sin. Early on, however, Patterson was concerned that Ham did not offer an invitation at these initial meetings. The evangelist responded that he wanted the people to be sure they knew what was at stake in following Christ before they made a decision. As the weeks progressed, Ham preached on salvation, and finally on separation.[13]

The controversies that had followed Ham to every city where he held meetings heated up in Charlotte in late fall as the evangelist found his target to preach against in some unruly local high school students. He caught wind of illegal misdeeds occurring at Central High School from the confession of a person in the inquiry room, where those who responded to the invitation would seek prayer and counsel. Allegedly, some students were going to a secret brothel across the street from the high school during their lunch hour. Along with his legal counsel, Ham had gathered affidavits from witnesses and began preaching about the activity in his services.[14]

The accusations went both ways, with Ham's critics accusing him and his piano player, Rawley Tredway, of gross immorality of their own—and even sending prostitutes to their hotel rooms to try to catch them in the act.[15] The plot failed, and the accusations against Ham appeared baseless, but his allegations against the high school students were not.

The swirling controversy also led to opposition from members of the Atheist Club at Central High School, who organized disturbances at the meetings.[16] None of this opposition fazed Ham, who was hardened by years of discord surrounding his ministry.

As Billy began to read about the immorality at the high school and heard about how Ham held up against his critics as a "fighting preacher," he became intrigued about the ringleader of this supposed circus.[17] His interest was piqued enough to go see for himself.

⟞⟝

Despite the ongoing controversies, Mordecai Ham's services were having a significant spiritual impact on the Charlotte community. Billy's parents and many of his friends had already been to meetings at the tabernacle. When Billy finally decided to go in November 1934, he quickly got a sense of the "fighting preacher" he had heard and read so much about.

As Billy sat amid the largest crowd he had ever seen in his life, and Mordecai Ham preached against sin, Billy began to wonder how the preacher could possibly know so much about him. Had Ham spoken to his mother? He was also impressed when Ham broke out into a hymn in the middle of his message: "The toils of the road will seem nothing, when I get to the end of the way."[18]

Billy was deeply convicted of his sin that first night, and he went home pondering the preacher's message as he looked across the fields of his father's farm. He felt drawn to return for several nights. One night, he felt under such conviction that he hid his face behind the hat of a woman who sat in from of him to escape the glare and pointing finger of the evangelist.[19]

Billy also made a connection at the meetings with two high-school-age peers who became lifelong friends: T. W. Wilson Jr.—or "T" as he was called—and his brother, Grady. The Wilson brothers were students at Central High School and attended

Caldwell Memorial Presbyterian Church; Billy was at Sharon High School and attended Chambers Memorial Reformed Presbyterian Church. Even though their fathers were friends through the Christian Business Men's Club, their paths had never crossed.

Like the Graham family, the Wilsons were a family in spiritual process. The father, T.W. Sr., had been converted at the 1924 Billy Sunday meetings, and their mother and the two brothers were converted in subsequent meetings—Grady and his mother in meetings led by George P. Stephens.[20] Even though Grady and T.W. had made commitments early in their lives, they struggled in their faith, and Grady in particular felt under deep conviction during Ham's preaching.

To escape the eyes of the convicting preacher, Billy and Grady decided to sit in the choir behind the podium—though neither could carry a tune. What they did not realize at the time was that it was not Ham's eyes they were trying to avoid.

On one particular night, Mordecai Ham delivered a message from Romans 5:8 (KJV) on the love of God: "But God commendeth his love toward us, in that, while we were yet sinners, Christ died for us." Afterward, Ham gave the invitation, and his song leader, William Ramsey, led the congregation in singing "Just As I Am" and "Almost Persuaded." During the second hymn, Billy left his seat in the choir, placed his feet on the sawdust trail, and committed his life to Christ.

Two things happened when he stood before the podium. First, as he looked around, he saw a woman weeping, and he wondered if his own response was genuine, because he felt no inclination to tears. Second, a tailor named J. D. Prevatt came up to him, also weeping, put his arm around Billy, and explained the plan of salvation to him.

The layman led Billy in a prayer and finally asked him to say a prayer himself.

When Billy filled out the response card, he checked "recommitment," uncertain of what his response meant. All he knew was that he was committing himself fully to the Lord.

That night, he returned to his home, where for the first time in his life he knelt down on his own initiative and prayed to God beside his bed. On that day in November 1934, there was a drastic change in the life and heart of Billy Graham, and there would be no turning back.

The Ham-Ramsey meetings were filled with spirited fighting, intrigue, and passion, but in the end they represented something of what Mordecai Ham hoped for and promised—a fight for the souls of men and women. The city of Charlotte was radically affected by the meetings, and the impact would eventually reverberate throughout the world through the commitment of an unwitting future evangelist.

The prayers of the men and women on the Graham dairy farm that spring were being answered. But there was still more work to be done in the heart and maturation process of the young man who would be called to preach the Gospel around the world.

CHAPTER 3

UNUSUAL FIRE

*"It was [at Bob Jones College] that
I first learned about evangelism."*
BILLY GRAHAM

The Ham-Ramsey meetings set Billy Frank Graham on a new course for his life, but more decisions, more commitments, and an ultimate surrender to the Lord's call on his life lay ahead.

As a high school student, he still lacked a clear direction and focus. His energy and love for life were not tempered by his conversion in 1934, but they would be challenged by the rigorous and suffocating environment he found in the fall of 1936 as a freshman at Bob Jones College, thirty miles east of Chattanooga in Cleveland, Tennessee.[1]

Since making his decision for Christ in November 1934, Billy got his first chance to share his newfound faith when he went with evangelist Jimmie Johnson to visit the jail in Monroe, North Carolina. While Jimmie was speaking to the men there, he surprised Billy by saying, "Here's a fellow who'll tell you what it's like to be converted."[2] And Billy did.

Perhaps the first evidence of fruit from his public ministry came when he went with a group to a home for troubled girls. Billy again gave a brief testimony. After the service—which likely included other testimonies—several girls made professions of faith.[3]

The young convert was beginning to grow spiritually, and his future began to come into focus as he became acquainted with several mature Christians who were graduates of Bob Jones College. Evangelists Jimmie Johnson and Fred Brown both stayed with the Grahams while holding revival services in Charlotte, and they planted the idea in Billy's mind to go to their alma mater.

That idea took root in Billy's mind when Bob Jones Sr. came to speak at Sharon High School during Billy's senior year. He was impressed by this winsome preacher whose stories came to life and whose quick responses to questions gave confidence to the inquisitive students.[4] Billy and his family decided that he should go to school at Bob Jones College.

Billy graduated from high school and spent the summer in a way that could not have served as a better contrast to what he would face at Bob Jones College—he was a freewheeling, traveling salesman of Fuller brushes and was treated as an independent adult. He spent the summer of 1936 as a successful salesman, sleeping in motels, roaming South Carolina towns, and knocking on doors to sell the luxury cleaning brushes. This manner of life fit his free-spirited, independent nature. As he would soon discover, Bob Jones College did not.

When Billy, Grady, and T. W. made their way together to Cleveland, Tennessee, to enroll at Bob Jones College, Billy and Grady eagerly and joyfully hatched a plot to take over the leadership of the freshman class. When nominations were taken for class officers, Billy would nominate Grady for president, and Grady would nominate Billy for vice president.

When the time came, Billy stood up, nominated Grady, and made a nice speech, extolling Grady's virtues and why he would be a great leader for the class. The nomination was accepted, the class voted, and Grady was elected to the office of president.

As president, Grady was now asked to preside over the rest of the meeting. As he asked for nominations for vice president, he instantly realized the bind he was in. His new position made it inappropriate, if not against the rules, to make a nomination. As Billy sat waiting for his friend to fulfill his side of the deal, he saw time running out with no nomination. He looked at Grady with eyes of desperation, even pointing at himself to be sure his friend had not forgotten their agreement. But Grady's hands were tied, Billy would not be nominated or elected to class office, and the plan to take over the freshman class fell apart.[5]

If Billy was offended, perhaps he would get his friend back during New Talent Night, when freshmen could show off their abilities. Billy and Grady once again schemed. Even though neither one could sing in tune, they decided they would get up and sing "Just Inside the Eastern Gate" as a duet. When their time came to sing, Grady went to the front, but Billy was nowhere to be found. Grady gamely cleared his throat and began to sing a solo. As he sang, T. W. kicked his foot and told him to stop. As T. W. said, "I am so embarrassed that I wish I was inside the Eastern Gate right now!" Grady quit, returned to his seat, and found Billy hiding underneath the chair.[6]

Bob Jones College was the brainchild of Methodist evangelist Bob Jones, who was born in 1883 in South Alabama as the eleventh of twelve children of a Primitive Baptist mother and Methodist father. At eleven years of age, he was converted in a Methodist church. Almost immediately, he became an evangelistic and preaching prodigy.

Jones ministered almost exclusively as an itinerant evangelist for the first two decades of the twentieth century, until he became extraordinarily concerned with the infiltration of modernism in the nation's schools in the 1920s. In particular, he felt that Christian schools that were accommodating modernism were compromising their very souls. The Scopes Monkey Trial in 1925, tried by Jones's friend William Jennings Bryan, only served to confirm his fears about the pervasive influence of modernism, as seen in the teaching of evolution.

In 1927, Jones took things into his own hands, starting an interdenominational, coeducational, and orthodox school (with emphasis on the *orthodox*) in Bay County, Florida, along the Florida panhandle. In 1933, he moved the school to Cleveland, Tennessee, because of rising real estate prices along the Gulf Coast.

The school provided education for both high school and college students and was founded upon a distinct antimodernist mind-set. Any hints of modernism—real or perceived—were quickly denounced, and the "perpetrators" were cut out from the world controlled by Bob Jones. The school's creed stated that they were "combating all atheistic, agnostic, pagan, and so-called scientific adulterations of the gospel."[7] The school motto proclaimed that "whatever the Bible says is so."

Those who could remain within this system of thought and could live with Jones's controlling personality and restrictive atmosphere would find a deep love for him. Those who could not often became deeply embittered against him. Billy found himself tossed in and out of the two extremes.

In the fall of 1936, enrollment had topped four hundred students, and there was reason for excitement in the school.[8] Three new buildings had been completed over the summer—a new auditorium, a new gym, and a newly renovated classroom building.[9] Bob Jones—or "Dr. Bob," as he was affectionately known by the students—had just returned from a summer of fund-raising. Upon his return, he raised an additional $2,500 from students and faculty.[10]

The first week of the new school year was dedicated to services, with three nights of meetings where Dr. Bob spoke. With an opening encouragement for the new students, and a taste of what was to come, the school's leader told the students to "play the game fair and square" and to be honest with themselves so that they would not "disappoint [their] parents back home by not doing [their] best."[11]

Dr. Bob had been grooming his son, Bob Jr., from birth to follow in his footsteps. By 1936, at the tender age of twenty-four, with a master's degree in history from the University of Pittsburgh and an honorary doctorate from Asbury College, Bob Jr. served as the school's treasurer, secretary, head of the history department, and acting president in his father's absence.[12]

Bob Sr. wrote to a friend, "I am not an educator. I am an evangelist."[13] He left the school's academics and administration in the hands of others, though they were ever under his watchful eye. He found his son to be an able administrator, as well as someone in whom he could place his unconditional trust.[14]

The first week of religious services proved fruitful. On the first night, Bob Jr. invited second- and fourth-year students to share testimonies about "Jesus and Bob Jones College," to an "overwhelming response."[15] The local paper reported that the first week yielded thirty decisions to accept Christ.[16] Students also testified in the school newsletter, which was sent out to potential donors with comments such as these:

"Since coming to this college I have received the assurance of salvation."

"I came here an atheist. I have found God and am going to be a preacher of the Gospel."

"Before coming to this college, I was inclined to be a religious fanatic, and thus did more harm than good. Now my religion is more practical and I can be of more use to Jesus Christ."[17]

To say that one tempered his fanaticism while at Bob Jones would surprise any modern reader, but Dr. Bob was intent on making his students' faith authentic. At Bob Jones College, he wrote, religion was a "natural thing—not strained or overly pious."[18] Students were being shaped, and lives were being changed.

◁━

Though guest speakers were not a regular occurrence at the daily chapel hour—where Dr. Bob or one of his in-house, appointed associates did most of the speaking—the fall of 1936 did bring a handful of outsiders, beginning on October 14 with R. E. Neighbour, a prolific church planter and pastor.[19] Jones also invited business leaders such as A. K. Harper, founder of Harper Brush Works of Fairfield, Iowa—a competitor of the Fuller Brush Company, for whom Billy had worked the previous summer.

In late November and early December, two services were devoted to events that had transpired in Russia over the past twenty tumultuous years, with Countess Irina Skariatina and Nikita Ignatievich Saloff-Astakhoff, who brought tales of imprisonment, torture, and martyrdom to the American consciousness.[20]

And, of course, there were also preachers and theologians, such as R. G. Lee, pastor of the fast-growing Bellevue Baptist Church in Memphis, Tennessee, and John R. Riebe of the Moody Bible Institute.[21]

Bob Jones and his preaching were the heart of the chapel services. But Dr. Bob was in and out of Cleveland, Tennessee, that fall, holding evangelistic meetings—which were also used for promotion and fund-raising for the growing school, leaving the school and chapel services in the hands of those he trusted.

He wrote to a friend, explaining his vision and view of his abilities during this time: "I can 'blow into' the college about one week in three and set it on fire, 'pep it up,' generate enthusiasm, keep things on a high pitch, and then go out into the world and preach the Gospel and contact the people over the radio and come back home and set the college on fire again."[22] Though he was often absent, it was clearly Bob Jones's school.

Bob Jones College, which in more recent years has come to be known as "an unusual university," was, in many ways, more radical than other fundamentalist institutions. But in other ways, Bob Jones Sr. was able to see beyond some of the overreactions within the fundamentalist movement. One of these ways was in the arts.

Whereas even some more moderate institutions, such as Wheaton College in Illinois, banned theater productions in the 1930s, Bob Jones Sr. embraced the arts, and Bob Jr. became an accomplished actor.[23]

If theater pushed the fundamentalist envelope, the invitation of magician McDonald Birch and his wife, xylophonist Mabel Sperry, pushed the envelope even further.[24] Jones was able to see the difference between illusion and magic where others could not.

In October 1936, Bob Jones Jr. showcased his acting talent with a production of Shakespeare's *Macbeth*, in which he played the title role. The local paper spoke of Jones's ability, saying that it "rivals famous Shakespearean actors of the day" with productions on par with what "you might see in big cities."[25] The entire campus was invited to participate in the production,[26] and Billy did.

The heart of the Joneses' passion for art can be seen in their vision that "dramatics are not being presented to teach the students how to become adept in Thespian art, but to teach them appreciation for art, literature, and history."[27]

Billy was cast in a minor role for the production of *Macbeth*, as a soldier, speaking once in a chorus of other soldiers; but he also may have played a lord, a gentleman, an officer, an attendant, a messenger, or an apparition—all of which were nonspeaking roles.

Not only did Billy get involved in the theater production during his freshman year, but he also participated in the Chi Delta Theta Literary Society—a fundamentalist version of the corrupted fraternity system at other schools. Joined also by Grady Wilson and Billy's roommate, Woodrow Flynn, the society existed to create "higher ideals of Christian living, higher standards of manhood; to develop literary talents; to foster clean speech, clean living, clean scholarship, and clean sports."[28]

Bob Jones College fostered an environment that would shape the young Billy Graham and the students around him. Students and faculty alike had a love and respect for Bob Jones that went deep into their hearts. The 1936–1937 yearbook sums up their admiration: "Dr. Bob, though an evangelist, teaches a practical philosophy of life to hundreds of young people by both precept and example. His sympathy, humor, and helpfulness inspire the students to walk cheerfully on their uphill path of learning and not to falter until the goal is reached."[29]

For Billy's part, he later said that Bob Jones College was where "I first learned about evangelism. It was there that I received my passion for the souls of men and began to realize the desperate need of a world outside of Christ."[30]

Despite the positive impact that the college seemed to have

on Billy's life, his admiration for Dr. Bob and the school was soon outweighed by his discomfort with the founder's personality and the environment he established. It wasn't long before Billy was thinking about leaving behind the "unusual fire."

CHAPTER 4

SINGED

"Our college has a reputation of being strict."
BOB JONES SR.

"Environment is a good thing," wrote Dr. Bob in a December 1936 edition of the school newsletter, "but environment cannot do anything for any man unless he has an affinity for his environment. A hog in the parlor is not changed by his surroundings. The hog changes his surroundings."[1]

Though Dr. Bob probably did not have Billy Graham in mind when speaking of hogs, to say that Billy did not have an affinity for the environment of Bob Jones College was an apt description of the free-spirited freshman from Charlotte.

Every aspect of life on campus was highly regimented for the students at Bob Jones College. Jones himself warned the students, "Our college has a reputation of being strict."[2] Billy put it another way: "There were demerits for everything."[3] There was even a "snitch rule," as some students called it, whereby second-year students and above were responsible to call out underclassmen for offenses (before they happened), or to report them to the school authorities (after they happened). Those who didn't abide by this standard would be considered "disloyal" and might themselves be referred to the faculty committee.[4] And there was certainly plenty to snitch about.

Dorm life was stifling to an energetic and active young person like Billy. Waving or shouting from the windows and loitering in the hallways were prohibited, and there were also daily cleanliness inspections. Quiet hours began promptly at 7:00 p.m. and were strictly enforced, and students were expected to "rise promptly" at the ringing of the bell at 6:30 a.m.[5]

This rigid structure must have been shocking for Billy, who had spent the summer with his own relatively carefree regimen. From dorm life to dining, from classes to work, and from church to their social lives, students were under the watchful eye of Dr. Bob and his subordinates.

Perhaps most suffocating of all for Billy was the dogmatic intellectual climate, which discouraged thinking for oneself or raising genuine questions or doubts.[6] From classroom to chapel, Dr. Bob's views were to be adhered to.

Chapel was held Monday through Saturday, and Dr. Bob spoke five days a week when he was on campus. This may have been only slightly unusual for a fundamentalist school of that era. Bob Jones Sr. was a winsome speaker and endeared himself to many as he spoke. But others were hurt by being called out as "offenders" from the pulpit.[7]

What marked the school out as unusual was its treatment of students and their choice of churches. Dr. Bob believed that students should maintain their denominational affiliations but not necessarily attend their own churches. Therefore, all students—except for ministerial students who were serving in local churches—were required to attend an on-campus Sunday school, which was divided up by denomination, followed by an all-campus Sunday morning worship service. This all but destroyed any other church involvement.

Furthermore, students were required to attend a Sunday afternoon vespers service, put on by the speech and music department, which included a "sacred program" or drama. Only after students had attended these services were they encouraged to go to a Sunday evening service at a local church.[8]

For many—perhaps even for the majority of the students—this structure and control worked well. For Billy, however, it made him question his spirituality. In a letter to his mother, he wrote, "I know that I know Jesus Christ, but I've lost my feeling. I can't seem to get anywhere in prayer."[9]

Billy's discomfort with the environment was exacerbated by a fall bout with the flu (which may have just been melancholy),[10] and by the struggles of one of his roommates, Wendell Phillips, who was even more unhappy than Billy.

Their discontentment became even more acute when they were disciplined for leaving campus without proper permission in order for Wendell to preach at a local church.[11] They were caught, and what followed were three meetings with Dr. Bob before Billy's eventual withdrawal from the school the following January when the first semester drew to a close.[12]

One of those meetings was called by Bob Jones Sr., who suspected that Billy and Wendell were teetering on the edge of disloyalty to him and the school. For his part, Billy sat nervously biting his nails as Dr. Bob lectured him and Wendell for their wavering commitment to the school.[13] Wendell, on the other hand, responded with some sharp words for Dr. Bob, the strong disciplinarian whose temperament and pride would not tolerate such insubordination. Shortly thereafter, Wendell withdrew from Bob Jones College (before his imminent expulsion)[14] and transferred to a small Bible school near Tampa, Florida, called the Florida Bible Institute. He began sending reports to Billy that the school was filled with strikingly beautiful scenes, sunshine, oranges, relative freedom, and pretty girls, and he encouraged Billy to join him there.[15]

Billy's mother, who was aware of her son's discontentment, had noticed an advertisement in *Moody Monthly* for the same Florida Bible school, and she deduced that it must be a "good Fundamentalist school" if it was advertised in that publication.[16]

The Graham family had planned a Christmas vacation to visit family in Orlando, and it turned out to be a wonderful opportunity to get a taste of the climate and Florida environment. Billy fell in love almost instantly. In contrast to the chill, damp winter climate of Cleveland, Tennessee, Florida's warm December air was refreshing.

When the Grahams returned to Charlotte, a visit to the doctor confirmed what Billy was already thinking: he needed a less strenuous atmosphere to fit his free spirit.

Billy returned to Bob Jones College, on the advice of Bob Jones Sr., to finish his first semester, which ended following the Christmas holiday. In a meeting with Billy around that time, the evangelist-turned-educator barked, "If you throw your life away at a little country Bible school, the chances are you'll never be heard of. At best, all you could amount to would be a poor country Baptist preacher somewhere out in the sticks." Then, as Jones continued his admonition to Billy, he changed his tune to offer some encouragement: "You have a voice that pulls. Some voices repel. You have a voice that appeals. God can use that voice of yours. He can use it mightily."[17]

In a final letter to Billy's father, Bob Jones Sr. wrote, "I have advised Billy to go down to Florida to the Bible Institute and take his work regularly and orderly. I have advised him that Wendell is not the type of fellow he should have with him. . . . As one father to another, and as a Christian brother to another, I advise you to write Billy to go to Florida. . .and that you do not want him to go with Wendell."[18]

To the president of the Florida Bible Institute, who was reluctant to accept dissidents from Bob Jones College, Dr. Bob wrote, "There are two fellows coming down from my school that are going to be in your school. One is not worth the salt that goes in his food, but the other is a good fellow from Charlotte, North Carolina, [who] comes from a good family, and if you hold his feet to the fire, someday he might amount to something."[19]

Billy had stood too close to the fire that was Bob Jones—and he simply got singed. When he arrived at the Florida Bible Institute, they took to heart the advice of Bob Jones and held Billy's feet to the fire. But in Florida, that fire would move from his feet to his heart.

PART 2

IGNITING THE FIRE:

FLORIDA BIBLE INSTITUTE
(1937–1940)

CHAPTER 5

THE MIRACLE SCHOOL

"That'd make a good Bible school!"
WILLIAM THOMAS WATSON

In January 1937, Billy Graham officially withdrew from Bob Jones College and made his way with his father to the Florida Bible Institute in Temple Terrace, Florida.[1] Upon his arrival on campus, it was clear that all that Wendell Phillips had promised was true. The campus was stunningly beautiful.

To get to the school, one drove through miles of orange groves into a landscape right out of a fairy tale—with moss-draped trees and thick vines worthy of Billy's boyhood hero, Tarzan. If the area's surreal lushness was not impressive enough, the school itself—a multiple-story, Spanish Colonial–style building—and its ideal location along the meandering Hillsborough River and Temple Terrace Golf Course, were enough to stun even the most ardent, miracle-believing Christian. The setting looked more like a wonderland resort than a Bible school—let alone a fledgling, five-year-old Bible school with fewer than fifty students.

The founding of the school, by evangelist William Thomas

Watson, had been nothing short of miraculous. Watson was the pastor of the St. Petersburg Gospel Tabernacle, which he had started in 1924 under the auspices of the Christian and Missionary Alliance (C&MA)—initially not as a church but as a center for evangelistic meetings in the South. His vision for a school to train evangelists, pastors, and missionaries had been brewing since early in his ministry. As he drove with friends throughout the St. Petersburg and Tampa area in the 1920s and early 1930s, Watson would often look at buildings that had been vacated as a result of the Great Depression and say, "That'd make a good Bible school!"[2]

In February 1932, Miss Jessie Reinhart, a faithful charter member of the Tabernacle, unintentionally set in motion the events that would culminate in the founding of the school. She was going to visit the renowned hymn writer Judson W. Van DeVenter in Temple Terrace, just north of Tampa, and asked Watson, "Would you like to go with us?"

"I sure would!" Watson blurted out. He rarely passed up an opportunity to rub elbows with spiritual giants.

On their visit with the gentle, spiritual hymn writer, Watson saw a pink stucco building all boarded up. It had been the main clubhouse and resort of the Temple Terrace Golf Club but had fallen victim to the tough economic conditions. Ever the ambitious visionary, Watson turned to Van DeVenter and repeated his oft-spoken phrase: "That'd make a good Bible school!"

Van DeVenter optimistically shot back, "Maybe it'll be gotten yet!"

They went to speak with the caretaker of the facility to see if they could find out more about it and take a tour of the building. It was a former hotel with forty rooms (each with a private bath), a grand lobby, and plenty of room for dining and classrooms. The facility also included a building that had housed the hotel's servants—a perfect place to house students.

Watson asked the caretaker, "Do you have the name and number of the owner so I might contact him?"

"It is owned by August Heckscher from New York," the caretaker replied. "But giving you his number won't do you any good. He does all his business through lawyers." Watson's heart sank, and he wrote off the idea of acquiring the building for his school. He returned home to St. Petersburg without following up on the inquiry.

Two weeks later, Watson received an unexpected telegram from Heckscher's secretary. It read, "Mr. Heckscher will be in Temple Terrace tomorrow afternoon if you would like to meet him." Excited but still skeptical, Watson returned to Temple Terrace and met with Heckscher, whom he learned was a German Jew. He told him his vision for a Christian Bible school. He also told him plainly that he had no money for the building or for the school.

The New York businessman replied, "Well, I'm not interested in finding out about your money. I just want to talk with you."

"Well, I can talk!" Watson blurted. And talk he could.

Watson had been born into poverty in 1901 in Lumberton, North Carolina, and had been deathly ill—weighing only three pounds when he was two months old. A doctor making a house call told Watson's mother and father, "There's no hope. Let him go or else he is already gone."

The doctor left the heartbroken mother to grieve, but instead she cried out to God, "Lord, if You spare him, You can have him. Just show me what to do!" Right then, she got the idea to wet a piece of cotton and place it on the sickly baby's lips. When she did, his tongue came out and he began to return to health. Watson would later reflect, "And my tongue's been out ever since!"[3]

Watson was converted in an evangelistic tent meeting at the age of fourteen and joined the local Christian and Missionary Alliance Church. When he was sixteen, he entered into the Toccoa Falls

Bible Institute, run by Dr. R. A. Forrest, who became a lifelong mentor to him. As a student, he began holding revival meetings of his own, and in 1921 entered Nyack Missionary Training Institute in New York, which was one of the first Bible schools in the nation.

After graduating from Nyack in 1922, Watson went south to minister in northern Florida, where he teamed up with an earlier Nyack graduate, John Minder. They founded a C&MA church in Melrose, Florida, but soon both felt called to start Gospel Tabernacles in the Tampa area. Watson went to St. Petersburg, and Minder went to Tampa.

Watson built a four-thousand-seat tabernacle to hold evangelistic services, which drew the likes of Billy Sunday, Gypsy Smith, Homer Rodeheaver, H. C. Morrison, W. B. Riley, Harry Rimmer, W. R. Newell, R. A. Torrey, Mordecai Ham, Gerald Winrod, and others. Even with such big names in attendance, the church struggled to make payments through the difficult economic times, and the leaders soon realized they needed to be not just an evangelistic center, but a church that could care for the believers in the area.

From his time at Toccoa Falls and Nyack, on through his ministry as an evangelist and pastor, W. T. Watson's heart burned with the vision of founding a school. When he met with August Heckscher to discuss the use of the building in Temple Terrace, he was aware that the school would never be built unless the Lord built it. When August Heckscher, the real estate mogul and philanthropist, failed to flinch at Watson's lack of money and instead invited him to New York, Watson knew it was the Lord's doing.

Further, knowing that Heckscher was a German Jew with no Christian conviction was a further sign that the Lord was moving mountains. But perhaps the greatest sign of all was the unfathomable deal that Watson and Heckscher reached: no down payment and no payments or interest for ten years. It was a miracle indeed.

Watson's vision for the Institute was clearly shaped by his experiences at Toccoa Falls and Nyack. Indeed, Nyack had been an inspiration for the founding of no fewer than thirty Christian and Missionary Alliance Bible schools across the nation,[4] and was clearly a visionary impetus for the Bible school movement in general. Watson adopted much of the vision and philosophy of the schools, but he wanted the new school to be nondenominational, and thus outside of his own denomination. This clearly offended the leaders of the Alliance, and they asked him to either make the Institute an Alliance institution or resign from his church. He would do neither, and his congregation stood with him as the church cut ties with the Christian and Missionary Alliance.

Watson was deeply hurt by what he felt was a betrayal by the denomination;[5] but despite the personal cost, he was convinced that the school needed to be nondenominational in order to train the most people possible for ministry. And so it was.

The Florida Bible Institute was committed, first and foremost, to the study of scripture. The Bible was the school's primary textbook.[6] Beyond the study of the Bible, there were few other options—only music programs and training for secretarial work.

Watson's vision was not merely for a commitment to scripture. He had a very low view of preachers who would not work. So a requirement that all students work was foundational to the running of the school. This served three main purposes. First, the students who were training for ministry would not become lazy, as Watson believed some were wont to do. Second, work was a way for any student to pay his or her own way through school. Watson strongly desired that anyone who wanted to come to the Institute could come—no matter the student's economic status. Finally, putting the students to work made the school itself function. It was the students who cleaned, cooked, and did the dishes. And when guests visited the school, it was the students who tended to their needs.

Not only was Watson's vision to put students to work, but he also wanted to get them quickly into practical ministry—a vision he surely picked up from Toccoa and Nyack. He believed that the sooner the students were involved in practical Christian service, the quicker they would develop a hunger for the Word of God.[7] Indeed, he believed that waiting to fully train students in the Bible before sending them out would lead to their losing their "cutting edge" and their passion.[8] Students at the Institute were sent out almost immediately to serve in local churches, missions—and even on street corners—to get their feet wet in ministry.

The faculty consisted of volunteers—local pastors, evangelists, music leaders, and Bible teachers. The curriculum included classes in doctrine, Church evidence, comparative religion, Bible analysis, Christian ethics, psychology, personal evangelism, prophecy, archaeology, homiletics, Bible synthesis, hermeneutics, and Church history, as well as introductory courses in Bible, Spanish, secretarial skills, and music.[9]

Even though the faculty were unpaid, the operating costs of the school could not be offset by the mere one-dollar-per-day tuition paid by the students, or by donations. Watson's hope was to appeal to wealthy snowbirds from the North who vacationed in Florida. It was his desire and vision to hold spiritually refreshing conferences during the winter. Not only would the conferences generate some income, but some of the guests might also become donors of the fledgling Institute and tell other prospective students about the school. Perhaps the most important purpose of all for the conferences was to bring in leading Christian preachers and evangelists from around the country to rub elbows with the students.

All these elements of Watson's educational vision—the inter-denominational spirit, the Bible-centered education, his view of students as workers who were involved in ministry, the dedicated faculty, and the winter conferences—served to profoundly shape the life and ministry of the young Billy Graham.

W. T. Watson created the environment in which Billy's faith and experience grew, but it was another man—John Minder, Watson's longtime friend and dean of the school—who had the greatest personal impact on Billy.

When Billy and his father pulled up to the school, John Minder—by an act of divine assignment—looked out his window, saw the new student, and went out to welcome him to campus. Little did he know that the investment he would make in this lanky eighteen-year-old would return dividends beyond his wildest imagination. Billy, for his part, had no idea how much Minder would stretch him in the coming years. It is beyond coincidence that the first person Billy Graham met when he arrived at the Florida Bible Institute would be his "father in the ministry."[10] It could only be a divine appointment.

No sooner had Billy settled into his new surroundings than the secretary of the school came up to him and asked, "Are you the new student, Billy Graham?"

"Yes, I am."

"Do you have a driver's license?" she asked.

"Yes, I do."

"We have some guests here and nobody to take them down to the Gasparilla Carnival. Could you please take them?"

Billy had never been to Tampa, and he knew nothing about the Gasparilla Carnival, a citywide festival honoring Tampa's pirate history and celebrating Florida's unique agriculture and arts.

Nevertheless, he agreed to chauffeur the guests—but it was certainly a case of the blind leading the blind. Years later, Billy joked that the school likely lost some prospective donors as a result![11]

Such an introduction to the school was matched by his first encounter with upperclassman Roy Gustafson. When Billy first met him, Roy was reading a small pamphlet. He put the pamphlet down and told Billy, "You're going to need this book. It's a special textbook that you will need for classes." Billy bought the book from him for one dollar, only to discover that it was simply a copy of the book of Romans that a fourteen-year-old boy from Clearwater had compiled. The "special textbook" scam became the first of many pranks that Billy would either perpetrate or be on the receiving end of during his time at Florida Bible Institute. But in this case, the prankster was someone who would become a dear friend and a member of Billy's ministry in later years.

The atmosphere of the campus was fun-loving and joyful, and there was no student more fun-loving and energetic than Billy. Pictures from the period show an exceedingly lanky young man. Indeed, he was always trying to gain weight—to no avail.[12] Many of his fellow students would have been shocked to know the grueling schedule he would keep for the next fifty years. Judging merely by his outward appearance and physique, one never would have guessed the boundless energy wound up within his skinny frame.

Early on, this energy seems to have been directed toward his love for baseball, a quest for girls, and his newfound freedom to play tennis, volleyball, and golf, or to swim or canoe in the water-moccasin-infested Hillsborough River. Not that he would ever entirely leave behind these interests, but in the next few months and years, his energy would be harnessed and channeled for the purpose of laboring for the Harvest.

The transition from Bob Jones College to the Florida Bible Institute could not have been better for Billy. Whatever the precise reasons for his departure from Bob Jones, he soon found several qualities of the Florida Bible Institute to be quite refreshing. First, the school's smaller size made it a much more intimate environment, with an evident love for one another among the students.[13] And though the Institute of course had its own set of rules, the more tenderhearted application of those rules seemed a better match with Billy's free spirit. Furthermore, the campus, climate, and atmosphere were vast improvements over what Billy had found in Cleveland, Tennessee. The next three and a half years at the Florida Bible Institute were the best years of his life.[14]

CHAPTER 6

INTO THE FIRE

"I'll never be a preacher!"
BILLY GRAHAM

Eighteen-year-old Billy's first semester at the Florida Bible Institute placed him close to the fire of great preaching and gave him almost unlimited ministry experiences and opportunities to see the wonderful workings of God.

The annual winter conference was held from January to March and brought some of the best preachers in the country to the school. These conferences had a deep impact on the students and attendees alike. But the influence of in-house preachers, such as W. T. Watson and other faculty members, was also significant. Dr. Watson was a dynamic speaker who poured himself physically, emotionally, and spiritually into his preaching.[1] Indeed, more than thirty years later, Billy could still recall the first sermon he heard Dr. Watson preach, on the text "Greater is he that is in you, than he that is in the world."[2] The lasting impression of Watson's preaching was also confirmed by the fact that he taught homiletics at the Institute.[3]

The school's rich preaching atmosphere was further enhanced by

Watson's determination to get students immediately into ministry. Teams were sent out wherever and whenever there was a need or opportunity—to churches, missions, and even trailer parks. And if no other opportunity was available, a street corner served just as well. On one of Billy's very first weekends at the school, he went with a team to hold a meeting on the streets of Sulphur Springs, a small town near Temple Terrace, just north of downtown Tampa. This group of students from the Institute was filled with veteran preachers and musicians—some of whom were graduating that spring. The Institute groups regularly held meetings on the surrounding streets— with musical instruments, singing trios and quartets, and one or more students who would preach. On this early occasion, the preaching privilege went to Charles Massey, a junior at the school. Billy was quite impressed with the music and the scene, but what struck him most was Massey's preaching. As he watched the upperclassman stride about and shout at people, Billy thought to himself, *I'll never be a preacher.*[4] Still, he knew that one day he would need to be ready.

Even though Billy was uncomfortable with the idea of preaching, other ministry opportunities soon came along. One early occasion was an invitation to teach about a dozen boys in a Children's Bible Mission class.[5] This ministry had been started in Florida in 1932 by Walter Jensen, a graduate of Moody Bible Institute. Jensen and his wife had heard of an enormous need for the Gospel in the South, and like many others, including W. T. Watson and John Minder, they viewed Florida as a ripe mission field. The Jensens' method was to teach the Bible to children in the public schools and to moti-vate them to memorize scripture by offering incentives such as books of the Bible, New Testaments, and even entire Bibles. The biggest prize, however, was the opportunity to attend a Bible camp.[6]

Billy's participation in these activities during his time at the Florida Bible Institute gave him firsthand experience and opened his eyes to important aspects of ministry. And no lessons were more significant than the ones he learned on prayer. During Billy's first year, Watson purchased a nearby building to continue to develop the school. The building had walls and a roof, but the interior was unfinished. The school needed to raise ten thousand dollars or risk losing the building to the bank.

As the deadline for payment drew near, the severity of the situation prompted Watson to call off classes so that the students, faculty, and staff could gather for a day of prayer to ask the Lord to provide for the enormous financial need. They met in the lounge of the main building and prayed all morning and through lunch. At about 1:30 in the afternoon, the school secretary tapped the president on the shoulder and told him there was a telegram waiting at Western Union.

When Watson received the message, he found it was from E. R. Kellog of Mount Vernon, Ohio, an old friend who had earned a fortune as the manager of a J. C. Penney store. Watson and Kellog were kindred spirits in that Kellog was connected with the Canadian Keswick movement, whose conferences were from the same stream as those that Watson put on at the Florida Bible Institute. Kellog and Watson had not spoken for some time prior to Kellog's sending of the telegram, and the wealthy retailer was unaware of any specific need at the school.

Watson scribbled down the message from the telegram, brought it back to the lounge, and said, "Folks, let's get up off our knees now; I've got some news for you." He read the telegram out loud: "Today I am mailing the Florida Bible Institute a check for $10,000." Cheers and praises immediately burst forth from the students and faculty gathered for the prayer time.

Kellog, they would later learn, had been driving through Ohio when he felt impressed to send the money to the school. As he drove, he felt a particular burden, not just to send the money, but to pull over and send an immediate telegram announcing his decision. He found the Western Union office, sent the telegram, and mailed the check.

This miraculous example of God's provision deeply affected the students and staff. For young Billy's part, the answer to prayer in such a marvelous way made him want to trust the Lord as never before, and it profoundly influenced his philosophy of ministry, money, and prayer throughout his life.[7]

Very early on, the dark-haired and vivacious Emily Regina Cavanaugh caught Billy's eye and captured his heart. Emily had enrolled at the Institute in the fall of 1936, while Billy was still at Bob Jones College. Her older sister, Inez, was a senior at the school, and her younger sister, Pleasant, was slated to begin her studies there the following year.[8]

The Cavanaughs lived in nearby Tampa, and that's where Emily had grown up. She was determined to become a missionary after being mesmerized as a young girl by the stories of adventure that her missionary neighbors from Africa told her.

The Cavanaugh girls had a gift for music. All three sisters entered the music program at the Institute, primarily establishing themselves as singers in all-female trios. They were so successful in their singing that they were invited to tour with Billy Sunday's song leader, Homer Rodeheaver—a fact that impressed Billy.

Even though Emily had a strong religious background and a musical talent that she dedicated to the Lord, she said that it wasn't until she was a student at the Florida Bible Institute that she really began to grow in her faith.[9]

It seemed that Billy and Emily were meant for each other. Before Billy had even arrived on campus, Wendell Phillips, his disgruntled friend from Bob Jones College, had already handpicked Emily for him. Billy was not disappointed. For her part, Emily was attracted to Billy, who was quickly growing out of his awkward youth into an increasingly handsome young man. But beyond his looks, she was also drawn by his charisma and energy, as well as his concern for, and awareness of, other people.[10]

As the two began spending time together, it became clear to the others, and to themselves, that they were an item. Billy was as happy as could be with the new environment in Temple Terrace, and he was even more excited about his budding relationship with Emily.

There were other reasons for Billy to be excited about his new surroundings. One of them was the dean of the Institute, John Minder. Minder was a thirty-eight-year-old bachelor whose single-ness afforded him the opportunity to invest most of his time and energy into the students at the school. Born in 1898 in Akron, Ohio, Minder was converted at an evangelistic tent meeting at his high school—the very last person to respond before the close of the meetings. After his graduation from high school in 1917, he went to Nyack Missionary Training Institute. The years at Nyack shaped Minder in deeply spiritual ways, and he had the privilege of being a student in C&MA and Nyack founder A. B. Simpson's final class, "Christ in the Bible," before Simpson's death in 1919.[11]

Minder finished at Nyack the semester before W. T. Watson completed his studies there. The two met, not at Nyack, but as volunteers at tent meetings led by Roscoe Stull, under the direction of R. A. Forrest, in cotton mill towns in Georgia and South Carolina.[12] Their hearts were united in ministry for many years thereafter.

After a year of postgraduate study in New York City, Minder reconnected with Roscoe Stull to start a Christian and Missionary Alliance church in Ensley, Alabama. He stayed there for only a short time before he and Stull moved on to hold tent meetings in north-central Florida and establish a church in Melrose in 1922. It was there that Minder invited Watson to participate in establishing the church. Minder also purchased ten acres at Lake Swan, with the hope of one day starting a Bible camp. He also built a home there, which he would keep for life.

In 1931, while he was the southeastern district superintendent for the C&MA, Minder realized his dream of creating a Bible camp. Many students from the Florida Bible Institute, including Billy Graham, spent time there during the summers and on vacations.

Minder's and Watson's work at the church in Melrose ended in 1924 when the two young pioneering evangelists and church planters took their well-worn tent to Tampa to hold evangelistic meetings. The result of the meetings was the founding of two churches: the Tampa Gospel Tabernacle, started by Minder, and the St. Petersburg Gospel Tabernacle, started by Watson. Minder stayed at the church for about five years before becoming associate superintendent, and then head superintendent, of the southeastern district of the C&MA, where he served from 1930 to 1934.

Watson remained at the St. Petersburg Tabernacle until he started his work at the Florida Bible Institute. In 1935, after Minder ended a successful radio ministry in south Georgia, Watson invited him to join the Institute's faculty.[13]

Minder's ministry experience was expansive and unique, but he learned through the years that there was no greater task than investing in young people to train them up as future ministers and preachers. In 1937, as Minder observed and got to know Billy Graham, he found a teachable young man in whom he could invest, which he did for the next three and a half years.

Minder began spending time with Billy and took him along on ministry trips. For Easter vacation in 1937, Minder invited Billy on a trip that dramatically changed the direction of Billy's life. The excursion was to Lake Swan, about 140 miles from Temple Terrace, where Minder had established the Melrose Gospel Tabernacle and Bible Camp.

On this trip, Minder introduced Billy to a longtime friend, the Reverend Cecil Underwood. The two had become acquainted in the early 1920s when Minder was church planting in Melrose, and they had kept in touch over the years.

Underwood was a busy man. He was the pastor of Peniel Baptist Church in Palatka, about thirty miles from Lake Swan, but he also had the responsibility to supply preachers for several Baptist churches in Putnam County. On top of these responsibilities, he also ran a painting company to supplement his meager ministerial income.

Being introduced to such a man during the Easter season would be a dangerous proposition for anyone—young or old—who did not want to preach. And it's likely that Minder was aware of this when he took Billy to visit Underwood in Palatka.

Ever the recruiter, Underwood turned to Minder and said, "Mr. Minder, would you preach for me tonight?"

As if he had just been waiting for the question, Minder shot back, "Billy's going to preach!"

Fear struck immediately in the heart of the unprepared student, and Billy exclaimed, "No, sir, I can't. I have never preached before, and I do not have a message."

But Minder would not let him pass up this opportunity to get his feet wet. He was determined to get Billy into the fire.

"You go ahead and preach. When you run out, I'll take over. We'll pray for you."[14]

Together they made the fifteen-minute drive up to Bostwick for the Sunday evening service on March 28. It was a brisk spring evening, and the small country church was warmed by a stove that sat near the front of the meeting hall. The congregation consisted of about thirty or forty rough-and-tumble, hardworking people. Even the piano player fit the description of a member of a "cowboy church," with his mouth filled with chewing tobacco. He would get up on occasion, open one of the side doors, and spit. If Billy had not been so nervous, the scene might have been amusing.

Though Billy did not have a message prepared to preach, he had been studying the sermons of great preachers and had a general grasp on a few outlines. After a time of singing, John Minder got up to introduce the student from the Florida Bible Institute, and then Billy stood up nervously to preach his first sermon. He rapidly delivered everything he had—all in less than five minutes, according to his recollection.[15] Minder remembered a "nice" message lasting ten to fifteen minutes in a meeting that had "a good spirit."[16]

Billy was less sanguine about how his message had gone and about the spirit of the meeting. Part of his feelings had to do with a conversation he had after the sermon, which he did not immediately share with his mentor. When Billy sat down, Minder went to the pulpit to tie up loose ends and call on the congregation to respond to the message. One man stayed in his seat but indicated that he was in need of prayer. So Billy went back to talk with him and pray. He introduced himself as a student at the Florida Bible Institute, which apparently turned the man off. The man looked Billy in the eye and barked, "Look here, young fellow. You don't have to think that just because you go to that school down there that you know everything."[17]

Billy was stung by the rebuke. If that was not enough, the man proceeded to completely humiliate Billy: "You will never be a preacher."[18]

This incident confirmed Billy's fears about preaching, but Minder encouraged him to press on—though Billy did not make him aware of the hostile encounter until much later. The event taught Billy valuable lessons, and he determined to never again be so woefully unprepared to preach.

When Billy returned to school after Easter vacation, he had the strange feeling that he had grown spiritually through his experience in Bostwick. Because John Minder had thrown him into the heat of the fire, he was now tempered and shaped—though not completely, of course—and he really hadn't gotten burned.

CHAPTER 7

SURRENDER

*"Lord, I'll go wherever You want me to go,
and I'll preach wherever You want me to preach."*
BILLY GRAHAM

Judson Van DeVenter was a gentle-spirited, eighty-year-old man in 1937 and was well loved by the students of the Florida Bible Institute. Not only had he been instrumental in the location of the school, but he was also an active participant and supporter. Though the seasoned hymn writer did not teach courses, his wife taught piano, and he regularly came to winter conferences and chapel meetings, resting on his cane as he stood to sing. He had a deep spirituality, tempered by years of faith and trust, which he imprinted significantly into the lives of the students.

As a young man in Sharon, Pennsylvania, Van DeVenter had been an art teacher and an aspiring artist, but he also had a heart for evangelism. He had volunteered as a follow-up counselor at evangelistic meetings at his church, and his friends began to notice his gift for counseling and encouraged him to enter the ministry. He resisted this call for five years. And then something happened, even more significant than his simply becoming an evangelist. He accepted God's call on his life and "surrendered all." As he later recalled, "I became an evangelist and discovered down deep in my soul a talent hitherto unknown to me. God had hidden a song in my heart, and touching a tender chord, He caused me to sing songs I had never sung before."[1]

The students at the Institute had the unique privilege of learning from and being inspired by this great man of faith. Billy and other students sometimes gathered in the Van DeVenters' living room for an evening of fellowship and singing.[2] They sang the classic hymns of the faith, but no doubt also sang hymns penned by Van DeVenter, such as "I Wandered in the Shades of Night," which was later renamed "Sunlight." But perhaps no hymn had more import than the one Van DeVenter wrote reflecting on his own surrender to the call of God to become an evangelist:

> *All to Jesus I surrender,*
> *All to Him I freely give.*
> *I will ever love and trust Him,*
> *In His presence daily live.*
> *I surrender all;*
> *I surrender all;*
> *All to Thee, my blessed Savior;*
> *I surrender all.*

In early 1938, Billy's own surrender to the call on his life had not yet come.

⇥

As a result of being saturated with the Word of God in classes and at chapel, Billy was growing spiritually. Even so, his priorities were still driven, not by the call of God on his life, but by his love of life, sports, and girls. The influence of sports in his life waned during his first year in Florida, but his love of girls did not.

As Billy became increasingly infatuated with Emily Cavanaugh, he spent as much time with her as he could. One of the first signs that Billy was perhaps moving a little faster than Emily desired came after he wrote to her proposing marriage in the summer of his first year at the Institute. Emily was not as confident of the relationship, and she was uncomfortable with the speed at which it was progressing. She asked for more time to consider the proposal. Billy could only wait—and hope.

It was several months before Emily told Billy that she was warming to the idea of marriage. The two had attended an African-American church together, and afterward she intimated that she was perhaps willing to marry him. He took this as more or less a full-fledged engagement, though he did not have a ring for her. His expectations and assumptions again ran wild. Emily's commitment, however, was more tentative.

While his relationship with Emily seemed to be progressing, Billy began to get more opportunities to grow in his preaching. He continued to go with groups of students to the streets of Sulphur Springs, and he preached occasionally at local churches. In addition to these regular opportunities, he held one of his first series of meetings at the Hope Mission in downtown Tampa over New Year's 1938. The mission was run by Carl H. Corwin, whose wife taught Spanish at the Institute.

One significant aspect of these meetings was that they were followed by conversations in Spanish led by another student. The city of Tampa was filled with Hispanic immigrants from Cuba and other nearby nations, so Spanish was an important ministry tool to reach the lost—especially at Hope Mission. These early meetings were among the first where Billy Graham needed to cross a linguistic barrier, and they reinforced within him the vision to reach the lost through any godly means.

Another important milestone for these meetings was that they were among the first ones that Billy actively promoted. He did this by printing flyers to be posted and handed out—a method he would continue to employ for much of his ministry.

Billy, of course, was not the only one of his contemporaries to use flyers to promote a preaching event. Indeed, the practice was quite common. Billy's mentor, John Minder, had been using flyers for many years to promote his evangelistic meetings. A Minder flyer from 1930 shows the structure, and even some of the language, that Billy replicated and adapted for his own flyers during the early years of his ministry. The Minder flyer, which included a picture of the preacher and information on the meeting time and location, had an eye-catching headline:

HAVE YOU HEARD THE
Minder Evangelistic Party
Sane, Sound, Spiritual, Soul Stirring Sermons
INSPIRING MUSIC[3]

Billy's flyer for the Hope Mission meetings was more rudimentary than Minder's flyers, but his confidence in the method of advertising would only grow, as would his confidence in promoting himself in order to reach more people for the Gospel of Jesus Christ.

Two regular ministry opportunities opened up for Billy in the winter and spring of 1938. The first was at the Tin Can Trailer Park, one of Tampa's largest trailer parks. Because of Tampa's warm winter climate, wealthy tourists from the north came, not only to stay in the area's hotels and resorts, but also to stay in their own parked trailers. In fact, such an influx of tourists came to Florida cities with their trailers that municipalities built parks and facilities to accommodate them. Many of the trailers were made of shiny tin and were aptly referred to as "tin cans." The yearly gatherings thus became known as "tin can conventions." The large parks, such as the one where Billy ministered, included recreational facilities, which Billy used for Sunday services. At the request of two women who had a vision for reaching the mobile crowd, Billy became the chaplain of the park and preached to groups of up to two hundred people from among the thousand or so trailers that descended on the area from around the country.[4]

As Billy's preaching ministry grew, his reports of the success of some of his meetings grew beyond the truth. At one point, he felt compelled to confess the fault to W. T. Watson, the president of the Florida Bible Institute. "Dr. Watson," Billy said in the privacy of the president's office, "I have been exaggerating the numbers of people who have been coming to hear me preach." Watson, for his part, tried to take Billy's confession seriously, but he had to fight the urge to burst out laughing. Billy was not the first, nor would he be the last, preacher to struggle with numbers inflation. Despite being tickled by Billy's pang of conscience, Dr. Watson knew the severity of all sin. So he collected himself and said tenderly, "Let's pray that the Lord would give you victory over this sin." They prayed over the issue, and Billy was able to leave with some relief.[5]

Billy's second regular ministry opportunity came through John Minder. In the summer of 1937, the Tampa Gospel Tabernacle was in a crisis. Finances were tight with a large building debt, and the pastor, W. E. King, had resigned in order to hold evangelistic meetings.[6] The church brought in a former missionary to South America and Spain, F. David Sholin, to serve as interim pastor. Finally, in November 1938, they asked Minder to return to the pastorate of the struggling church.

Minder brought not only his leadership experience, but also the excitement and fresh vigor of students from the Florida Bible Institute. He asked Billy to head up the Young People's group at the church, and Billy responded by teaching Bible classes on Sunday mornings—which he advertised as "Fundamental! Inspirational! Interesting!"[7]—and holding services on Sunday nights with the help of some of the other students, including his girlfriend, Emily Cavanaugh. This opportunity gave Billy not only ministry experience, but also a chance to spend time with Emily. Often, to Billy's delight, the group of students went to Emily's family's home for dinner before the evening meeting.[8]

It was also during this time that Billy felt compelled to be baptized as an adult—not as a repudiation of his infant baptism from his Presbyterian upbringing, but perhaps because of the expectation that Christian and Missionary Alliance ministers be baptized as believers.

Soon after Billy became the leader of the Young People's group, Minder asked him to preach at one of the regular services. After his first humbling experience at Bostwick, Billy was determined not to be caught flat-footed. Even though he knew he needed to be ready, he still wasn't sure exactly how to prepare. He talked to his friend Woodrow Flynn about his problem. Flynn gave Billy a sermon from Daniel 5 on Belshazzar's feast. Billy studied the sermon, made some changes, and preached it with much more ease than when he had preached at Bostwick. And indeed, he would preach from that sermon text dozens of times over the next ten years.

Though he was able to preach the sermon with more ease, he could not get too prideful just yet. As Graham recorded in his autobiography, when he came to the Aramaic handwriting on the wall, "*Mene, Mene, Tekel, Upharsin*," it came out of his mouth, "Meany, Meany, Tickle, Upjohn."[9] This amused his friends, who continued to tease him about it later.

On another preaching occasion at a different church, Billy was trying to grow in his dramatic effect as a preacher. As he warmed to the topic of the ancient world's wait for the Messiah, he yelled out:

"A thousand years went by, and no Christ!"

After pausing for dramatic effect, he added: "Two thousand years rolled by, and no Christ!"

Again he paused for dramatic effect.

After adding several thousand more years to his chronology, he heard his friend Wendell whisper from behind him on the platform: "Shut up!"

Billy was angry and asked Wendell about it after the service. Wendell told him that Bishop Ussher's chronology of the Bible put the age of the earth at six thousand years—in contrast to the millions of years espoused by evolutionists—and this was becoming an indubitable fact within fundamentalist circles. Billy had been working his way up to at least ten thousand years.[10] This experience was a good reminder for the young preacher to temper his dramatic effect with biblical and theological accuracy.

Billy also learned another important lesson in his early church preaching, thanks to the guidance and wisdom of his new mentor, John Minder. Billy had received an honorarium for preaching at a church and felt guilty. Getting paid to preach the Gospel seemed fundamentally wrong to him. For a couple of days, he kept the money in an envelope and would not touch it, but then he talked to Minder about it.[11]

Minder knew quite a bit about money and ministry. Twenty years earlier, when he had told his father that he was going to enter the ministry, his father had replied that he thought he was making a big mistake, because preachers don't make much money.[12] This proved to be true for Minder, who never drew a salary but instead depended on the Lord to provide through the meager offerings and gifts that Minder received from preaching. But receiving some pay for ministry was the only way one could live and remain in full-time ministry.

Whether or not Minder shared these experiences with Billy is not certain, but he did point the struggling young preacher to 1 Corinthians 9, which contains Paul's defense of ministers being paid for their service. The wise counselor shared Paul's concluding words on the matter: "Do ye not know that they which minister about holy things live of the things of the temple? and they which wait at the altar are partakers with the altar? Even so hath the Lord ordained that they which preach the gospel should live of the gospel."[13] With this scriptural guidance, Minder gave Billy a firm theological foundation on which to build his views on money in ministry.

Billy's work at the Tampa Gospel Tabernacle opened up doors outside of the church and helped him make connections within the Christian and Missionary Alliance as well. He teamed up with two other evangelists—Florida Bible Institute graduate Steve Cloud and Norman Vernon of the Chattanooga Bible Institute—for Interdenominational Evangelist Tent Meetings on March 5, 1938. These were Billy's first cooperative, interdenominational meetings, and they furthered Billy's understanding of advertising and promotion, with flyers that read, "See! Hear! Enjoy! These three young men with a burning message and their powerful appeal for Christian Living in Tampa."[14] This advertisement established a pattern for future promotions.

By the summer of 1938, the Tampa Gospel Tabernacle was

getting back on course under John Minder's leadership, and the fifty-member Young People's group had been much encouraged under Billy's leadership.[15] Billy was most certainly growing as a preacher as he gained experience, but the winter and spring of 1938 would teach him the greatest lesson he would ever learn—in a very painful way.

Looking at all of the preaching and ministry opportunities Billy had in his first year and a half at the Institute, one would be tempted to believe that he had taken off as a preacher and that there were no obstacles in his way to becoming world famous. But that would overlook two important facts. First, Billy was certainly a naturally gifted and charismatic person, but the frequency of his preaching was typical of any male student at the Institute. Not only were ministry opportunities encouraged for all students, but many times they were provided. Second, though the Lord had already chosen Billy for service long before Billy even considered ministry, Billy had not yet committed himself fully and unequivocally to the task of preaching the Gospel. His interests were, by his own admission, divided.

One competing interest was his relationship with Emily Cavanaugh, but this came to a crumbling halt in May 1938.

Almost from the outset, their relationship had an uncertainty about it. Emily's reply to Billy's proposal in the summer of 1938 was delayed, and her acceptance later that fall was tepid. But there were other indications of trouble as well.

Though Emily was attracted to Billy's charisma and energy, his energy at times expressed itself in seemingly immature ways. He was a cut-up and often played practical jokes. On one occasion, Billy was involved with some other students in putting a skunk pelt in the room of a student who had dished out his share of practical jokes. The student was not amused, however, and reported the incident to the supervisor, who called the rest of the students to find out who the perpetrator had been. Billy was quick to confess—in fact, the only one to confess.[16]

For Emily, stunts like these raised questions about the seriousness and direction of her boyfriend's life. But even if she had legitimate concerns about his maturity, there were also aspects of Billy's personality that she might have seen as positive qualities but didn't exactly appreciate. When Billy's friend Roy Gustafson left the Florida Bible Institute for Asbury Theological Seminary, he did not have many nice suits to take with him. His parents had died tragically shortly after he arrived at the Institute, and he had few financial resources.[17] Billy was an extremely generous individual—almost to a fault. When he saw his friend in need, he gave him two suits. Emily, for reasons that are unclear, was not exactly pleased.[18]

Billy picked up on the mixed signals, and it was confusing for him. One day he would come up to Roy and say, "Oh! Roy. I know I am in love!" But the very next day, he would say, "I'm just not sure."[19]

Billy's relationship problems with Emily came to a head in May 1938 at the end-of-the-year school banquet. The men would typically get corsages for their dates, and Billy spent extra money on a nicer, bigger corsage for Emily, believing she deserved the best.[20]

Later that evening, a confrontation occurred when Billy saw Emily without the corsage, which led them to have a talk on the school swing. There, Emily broke the news to him: she thought it would be better if they didn't date for a while. If the Lord wanted them to be a couple, He would bring them back together.

Through the years, and through many reports about the relationship, there have been numerous contradictory explanations for why Emily broke up with Billy. Some suggest it was because Billy was not serious enough about his call to ministry. Others adamantly deny that claim. Still others, including Billy himself, suggest that

Emily left him to be with classmate Charles Massey, whom she went on to marry. Others sternly reject this view, saying that it was only later that Emily and Charles began dating.

Discerning the reasons for love and breakups is a tricky business. The fact of the matter is that Billy wanted the relationship and Emily did not. God had other partners for both of them. Emily married Charles Massey and lived happily with him for the rest of her life. Billy needed to find someone who could endure his extraordinarily hectic life. But these future hopes were unseen to the heartbroken nineteen-year-old. Billy and Emily were broken up—amicably, thanks to Billy's graciousness—never to be together again.

That night, Billy turned to the only person he could for help— his mentor and friend John Minder. Minder spent most of that night with Billy as the young man wept, pouring out his heart as he sought direction in interpreting what had happened. Minder patiently listened and encouraged Billy, leaving him that night with these words from scripture: "Blessed be the Father of mercies, and the God of all comfort; who comforteth us in our affliction, that we may be able to comfort them that are in any affliction, through the comfort wherewith we ourselves are comforted."[21]

Even with Minder's kind and much-appreciated counsel, the pain did not go away. Billy wrote to his friend Wendell Phillips in dramatic hyperbole, "All the stars have fallen out of my sky. There is nothing to live for. We have broken up."[22]

The school year ended, but the turmoil had just begun. Billy became extremely contemplative in the coming weeks, taking long walks, filled with prayer, through the golf course. In his prayers, he struggled at first with why this had happened to him, but later he began to learn more about what the Lord wanted from him. The Lord wanted him to preach and to commit himself fully to the task. But Billy did not want to preach.[23]

One late, moonlit night, Billy finished one of his long golf course walks, during which he had been "arguing with the Lord."

"I can't preach. . . .I don't want to preach. . . .No church would have me," he cried out.

But the Lord "talked right back." *I can use you. . . .I need you . . . .You make the choice, I will find the place."*[24]

As Billy made his way back to the school, he stopped on the eighteenth green, which approached the main campus building. Tears welled up in his eyes as he fought with the Lord. He knelt and then prostrated himself as tears rolled down his cheeks. He cried out, "Lord, I'll go wherever you want me to go, and I'll preach wherever you want me to preach."[25]

Later, he wrote a letter to Wendell Phillips: "I have settled it once and for all with the Lord. No girl or friend or anything shall ever come first in my life. I have resolved that the Lord Jesus Christ shall have all of me. I care not what the future holds. I have determined to follow Him at any cost."[26]

Billy Graham had surrendered all.[27]

CHAPTER 8

FIRE IN HIS BONES

*"I seemed to hear a voice within me,
telling me that one day there would be many."*
BILLY GRAHAM

After Billy committed himself fully to the Lord to preach the Gospel, he expected to be flooded immediately with preaching opportunities. The opportunities, however, were a long time in coming—at least to the mind of a zealous young man ready to put his gifts to use. His wait would be weeks or months, rather than years, but the impatience exhibited in his life at this time demonstrates an urgency placed within his heart—a fire shut up in his bones, to use the language of the biblical prophet Jeremiah.[1] This fire continued to smolder as the Lord prepared His servant for the task ahead.

While the Lord was preparing him for the ministry, Billy did not sit idle. He began preparing himself. He was determined, of course, not to embarrass himself again in the pulpit, as he felt he had at Bostwick and with his other early preaching gaffes. But now there was another driving factor in his life. He was determined to please the Lord and to reach the lost. How could he most effectively communicate the truth of the Gospel of Jesus Christ to those who were in need of it?

Lacking the opportunity to preach, but wanting to prepare for the day when the opportunity would come, Billy gave himself over to practicing his sermons. He continued this exercise for the next few years—to the point of being obsessive in the eyes of some.[2] He was driven in part by the belief—as he had been taught by one of his preaching mentors—that any sermon worth preaching should be practiced at least twenty-five times.[3] But even Billy would later wonder if he had practiced too much.

Most of Billy's practicing was done outside, out of earshot of his peers. The serene environment of the Hillsborough River, which ran by campus, was one of his favorite spots to practice. He would find a spot on the bank of the river, lay his Bible and sermon on a cypress tree stump—sort of a makeshift pulpit—memorize a paragraph or two, and then preach it, all the while working on his diction, cadence, and mannerisms.[4] Other times, he paddled a canoe to a nearby island on the river to preach, or wandered through the Temple Terrace golf course.

Though he sought isolation to practice his sermons, his booming voice was bound to be heard by others. Local fishermen on the river looked in bewilderment as they heard him preaching, probably worried that this overly zealous preacher was scaring away their fish.

Besides preaching on the Hillsborough River, Billy sometimes practiced in the school auditorium. From time to time, the school janitor would be there cleaning while Billy practiced. Billy would stop mid-sermon and say, "Well, how was that?" The janitor replied with only a shrug and a grunt—not exactly the most encouraging response.[5]

Several of Billy's peers remember hearing him preach a little closer to campus, behind the school garage. Most thought he might be "going too far" in his practicing.[6] It was certainly an extraordinary habit—but then again, the students did not yet realize that Billy was going to be an extraordinary preacher. They would tease him when they caught him in the act of preaching to trees and animals, "Got any converts yet, Billy?"[7]

All his practicing of sermons raised important questions that would continue to be asked for years to come—especially in regard to the crafting of his diction, cadence, and mannerisms. There is always a danger of using technique as a manipulative tool—a dilemma that came to the forefront with his friend Charles Templeton in their Youth for Christ ministry a decade later. In later years, Billy defended himself against accusations of manipulative stagecraft: "If God expects me to give thought to what's in my sermons, as I know He does, isn't it likely He expects me to give some thought as to *how* to deliver them?"[8] Billy gave extraordinary thought to both the content and the delivery of his sermons.

Even as Billy came into his own as a preacher during his time at the Florida Bible Institute, he did not alter his fun-loving, cutting-up nature. At one point, Dr. Watson's four-year-old son, Bobby, was in the men's dormitory with the students. When Dr. Watson came looking for him, he found Bobby in Billy's room, propped up on a dresser, with Billy shaking his finger, mock preaching at him.[9] Bobby was quite amused by the playful young preacher.

Bobby grew in his affection for Billy. Many of the other students ignored the young boy, or found him a nuisance. But Billy showed a real interest in him, which would forever endear him to Bobby.[10] One day, when the Watsons needed help moving into a new home, Billy volunteered his services. As he played with Bobby during a lull in the moving process, Mrs. Watson called out, "Billy! Where are you?" When she came looking for him, Billy and Bobby hid together behind the door, until Mrs. Watson finally came into the room.

Then they popped out from behind the door and once again began to help.[11] This concern for and interest in the young, as well as the overlooked, continued throughout Billy's ministry.

⊹═

Even though most of Billy's sermon practice was done in isolation, his sermon crafting was often done in consultation with others. Whether it was the school secretary, who typed as he dictated, or his evangelist friend Jimmie Johnson, or roommates or other classmates, Billy always wanted the input of others on his sermons. When he was not using the outlines his friends gave him and making them his own, he was sharing his outlines with others, trying to craft a respectable sermon. Many have attested to being a part of this process, but they also suggest that their help was minor.[12] It was almost as if Billy just needed to talk though his sermons with others in order to work through them in his own mind.

⊹═

Billy spent the summer of 1938 in Temple Terrace, hoping to find ministry opportunities. He applied to churches, but none were interested in the young, inexperienced preacher. At a loss for how to proceed, he had to make his own opportunities. He went to downtown Tampa on Franklin and Fortune Streets to hold a prayer meeting in front of a local bar. The owner of the bar was not pleased to have a preacher driving away customers from his business, so he came out and demanded that Billy leave. When Billy refused, the owner pushed the lanky youth to the ground, scuffing some of his clothes. Rather than being disheartened by the experience, Billy was encouraged and grew in boldness. Indeed, he felt he was "suffering for Christ's sake."[13]

Billy waited and prayed for a time when he would finally be invited to preach. Until then, he prepared himself to be "a workman who does not need to be ashamed" (see 2 Timothy 2:15). Through the biblical and theological foundation established for Billy at the Florida Bible Institute, he learned to love the Bible—a love he has maintained throughout his life.

This love of scripture was a fulfillment of Dr. Watson's vision for the school. He wanted the students to be "saturated" with the Word of God.[14] And saturated they were. The curriculum was crafted for the purpose of teaching students how to study the Bible and then prepare to preach or teach scripture. The school unequivocally taught that the Bible is not just the inspired Word of God but is also inerrant in all that it teaches and in its historical descriptions. The faculty taught that the Bible could be trusted—indeed, that it *must* be trusted. The students were able to take this teaching and confidently enter into pulpits, certain of what they were preaching. Their interpretations, of course, were not infallible, but the Word of God was undoubted.

However, Dr. Watson was skeptical of overly academic training for a preacher. More important to Watson than education was the infilling presence and power of the Holy Spirit.[15] He had seen too many preachers enter into seminary, become educated, and lose their "edge"[16]—perhaps as a result of trusting in their learning or their degrees instead of in the Holy Spirit. As a result, Watson believed that learning Greek and Hebrew, the major languages of the Bible, was not necessary. Lexicons and concordances, if used correctly, could do enough for the preacher.[17] So the biblical languages, which Watson himself did not know, were not taught at the Institute.

Billy soaked up all he could learn about scripture while at the Institute. His foundation would be shaken in later years when he ministered with Charles Templeton, but it would always remain intact. As he began to fully trust in the full inspiration of scripture, Billy later said in reference to his Bible training at the Institute, "It became a rapier and a sword in my hand that I have used as a hammer as well as a sword to break open the hearts of men and to direct them to the Lord Jesus Christ."[18]

In addition to gaining a scriptural foundation, Billy also gained a theological foundation while at the Institute. A notebook of his from that period demonstrates a systematic theology that biblically examines all the major doctrines of the faith.[19] Billy's underlining and notes indicate his growing interest in biblical themes and topics. In particular, sections on sin and redemption are replete with underlining and notes, which clearly became the primary subjects of his evangelistic preaching.

Billy picked up other themes that he would later funnel to the rest of the world through his preaching and book writing. His view of the end times was shaped at the Institute, as well as his concern for the Church. But even as he was becoming associated with the Christian and Missionary Alliance—a movement that holds Christ as (physical) healer as one of its four pillars—his learning was tempered by a cautious, though open, view of the gifts of the Holy Spirit. Concerning questions about the gift of tongues, which came to the forefront through the explosion of the Pentecostal movement, Billy was impressed by one of his teachers who advised, "Seek not; forbid not."[20]

This biblical and theological foundation was not just to be absorbed, but also to be preached. And during this time at the Institute, Billy was taught important fundamentals of preaching. Mentor John Minder, who taught one of Billy's preaching classes, had a simple, three-pronged approach to preaching that influenced Billy.[21] First, according to Minder, a preacher must *know his subject*—the biblical text or doctrine being preached. Not knowing the subject, Minder believed, led to "half-baked sermons."[22] Second, the preacher must *believe his message*. Minder thought that believing partway or with reservations was fine for essay writing; but in preaching, you must believe fully what you preach. Finally, Minder taught that a preacher must *preach with conviction*. "If there's no fire in the preacher," Minder believed, "there's likely to be none kindled in the people."[23]

Billy followed Minder's simple approach and philosophy to a tee. Though he always lamented the fact that he did not know enough about scripture, he consistently strove to learn more through study in order to know about what he was preaching. As for the second and third prongs, few would ever doubt the sincerity of Billy's beliefs about what he preached, made certain by the way that he preached with absolute conviction, particularly early in his ministry.

Beyond his views on preaching, Minder's views on evangelism also filtered down into the ministry of Billy Graham. We get a peek into Minder's thinking on the subject later in his life, when he writes, "The major weakness of modern-day evangelism is the failure to tell the seeker how to be saved and how to have a vital personal relationship with Christ."[24] These two aspects—the offer of a clear road to salvation and the discipleship of believers—became central to Billy's lifelong ministry.

⊣⊨

The preparation that Billy gained during his time at the Florida Bible Institute put his life and ministry on a firm foundation of scriptural faith, which would be tested but never destroyed. And in the summer of 1938, after committing himself to preach the Gospel, Billy waited for preaching opportunities for the last time. His ministry was about to take off.

His first post-commitment preaching opportunity came one Saturday while he was out mowing the Institute lawn. Carl Corwin, the leader of the Hope Mission in Tampa, where Billy had preached his first series of meetings the previous winter, pulled into the drive. Knowing that Corwin might be looking for a preacher for that evening's services, Billy ducked behind a bush, knelt down, and began to pray that Mr. Corwin would ask him to preach. When Billy got up from his knees, he was delighted to find that the mission director had indeed come to invite him. That night, when Billy preached to the two dozen or so young people in attendance, it went well enough that he was invited back the next Saturday and many times after that. Finally, the burden for preaching that had been swelling up within him had found an outlet, and the floodgates were about to open for this young preacher who was called to be a harvester of souls.

Billy's first church preaching assignment after his surrender was scheduled for mid-August at Capitola Baptist Church just outside Tallahassee. The small church was pastored by twenty-two-year-old A. V. Pickern Jr., and Billy was ready to heavily promote the meeting with flyers that he had printed for the occasion, just as he had for the Hope Mission meetings the previous winter. The flyers incorporated some of the same elements from the mission meetings, but also drew upon his interdenominational tent meeting with the C&MA. "HAVE YOU HEARD the Young Man with A Burning Message?" the flyer blared. Billy was growing bolder in his promotion, and indeed confident in his identity. He was now "EVANGELIST BILLY GRAHAM."[25]

Billy was so excited about the meeting that he sent one of the flyers to his longtime friend Grady Wilson, who was still a student at Bob Jones College, and with whom he had maintained contact throughout these years. On the back of the flyer, he wrote, "Big Baptist church in the capital of Florida. Pray for me." However, even though Billy had already arranged for the promotion of the event—having hundreds of flyers printed for a church smaller than his overblown expectations—the meeting was canceled unexpectedly when A. V. Pickern abruptly left the church on the meeting date.[26] It was a fitting end to a discouraging but formative summer.

As Billy waited, he prepared by faith for the task of preaching, to which he knew he'd been called. His studies, his preparation, his practice—all would prove fruitful in the end. But even during this time, Billy was given a prophetic vision for things to come. One morning, as he preached outdoors to the trees, to the birds, to the insects, and to the creatures of the river, his voice reverberated as he called out loudly for sinners to come forward and repent. There was, of course, no one to respond. But as he waited, Billy later recalled, "I seemed to hear a voice within me telling me that one day there would be many."[27]

CHAPTER 9

A BURNING MESSAGE

*"Lord, I do not want to be a great preacher,
but I do want to be a great soul winner."*
BILLY GRAHAM

The summer of 1938 was a trying time for Billy. His heart had been broken, he was wrestling with the Lord, and his ministry was slow to take off after he had finally committed himself fully to preaching the Gospel. But the Lord was preparing to open up doors for him that would confirm the calling on his life. Indeed, ever since Billy had surrendered himself in obedience to God, the Lord was strongly supporting him.

Dr. Watson and John Minder encouraged Billy to preach wherever, and whenever, possible.[1] And when Billy was invited to preach, he took every opportunity.[2] Indeed, there was always a message burning in his soul.[3]

Even though Billy worked hard to refine himself as a preacher—spending countless hours preparing and practicing sermons—his concern was never to be a great pulpiteer. One of his late-night prayers illustrates his deep passion: "Lord, I do not want to be a great preacher, but I do want to be a great soul winner."[4]

In the fall, Billy continued with his work at the Tampa Gospel Tabernacle, but his main drive was toward evangelistic meetings, where he began to see some fruit for his labors. He was invited by the father of one of his classmates to preach at Venice Baptist Church on the Gulf Coast in Venice, Florida, some eighty miles south of Temple Terrace. For a song leader, the young evangelist took along his classmate Ponzi Pennington, a gifted singer with whom Billy would minister in several meetings over the coming months and years.

On the day of the service, Billy and Ponzi had the afternoon free before the evening meeting, so they decided to devote themselves to prayer. The small church met in a converted meat market, and the service drew about eighty-five people. To the delight and surprise of the two young evangelists from the Institute, thirty-two responded to the invitation to "commit their lives to Christ."[5] Billy was becoming convinced, not of his ability to preach, but of the effectiveness and necessity of prayer.[6] He had seen the miraculous working of prayer in the provision of ten thousand dollars for the Florida Bible Institute more than a year before, and now he was seeing a miracle of a different kind—the salvation of many souls through his preaching.

The Lord continued to use Billy as he began his first whirlwind of meetings in Putnam County in north central Florida—the region where he had preached his first sermon at Bostwick. The Reverend Cecil Underwood, John Minder's friend from Palatka, had arranged some meetings for Billy, the first of which was at Peniel Baptist Church, where Underwood was pastor. Peniel (which, for locals, rhymes with *denial*) was Billy's launching pad to other churches in the region and became an important church in his early ministry.

Billy was not the only young preacher to hold meetings in the area. Earlier, Institute graduates Roy Gustafson, Howard Street, and Howard Rich had held a month-long revival campaign at Peniel with great success.[7] By and large, the small country churches in the area warmly received the young, zealous preachers and musicians from the Institute, but Billy in particular began to distinguish himself as an extraordinarily successful evangelist, drawing larger crowds and seeing many commitments.[8] He was touted by Cecil Underwood in the local paper as "a young preacher of unusual ability" and was "in great demand during the summer vacation period."[9] (This last claim might be an embellishment of the reality.) Very early on, it was becoming clear that Billy was unusually anointed.

While Billy ministered at Peniel, he met a young lady named Irene McManus, a recent high school graduate who was struggling with her identity and purpose. She loved children and served her church as an organist and piano player, but like many new graduates, she struggled with God's call on her life. But more than that, Irene had been a bit of a misfit from early on in her life.

At the age of two, she had contracted polio—a crippling disease that affected millions of children in the United States during the first half of the twentieth century. She survived the potentially deadly disease but had to learn how to walk using leg braces, which she wore through several years of school before finally shedding them in early adolescence. Still, she lived with a pronounced physical disability for the rest of her life.[10]

Though Irene was uncertain of herself and her own abilities, Billy instantly put her at ease and began to encourage her to use her gifts and passions in service to the Lord. In particular, she had a passion for children and for teaching them the Bible. She used her gifts as an organist and piano player when she went with Billy to some of the surrounding churches. As he got to know her, he encouraged her to begin studying at the Florida Bible Institute.

Irene immediately objected to the idea. Her family was poor and had been hit most recently by the dire economic circumstances of the late 1930s. She felt she could never afford the schooling. Still, Billy persisted in encouraging her to go to Bible school. Finally, she agreed to at least explore the possibility, and in faith decided to enroll. When she did, she found that her tuition was paid, though she never learned who covered the costs. She always suspected that Billy was, at the very least, instrumental in working it out.[11]

After Billy preached for a time at Peniel Baptist Church, the Reverend Cecil Underwood and his congregation began to support Billy and arranged for several of his next meetings. The first of these meetings were across the St. John's River at East Palatka Baptist Church. These were important meetings in several ways. First, along with their being his first series of meetings, he also had the opportunity, in the mornings, to speak over the radio in St. Augustine, accompanied by Irene McManus and a women's trio. These meetings were also important to Billy's blossoming ministry because they were covered by the local media—which gave the meetings free publicity, and gives us our first documented glimpse into Billy's early preaching.

The meetings began midweek and were intended to run into the first half of the following week. On Sunday night, in the midst of the revival, Billy was obligated to return to Tampa for his Young People's group meeting at the Tabernacle—an inconvenience that would prove providential.

The first several revival meetings had been dispiriting for Billy for several reasons. First, while in Palatka waiting for the evening meetings, Billy practiced his sermons throughout the day in vacant churches or along the streets. By the time he came to preach in front of people at the church, he had already worn himself out.

Perhaps more discouraging was a persistent disturbance during the meetings. As Billy preached those first few nights, one of the youths who was seated at the back of the church repeatedly interrupted the service with his cutting up. Billy was at a loss for what to do, but after about three nights, he finally decided that if this particular young man acted up again, he would call him out from the pulpit.

That night, when the boy again disrupted the service, Billy stopped and said to him, "You've been disturbing this meeting every night since I've been coming here. Now I want you to stop it, and I want you to stop it right now."[12] Then Billy threatened to physically throw the young man out if it happened again. At that, the son of one of the church leaders got up, shook his fist at Billy, and stormed out of the building.[13] To Billy's relief, the meetings were not interrupted again. But his confidence was shaken. He went home to Tampa on Sunday with doubts about whether to return to East Palatka the next week. He raised his concern with his mentor, John Minder, saying, "Those people don't want to hear me."

Minder encouraged Billy, "You go back. You pray and trust God, and God will honor His Word."[14]

Billy decided to return on Monday night, finish the meetings, and then go to Charlotte with Minder to visit his family and take a little vacation.[15] When he arrived in East Palatka for the evening service, he found that a good-sized crowd had assembled.[16]

Perhaps the size of the crowd had been influenced by the effusive articles about the meetings in the local newspaper. The articles included quotes from Billy's sermons, which reveal the young evangelist's burning message. An article with the headline "Revivalists Hear Tampa Minister" includes this excerpt from Billy's sermon titled "God's Blockade": "The road to Hell is blocked with many godly influences. . . . If you go to Hell, it will be your own deliberate choice as God is [doing] his best to keep you out of there."

Billy continued: "[The person who goes to hell] must climb over the Bible, a mother's influence, and prayer, the Holy Spirit, the mountain of reason, and the cross of Christ."[17]

The young evangelist's preaching often included prophetic boldness. After a message in which Billy warned that church members were "headed for the same hell as bootleggers and racketeers unless they get right and live right," the local newspaper reported that "young Graham does not mince words."[18]

Billy continued with his forceful approach, asserting that the Church had "nothing to offer the average citizen" because it was filled with people who cared "no more for God than the devil himself." Then he laid out the same vision for the Church that he would maintain—if not in message, then in practice—for the rest of his ministry. He concluded that the Church is the beginning and the end of the evangelistic task.

This vision demonstrates his passion to spiritually revive not just cities, but also the churches, and not to merely cast them off. Billy said, "What we need is a backdoor revival to empty our churches of the unholy element and fill them with people the world can respect; then we will see our churches filled again with people seeking something that will satisfy the longing of their souls."[19]

If the message printed in the local paper did not inspire curiosity in people and bring them to the meetings, then the accounts of those in attendance certainly did. As the paper reported in a separate article: "Old-timers say that last night's meeting in East Palatka was the greatest meeting in the history of the church."[20] Yet another article reinforced the effectiveness of the meetings, claiming that Billy was "causing quite a sensation" at the meetings.[21] Indeed, the crowds were growing, and people were responding to Billy's invitations. In fact, interest in the meetings grew so much that people began to ask Billy to extend the revival.

This raised an issue for Billy. How could he close meetings that God seemed to be using to bring people to himself? On the other hand, he had committed to his family to be home on Thursday. The issue tore at Billy. So he called up his mentor, John Minder.

"Mr. Minder," Billy said, "I don't know what to do!"

"Well, what's the matter now?" Minder asked.

Billy explained the predicament—a markedly different issue than he'd raised just a few days earlier, when he had wanted to quit the meetings.

"These people don't want me to stop. What should I do?"

Minder's response shows an approach to his relationship with Billy that was both wise and empowering.

"Well, that's up to you," Minder replied. "You are of age now, and you have come to a time when you've got to make a decision for yourself. The thing for you to do is pray and see what you feel the Lord wants you to do, and then do it."[22]

Clearly, Billy wanted to extend the meetings, but he felt obligated to be with his family. Minder said, "You've been away from home for over a year now, and I don't think it will bother them very much a day or two either way, especially if they know that you are doing what you feel the Lord wants you to do."[23] With the careful guidance and wisdom of his mentor, Billy decided to extend the meetings and announced that he would be preaching messages titled "Who's Who in Hell," "A Love That Saves," and "The Way to the City."[24]

Meanwhile, the local paper printed still more of Billy's messages, one of which he preached to a "nearly full" church of about 150 people. The sermon, titled "The Old-Fashioned Gospel," included these words:

Some people say that I am old-fashioned because I believe in the old-time religion. Well, maybe so, but it's the old-time gospel that is going to take us to heaven. I would rather go to heaven a little old-fashioned than to hell with all the modern society attached to me. I thank God I stand on the Bible four square and say without apology I believe in the old-time religion. I believe actually what Paul said is true, that only by believing on the Lord Jesus Christ can a man be saved. The world will tell you today that if you join a church, be baptized and quit your bad habits, then you will go to heaven, but my Bible says that there is no name under heaven whereby a man can be saved except through the name of Jesus.[25]

By the last night, the crowds had grown so much that the church was filled to the brim and loudspeakers were placed on the outside of the church.[26] John Minder came up for the last service and sat in the front row with Billy. Before the meeting started, Minder noticed that Billy was squirming.

"What's wrong?"

"Well, I've been telling people I was going to preach on the Second Coming, but I don't have a sermon." All of his sermons had been exhausted, and so was he. So, as the congregational music went on, Billy and his mentor put their heads together and talked through a sermon outline, which Billy then took and preached "like an old soldier."[27]

By the end of the revival meetings, about eighty people had made decisions for Christ—an impressive demonstration to Billy that he was indeed called to evangelism. And many of those people joined East Palatka Baptist Church.[28] Billy also organized a Young People's Club at the church,[29] demonstrating once again his concern for youth as well as his organizational prowess.

In the wake of Billy's East Palatka meetings, and after he had returned from visiting his family, he held meetings fifteen miles south of Palatka, at First Baptist Church of Pomona. The church, at that point, was without a pastor, but one of the church's founders, William Mew, had been diligent to bring in good preachers to fill the pulpit. Having caught wind of the success of the revival meetings in East Palatka, the church brought in Billy to hold meetings there as well.

Billy advertised for these meetings with a new promotional phrase and program. He called it the Eight Great Days of Revival Meetings, a phrase he emblazoned on flyers, inviting the people of Pomona to "hear the dynamic youth evangelist."[30] He brought with him Irene McManus and singers from Peniel's Young People's group; Roy Gustafson, who played the trombone; and classmates from the Institute, including Ponzi Pennington, the friend with whom he had held meetings at Venice Baptist Church.[31]

At Pomona, Billy intentionally included a children's program, holding meetings after school in the school's gym.[32] The children were drawn to him, as he took a genuine interest in them. A few of the girls even had not-so-subtle crushes on him. A little girl named Irene, about five years old, climbed up in Billy's lap as he told her Bible stories. She looked up at him, thinking not so much about the stories, but about how good looking he was—comparable to any movie star in her opinion. She asked him, "Will you marry me?" At the time,

Billy had no girlfriend, so he told her that he would marry her.[33]

Not only did Billy and his group hold meetings for children, but he also held youth meetings every night at 7:00, just before the main service at 7:30. He continued to refine his sermons, which he used again and again.

The meetings were very successful, though the number of decisions is unknown. The revival brought several souls to the Lord and was a "great historical and spiritual event" for the church.[34]

On the last night of the meetings, Institute president W. T. Watson came to hear Billy. At the time, Billy felt that maybe he should extend the meetings. There was one problem with that—classes at the Institute were in session the following day. He spoke with Dr. Watson about it, arguing that the Lord was using him to save souls. It did not make much sense to him to go back to school when souls were being saved. But it seemed to Dr. Watson that Billy had missed enough school, and he convinced the young evangelist to close the meetings.[35]

After Billy returned to the Institute and caught up on some of his studies, he wrote to thank Mr. Mew, whom he called "the sweetest Christian any of us have ever known."[36] In the letter, Billy looks back on the meetings as a time when "the Lord was really with us." He also looks forward to the future day when those who were saved will be gathered around the throne of God, singing "Saved by Grace."[37]

Billy also arranged to return to Pomona—not to preach, but to visit his old roommate, Woodrow Flynn, who, on Billy's recommendation, was going to be Pomona's new pastor.[38]

Even while Billy's message was spreading like wildfire throughout Putnam County, there were still undercurrents of opposition. In particular, there were two issues that raised questions among the

Baptists in the area. First was Billy's age—he was just twenty years old in November 1938. Billy's youthfulness particularly bothered the more seasoned preachers and deacons, who thought they were more qualified to preach than Billy or the other students from the Institute.[39] For this issue, Billy could only abide by 1 Timothy 4:12: "Let no one look down on your youthfulness, but rather in speech, conduct, love, faith and purity, show yourself an example of those who believe."

The second issue was more significant in the eyes of most of the local Baptists: quite simply, Billy was not a Baptist. This concern was raised early in one of his revival meetings when someone asked which Baptist church he belonged to. Billy told them that he had grown up Presbyterian and was currently involved in the Christian and Missionary Alliance—neither of which met the standards for the local Baptists. As a result, Cecil Underwood, pastor at Peniel, encouraged Billy to be baptized by the church and become a Baptist.

This presented a quandary for Billy. He had already been baptized by John Minder, to settle questions in his own mind about the validity of his infant baptism; but now he was being asked to question his adult baptism as well, because it had not been done in the "right" church. In the end, Billy decided that a more important issue was at stake than the effectiveness or validity of his baptism: his sphere of ministry, and therefore the lost souls he might otherwise be able to reach.[40] He decided that if he refused to be baptized, the decision could hinder the work the Lord was clearly doing through him. His decision to be baptized a third time was more a matter of expediency than conviction—a charge that critics would level against him for the rest of his ministry.

Even if expediency was the driving factor in his third baptism, it wasn't as if it violated his convictions, which were already more closely aligned with the minimalist doctrines of the Baptists than with the more polemical beliefs of the Christian and Missionary Alliance. The Baptist tradition, and its Bible-based, non-creedal system (at least explicitly) gave Billy a wider platform within mainstream evangelicalism than the C&MA ever could. Billy found a home in the Baptist tradition that he would retain for life, even while keeping a foot within the Christian and Missionary Alliance.

On December 4, 1938, Billy Graham was baptized at Silver Lake, a few miles from Peniel Baptist Church. He had expected it to be an uneventful act, but it turned out to be a "great spiritual experience,"[41] confirming his decision to become a Baptist.

The baptism was a spiritual blessing for Billy for another reason as well, because a half dozen converts from his meetings were also baptized, a small representation of the eighty people who received Christ in the meetings he had held at Peniel.[42]

After his baptism, Billy hurried back to Temple Terrace to catch up on his schoolwork, which he had been neglecting in the midst of his revival meetings, and which he had to finish before the Christmas holiday.[43]

Unlike his schoolwork, Billy's ministry did not stop for the Christmas vacation. At the New Year, Billy held a meeting at Piney Knob Baptist Church in Rutherfordton, North Carolina. The meeting was advertised in the local paper as featuring Billy Graham, along with "two from Bob Jones."[44]

Billy's family came to hear him preach for the first time. His mother, Morrow Graham, thought he was too young to be preaching to congregations like he was, and when she heard him, she was sweating and nervous about what he was going to say.[45] His sister Catherine thought, like many others in the early days, that Billy spoke "awful loud." After the service, she reproached him, "You are talking as though you were talking to a thousand people."[46]

Billy replied with a smile, "Well, maybe one day I will."[47]

The "awful loud" young man with the burning message returned to Florida for the spring semester with what appeared to be a stronger concentration on his studies, given the lack of revival meetings during that period. But his continued growth as a preacher did not stop. In January 1939, Billy cemented his association with the Baptist tradition by seeking ordination from the St. Johns River Baptist Association to the Gospel ministry at Peniel Baptist Church.

His ordination was opposed by two old-timers who thought he was too young.[48] As a candidate for ordination, Billy was grilled by the ordination council, which was filled by local ministers. After intensive questioning on issues of doctrine, the Bible, and practical ministry, Billy became frustrated with one of the men who seemed determined to discern every little biblical or theological detail lacking in Billy's system of beliefs. Billy finally lost all patience and said, "Brother, you've heard me preach around these parts, and you've seen how the Lord has seen fit to bless. I'm not an expert in theology, but you know what I believe and how I preach, and that should be enough to satisfy you."[49] Fortunately for Billy, the man chuckled and agreed most heartily to ordain him.

Billy Graham was ordained at a service at Peniel Baptist Church. Irene McManus played the piano, and Woodrow Flynn, Billy's friend and the new pastor of Pomona Baptist Church, preached on 2 Timothy 2:3: "Thou therefore endure hardship as a good soldier of Jesus Christ."[50] The local ministers laid hands on Billy, and he was ordained as a Baptist minister, an association he would retain for the rest of his ministry.

CHAPTER 10

JESUS ONLY

"My roots are very deep in [the Christian and Missionary Alliance] and what [it stands] for and what [it] believe[s]."
BILLY GRAHAM

Despite the flurry of revival meetings in 1938, and Billy's baptism and ordination by the Southern Baptist churches of north Florida, most of his ministry opportunities—and certainly the distinctive influences on his life, thought, and spiritual development—between 1938 and 1943 came through the Christian and Missionary Alliance.

When Billy had transferred to the Florida Bible Institute, he stepped into an environment birthed out of the C&MA movement, which was injecting a much-needed shot of evangelistic and missionary vision into the Church in North America. Billy had already picked up on this vision from the evangelistic meetings of Mordecai Ham—and even from Bob Jones and the evangelistic ethos of the 1930s. But the Alliance flooded the mind and heart of the budding young evangelist with its emphasis on deep spirituality exhibited in service to God.

A primary source of this influence came through John Minder

and the C&MA Tampa Gospel Tabernacle, which he had founded to be an evangelistic and spiritual center for Tampa, with no denominational bias. Much like W. T. Watson's vision for the St. Petersburg Tabernacle, Minder's goals were in line with the spirit of the early days of the C&MA.[1]

When Minder returned to the Tabernacle as its pastor in 1937, the church had taken on dangerous levels of debt and had lost some of its initial zeal. Over the next several years, Minder worked to get the church back on a sound financial footing, renew its vision, and renovate the two-thousand-seat, Spanish-style stucco building at Jefferson and Armenia Streets in West Tampa.

Billy's leadership of the fifty-two youths enrolled in the Tabernacle's Young People's group was going well—so well, in fact, that he was named associate pastor and was asked to take over the preaching and pastoral duties when Minder left town for two weeks to attend the C&MA council meeting in Oakland, California. The *Tampa Daily Times* made note of this development with what was perhaps Billy's first newspaper article with his picture.[2] Almost as interesting as his new title of associate pastor is how the young minister was named: W. F. Graham.

The struggle over what to be called was not surprising. He had grown up being called Billy Frank, which in casual circles had been shortened to simply Billy. But this was an age of formality, in the South in particular, and casual was not the norm. Great preachers of the era often used initials for their names, including men within Billy's circle such as R. G. LeTourneau, R. G. Lee, A. B. Winchester, H. C. Morrison, R. E. Neighbour, W. R. Newell, E. J. Pace, R. R. Brown, W. I. McGarvey, H. M. Shuman, and W. B. Riley, as well as the Institute's own W. T. Watson and J. W. Van DeVenter. Even when a preacher was referred to by his first name, it was most often followed by his middle initial.

Furthermore, for the twenty-year-old evangelist, W. F. Graham sounded a bit more dignified than Billy. Billy Sunday had pulled it off, but even that comparison was intimidating to the young Mr. Graham. In the end, the name W. F. Graham would fall by the wayside. But at this early stage, he continued to struggle with different formulations of his name. It wasn't until years later that he finally settled on the name that would be most fitting: Billy Graham.

In addition to the local opportunities within the Christian and Missionary Alliance, Billy began to make statewide, and even regional, connections. Every Labor Day weekend, the Florida State Young People's Association gathered for a rally.[3] In 1938, the rally was held in West Palm Beach. Billy delivered a message in the afternoon and was elected vice president of the association. The following year, he was reelected as vice president during the rally in Tampa and spoke on the afternoon of the first day—not exactly the keynote speaker.[4]

Beyond Florida, Billy traveled with John Minder to Birmingham, Alabama, in October 1939 for the Southeastern District Prayer Conference. Minder had begun his ministry in the city of Ensley, on the outskirts of Birmingham, and Robert Adams, a Birmingham native and Florida Bible Institute graduate, was now the associate pastor of the Birmingham Gospel Tabernacle under Glen Tingley, who had moved the Tabernacle that Minder had started in Ensley to Birmingham. Tingley also directed the Birmingham Bible Institute. The meeting's main guest speaker was H. M. Shuman, president of Nyack Missionary Training Institute and editor of the *Alliance Weekly*. Shuman spoke daily, supplemented by various evening speakers.[5]

In late May and early June 1939, Billy was once again given the opportunity to take over duties for John Minder at the Tampa Gospel Tabernacle when Minder went to St. Paul, Minnesota, for the annual church council. Once again, the *Tampa Daily Times* reported the news, referring to Billy as W. F. Graham. The opportunity to run the church in Minder's absence gave Billy experience, not just in preaching, but also in ministering to the sick in hospitals and in canvassing the neighborhoods. And the interim job came with another perk: access to his mentor's personal library, where Billy immersed himself in the writings of many men who had shaped the life of John Minder.[6]

When John Minder returned to the church, he found what he described as a "mini revival."[7] After one series of meetings at the Tabernacle, Billy wrote a letter to his parents, which read, in part:

> *I preached Sunday night to a larger crowd than usual. Sunday it seemed that heaven opened up and fell on the meeting. Never have I preached with such freedom. Sunday morning five rededicated their lives to the Lord, and Sunday afternoon five grown men made a profession of faith in our blessed Savior. Sunday night, two grown young people found Christ. Several said it was one of the best days the Tabernacle had seen in a long time.[8]*

Later in the letter, Billy added, "God forbid that I should not boast only in Him."[9]

The Tampa Gospel Tabernacle also afforded Billy the opportunity to try his hand at writing. The church published a monthly newsletter called the *Tabernacle Messenger*, which told of events in the church and also included devotional writings. John Minder was never a great writer, though he wrote poetry in private. Still, Minder knew the power of the pen. In one of Billy's earliest published writings, the young associate gave a dramatic description of the conversion of the Philippian jailer in a piece titled "A Midnight Cry." Billy did more than simply describe the events found in Acts 16. He pushed back on the reader with probing questions: "Are you seeking satisfaction? Are there burdens pressing you down? Are there trials too hard to go through alone? Does your conscience hurt you because of sins committed? Jesus Christ is the answer to each of these questions."[10]

In June 1939, the Tampa Gospel Tabernacle celebrated its fifteenth anniversary with a week of services, culminating in the burning of $25,000 worth of bonds to celebrate the retirement of some of the church's vast indebtedness. Julian Bandy, the Tabernacle's original associate pastor, returned after a ten-year absence to serve as a guest speaker. In 1939, Bandy was a minister in Asheville, North Carolina, and was quickly climbing up the ranks of the C&MA.[11] The Reverend R. A. Forrest, president of Toccoa Falls Bible Institute, also spoke at the meetings.[12] Under John Minder's leadership, the Tampa Gospel Tabernacle was climbing out of debt and being spiritually renewed.

In addition to the opportunities that Billy had to pastor the Tampa Gospel Tabernacle for a couple of weeks during the summers when he was attending the Florida Bible Institute, he also spent time at John Minder's Christian and Missionary Alliance camp at Lake Swan in Melrose, Florida. The scenic camp, set on ten lush acres, had somewhat crude buildings and a lake whose waters were cool but not too cold for swimming and boating. Like the Institute, the camp was maintained by students who cooked, did dishes, and cleaned.

Minder founded the camp in 1931, near the church in Melrose that he and Roscoe and Ruth Stull had planted in the early 1920s. Like the Tabernacles he had established, Minder wanted the camp to remain affiliated with the Christian and Missionary Alliance, but he also wanted it to minister across denominational lines. So in addition to hosting yearly Lake Swan Bible Conferences for the C&MA, the camp also hosted groups from other denominations.

During his first two summers at Lake Swan, Billy was not a key speaker. Seasoned preachers, such as John Minder and W. T. Watson, preached to the adults, and upperclassmen from the Institute led the Young People's meetings. Billy went to help in whatever capacity he could—doing dishes, directing youth, and perhaps even speaking to the youth. But just as there was a joyful and free spirit at the Institute, the camp gave the students plenty of opportunity to enjoy themselves—with no homework over their heads but still lots of work to do.

In the summer of 1939—Billy's last summer in Florida—he was in charge of the Young People's group at Lake Swan Bible Conference, which ran from June 25 to July 4, with Ponzi Pennington leading music. The one hundred or so young people in attendance took to Billy's preaching, and by the end of the time, nearly every young person had made a profession of faith.[13]

After the ten-day conference ended, Billy left Lake Swan until the beginning of August. During that time, word began to spread that J. W. Van DeVenter was on his deathbed in Temple Terrace. On July 17, a group of students, faculty, and friends, including Billy, gathered at Van DeVenter's bedside. As the beloved eighty-three-year-old hymn writer lay dying, Billy and the others took turns holding him and offering words of comfort. Finally, while in the arms of his friend W. T. Watson, Van DeVenter entered into the Lord's presence.[14]

Billy returned to Lake Swan for the Baptist Boys Camp and gave morning talks or "Our Bible" drills. In the evening, around the campfire, he delivered a Pathfinders Series, which consisted of biographical sketches of pioneering missionaries such as David Livingstone.[15]

The Christian and Missionary Alliance offered Billy a wonderful opportunity to preach in churches and at conferences and camps. Little did he know that this was just the beginning of a flurry of opportunities.

Beyond Billy's service within the denomination, he was shaped by the theology espoused by the C&MA movement—and, even more important, by the spirituality and evangelical emphasis of its theology.

The C&MA was more a movement than a denomination in the 1930s; it didn't become an official denomination until 1974. Founded in 1898 by Albert B. Simpson, the Alliance rested on four doctrinal pillars, called the Foursquare Gospel.[16] More than mere doctrinal beliefs, these pillars were a genuine impetus for virtually all of the work done within the Alliance. It was also these pillars that distinguished the movement from mainstream evangelical Protestantism, and from which Billy eventually, if not initially, shied away from in his preaching. The Fourfold Gospel holds Christ as Savior, as Sanctifier, as Healer, and as Coming King. The Alliance believed and taught that the fullness of Jesus—and Jesus alone— through the indwelling power of the Holy Spirit was able "to meet and satisfy every need of spirit, soul, and body."[17]

PILLAR ONE: CHRIST AS SAVIOR

Of the four pillars, Christ as Savior was the most palatable to evangelicals. This conviction refers to the penal substitutionary atonement of Christ—that is, that Christ suffered death on the cross in order to pay for people's sins, taking on Himself the punishment deserved by sinful humanity. This view fits within the mainstream of evangelical Protestantism. However, in accepting an Arminian concept of the universality of the Atonement, C&MA founder A. B. Simpson rejected his Presbyterian roots. According to Simpson and members of the Alliance, Jesus Christ was Savior to "whosoever" would receive the Gospel of Jesus Christ by faith. Flowing out of this conviction was the drive to reach the whole world—near and far, rich and (especially) poor—with the good news of salvation, which is found in Christ.

The penal substitutionary view of the Atonement and salvation confirmed what Billy already believed. It was taught by the main proponents of the fundamentalist movement. Though the Arminian elements of the universality of the Atonement certainly rubbed against Billy's Presbyterian upbringing, whatever dissonance he felt about such issues was of secondary importance to the message of substitutionary atonement, which he believed and taught most emphatically as an evangelist.

Pillar Two: Christ as Sanctifier

The second pillar, Christ as Sanctifier, had a more complex bearing on Billy's spiritual formation. According to the Alliance, sanctification is an *event* that happens *after* salvation, rather than instantly at the time of salvation.[18] In other words, even though a person might be saved, or justified, he or she could also have a later experience of sanctification. This meant that even though a person might be saved from hell, he or she must also be delivered from sin. This event, or process, is called *sanctification.*

This notion of subsequent sanctification was extraordinarily controversial. It found its roots in the holiness movement popularized by John Wesley in the eighteenth century and was adopted by most revivalists in the United States, including Charles Finney and D. L. Moody. But by no means were these evangelists' views on sanctification unified, and many holiness advocates veered into rank heresy in their teaching.

To add to the fires of controversy, the advent of the Pentecostal movement in the early twentieth century—influenced in part by the teachings of A. B. Simpson—brought to the forefront a subsequent work of God called "the baptism of the Holy Spirit." The Pentecostal perspective came with an even more controversial claim—that the baptism of the Holy Spirit was *always* marked by speaking in tongues. No teaching aroused more emotional division in the early twentieth century than the Pentecostal doctrine of speaking in tongues.

The Christian and Missionary Alliance, and Simpson himself, never held the teaching that sanctification, or the baptism of the Holy Spirit, was marked by speaking in tongues. Their view of Christ as Sanctifier was that a regenerated believer received the Holy Spirit for two purposes: empowerment for service and for living a life of holiness. This view played out in different ways among members of the Alliance. Some spoke in tongues, while others did not. In general, members of the Alliance were less concerned with the event, or even the experience, of sanctification than they were with the Person of Jesus Christ and His deep and abiding presence in the lives of believers through the Holy Spirit. This was called the Deeper Life.[19]

Billy encountered this issue at the Institute, and how he dealt with it gives insight into his thinking. One evening, he attended a "brush arbor revival meeting," at which the preacher zealously asked individuals in the audience, "Have you been baptized with the Holy Spirit?"

When the preacher turned to Billy and asked, "Young man, have you been baptized with the Holy Spirit?" Billy said, "Yes, sir," just as others had before him.

"*When* were you baptized with the Holy Spirit?" the preacher persisted.

Though none of the others had been asked for such details, Billy responded anyway: "The moment I received Jesus Christ as my Savior." This answer is in stark contrast to C&MA teaching.

"That couldn't be," the perplexed preacher blurted out, before moving on to question others.[20]

This interaction reveals some fissures between Billy and the C&MA. Although the Alliance generally avoided the Pentecostal language of "baptism of the Holy Spirit," the view that sanctification was an event after and separate from justification was at odds with Billy's contention that he had received the baptism of the Holy Spirit at his conversion.

Billy had earnestly sought a "second blessing" for himself during the early years of his ministry.[21] But in later years he roundly rejected the doctrine, which he had come to believe resulted in seeking *experiences* rather than maintaining faithfulness to biblical teaching.[22] But even if he had questions about the Alliance's teaching on sanctification, their emphasis on pursuing holiness and a deeper spiritual life pulsated throughout his views, and the doctrine clearly shaped his deep and zealous spirituality.

PILLAR THREE: CHRIST AS HEALER

The third pillar of the Alliance, Christ as Healer, was held in "strict subordination" to the first two pillars, *salvation* and *holiness*.[23] This explicit subordination allowed members of the Alliance to adopt varying degrees of belief about the doctrine of divine healing. According to C&MA founder A. B. Simpson, the Atonement made physical healing possible, because sickness and disease were the result of Adamic sin, and Christ's death destroyed not only the *spiritual* power and effects of sin, but also the *physical* power and effects of sin. This victory, however, was not universal. Just as salvation must be received by faith, so too must divine healing be received by faith. Though modern Pentecostalism looks to Simpson as a source for its doctrine of the gift of healing, Simpson himself focused his teaching almost entirely on the Source of the healing—Christ Himself—and the subject of the healing: those in need of healing (and their faith).[24]

In Billy's direct experience, his mentor, John Minder, was committed to each of the four pillars in the establishment of the Tampa Gospel Tabernacle, and Minder even attested to miraculous healings within his ministry.[25]

If Billy ever held the Alliance teaching on healing, there is no evidence of it in his preaching or writing. Indeed, in his later writings on the work of the Holy Spirit, he taught that healing could come to one who received the gift of faith for that healing (which is in line with Alliance teaching); but, in contrast to A. B. Simpson, he did not believe that healing was available to all. Sickness, Billy came to believe, could be used by God in ways that health could not, in order to bring glory to God.[26]

By not fully embracing the second and third pillars of C&MA doctrine, Billy perhaps showed one of the underlying reasons for his association with the Baptists rather than with the C&MA.

PILLAR FOUR: CHRIST AS COMING KING

Most emphatically, in his early ministry, Billy adopted as his own the final pillar of the Alliance: Christ as Coming King. Like the third pillar, Christ as Healer, this doctrine was held in subordination to the first two pillars within the Christian and Missionary Alliance. Even so, it is within this doctrine that the evangelistic and missionary impulses of the Alliance rested, because members of the C&MA believed that Christ's return would be preceded by the Gospel being preached throughout the world.

In speaking of Christ as Coming King, this pillar describes the Alliance's hope for the personal, premillennial, and imminent return of Christ. That is, that Christ will return physically (as opposed to just spiritually) to establish His kingdom, and that He could come at *any* time.

This view stands in stark contrast to postmillennialism, which teaches that Christians—the *spiritual* body of Christ—are to usher in the kingdom of God, and then the Lord will physically return. This postmillennial view retains an optimism for the moral potential of humanity and of Christians in particular. Its fullest expression perhaps can be found in the naming of the periodical the *Christian Century*, which was established in 1900 on the belief that the twentieth century would fulfill this utopian vision.

Billy forcefully rejected the *Christian Century* and its optimistic viewpoint, particularly in his founding of *Christianity Today*, which countered the *Christian Century*'s liberal vision.

Most early-twentieth-century fundamentalists accepted the doctrine of the premillennial return of Christ—shaped most markedly by the influence of John Nelson Darby and Cyrus Ingerson Scofield, who countered the thinking of the previous century, in which postmillennialism had reigned. Darby and Scofield captured the minds and hearts of those in the fundamentalist movement and brought the end times to the forefront of believers' thoughts for the twentieth century.

If postmillennialists have an optimistic view of humanity, then premillennialists have a pessimistic one, believing that this world is growing increasingly evil and can only be redeemed by the physical return of the King, the Lord Jesus Christ. This return will be the glorious culmination of human history, and the day for which premillennialists long, when they will meet their King.

Virtually all premillennialists believe that the return of Christ is imminent, but A. B. Simpson taught emphatically that the scriptures lay out *conditions* for that return, the most important of which flowed from his interpretation of Matthew 24:14 (KJV): "This gospel of the kingdom shall be preached in all the world for a witness unto all nations; and then shall the end come."

Simpson and the C&MA taught that Jesus would not return

until Christians had reached the entire world with the preaching of the Gospel—the *evangelization* of the world. Though not entirely unique to the C&MA, this teaching became the linchpin of Alliance teaching and was the driving force behind its zealous missionary and evangelistic impulse. This emphasis so deeply penetrated Billy's thinking that, for a time in his early ministry, he believed that the entire world would receive the Gospel of Jesus Christ—a view that went beyond evangelization of the world to worldwide acceptance of it. He later rejected this view as bad theology.[27]

Beyond the Fourfold Gospel, there were other significant ways in which the Alliance influenced Billy. Nyack Missionary Training Institute, the C&MA's flagship school, had served as a loose model for the Florida Bible Institute; and the Tampa Gospel Tabernacle and St. Petersburg Tabernacle, founded by John Minder and W. T. Watson respectively, were outflows of A. B. Simpson's New York Gospel Tabernacle. Also, the *Alliance Weekly*, the periodical of the C&MA, was a rich magazine that not only spread its theological viewpoint, but certainly impressed Billy with the power of the pen. Indeed, Billy used the periodical at least once in the next few years to report on an event where God had worked powerfully.[28]

Though Billy could not wholeheartedly accept everything within the C&MA's doctrine, this was more than made up for by the precious spirituality he learned and the godly mentors and friends he made within the Alliance. Indeed, within the movement he encountered a unique set of people who were absolutely and completely set apart for service for the Lord and who were committed exclusively and exhaustively to evangelism and missions.

As Billy would later attest, his spiritual roots were deeply entwined with what the C&MA taught and believed and with what those beliefs led to—namely, an unquenchable evangelistic impulse.[29] The

Alliance's Christ-centered theology left an indelible imprint on Billy's heart.

> *Jesus only is our message,*
> *Jesus all our theme shall be;*
> *We will lift up Jesus ever,*
> *Jesus only we will see.*
> *Jesus only, Jesus ever,*
> *Jesus all in all we sing,*
> *Saviour, Sanctifier, and Healer,*
> *Glorious Lord and Coming King.*
> A. B. SIMPSON

CHAPTER 11

AT THE FEET OF GIANTS

"Oh, if someday I could be a great preacher like him!"
BILLY GRAHAM

The Florida Bible Institute enveloped Billy in an atmosphere of the best of American evangelicalism. W. T. Watson, John Minder, J. W. Van DeVenter, and other members of the faculty were invested in Billy, and he was deeply shaped by the Christian movements at the time, which at their core were concerned with the spread of the Gospel of Jesus Christ.

Upon entering the Institute in the winter of 1937, Billy immediately encountered what would become another important influence during his time in Temple Terrace—winter conferences, which drew evangelical leaders from across North America as well as wealthy attendees from the northern United States, affectionately called "Yankee tourists."

These conferences, which W. T. Watson believed would help all participants in profound ways, were a central part of his vision for the school. Speakers would find respite in the beautiful setting of Temple Terrace, as well as much-needed collegiality with other leaders.

Conference attendees would be enriched by a spiritual retreat, rather than merely vacationing in Florida's warm winter climate. The communities of Temple Terrace, Tampa, and St. Petersburg would experience the fervor of the Gospel, as meetings were open to the public and the speakers were often invited to preach in local churches as well.

But perhaps the greatest impact of the conferences was on the Florida Bible Institute itself. Not only did the conferences make the Institute a financially viable endeavor, but they also made the fledgling school a place where students would rub elbows with the leaders of evangelicalism.

These meetings had a profound effect on Billy after his transfer from Bob Jones. He wrote to his mother, telling her of the impact of the conferences and speakers on his life.

"I rededicated my life to the Lord Jesus Christ last night under the stars," Billy wrote early on. "Mother, I've been in tears for weeks over my past indifference."[1]

At the Florida Bible Institute, he was taking the faith as his own and began to realize why it was important to his parents. "Every time I go to these great meetings," he wrote to his mother, "I think of Daddy because he loves that kind of meeting so much."[2]

⊥≫

Students of the Institute were not only expected to attend the conferences, but in keeping with how the school itself was run, the conferences were facilitated by their hard work. They helped prepare and serve food, washed and dried dishes, bused tables, cleaned guest rooms, and acted as porters and golf caddies for the guests.

Billy was no exception, tackling his share of these often menial tasks. Not only did he work as the school's "first automatic dishwasher," but he also caddied for the golfers who visited. On one occasion, he caddied for the former director of the Bible department at the Moody Bible Institute, Dr. William Evans, who tipped him one dollar. Dr. Evans told the young student that if he applied himself, perhaps one day he too would be able to tip others.[3]

One of the ways Billy served guests and speakers in his first few weeks at the Institute was by shining shoes. One such speaker was W. B. Riley, president and founder of Northwestern Bible School in Minnesota.

Riley was seventy-five years old in 1937 and had already been an important spokesman for the fundamentalist movement, serving as the editor of the *Christian Fundamentalist* from 1891 to 1933. He had also been the pastor of the First Baptist Church of Minneapolis since 1897 and had founded his Bible school in 1902. By 1935, it had grown to include a seminary. Riley's influence as a leader of fundamentalism can hardly be overstated.

But Riley was also a phenomenal preacher, which proved instrumental in growing his church from some six hundred members to several thousand during his nearly half-century-long pastorate. This preaching gift was not lost on conference attendees, and Riley had been a regular speaker at the Florida Bible Institute conferences for years.[4]

Billy often described his experiences in letters home to his mother. In one such letter, Billy wrote that as he polished Riley's shoes, he looked up at the pastor and thought, "Oh, if someday I could be a great preacher like him!"[5]

Billy sat at the feet of giants. Little did anyone expect that, one day, he not only would fill the shoes of this giant, W. B. Riley—succeeding him as president of Northwestern Bible School—but also would become a giant himself.

＝

Other opportunities to serve did not always turn out so well. One day when Billy was waiting on guest tables, he came barreling through the kitchen door, yelling, "What will get coffee out of a dress?" He had just spilled the hot liquid all over the dress of the school's dean of women, Miss Sara Allred.

Sara was a lifelong friend of W. T. Watson's wife, Lucy, having grown up in the same hometown of Greensboro, North Carolina, and she was the maid of honor at the Watsons' wedding. When they started the Institute, they asked Sara to become the hostess.[6]

Her importance to the school was amplified when she became engaged to one of the regular speakers at the conference, Dr. Vance Havner, the "Will Rogers of the American pulpit." Dr. Havner earned this moniker with his quick, deadpan wit, which often tied up his audiences in knots.[7]

Needless to say, Billy saw to it that Sara Allred's dress was cleaned.

⊹≈

The conferences at the Institute were touted as the Florida Keswick Conferences from the 1920s until 1938. It was an advertisement for these conferences in a 1936 issue of the *Moody Monthly* that first made Billy's mother aware of the Florida Bible Institute. By Billy's final year at the Institute in 1940, the word *Keswick* had been dropped from the title, and the conferences were referred to as "the annual mid-winter Bible Conference of the Florida Bible Institute."[8] Some within the Keswick movement had apparently taken issue with the use of the name Keswick, as it was becoming a brand of sorts, and had asked W. T. Watson to remove the name from the conferences.[9]

Keswick is a town in Cumbria County, England, where, in the late 1800s, droves of spiritually hungry Christians gathered for conferences at which they longed for, and often received, a touch by the Spirit of God. With renowned speakers in the early days, such as missionary to China Hudson Taylor, the conferences gained a reputation that would carry forward all the way into the twenty-first century, igniting a spiritual renewal in England that, in turn, affected the entire world through Christian service and world missions. Amy Carmichael and Oswald Chambers are two influential writers whose spiritual depth can be traced to the Keswick movement.

The Keswick teaching had its own set of distinctions. As with the Christian and Missionary Alliance, the spirit and impact of Keswick was, and is, interdenominational. Speakers and participants alike came from a wide swath of Christian denominations. Also, like the Christian and Missionary Alliance, the teaching of Keswick included at its core the doctrine of subsequence—the belief that sanctification is an event that happens, and is received by faith, after justification.

As noted in earlier chapters, the Pentecostal movement refers to this "second blessing" as "the baptism of the Holy Spirit," which is manifest by speaking in tongues. C&MA teaching, by and large, had rejected Pentecostalism's insistence on speaking in tongues but taught that sanctification led to assistance toward a life of holiness and empowerment for Christian service.

The Keswick teachers often placed a more particular emphasis on sanctification, which was in line with the C&MA's rejection of the Pentecostal view of glossolalia as evidence of the baptism of the Holy Spirit. However, the Keswick emphasis often took matters a step further than the Alliance would, teaching that sanctification would lead to victory over sin. Some even taught the possibility of complete victory over all known sin. If God could reveal the sin, the Keswick teachers argued, He could—and would—also give the power to be victorious over it.

The movement in England was more generally referred to as the Higher Life movement. Its parallel counterpart in the United States was called the Victorious Life movement and was influential in the lives and teaching of many, if not most, fundamentalist leaders in the first half of the twentieth century. The Keswick influence was ingrained in the spiritual makeup of both British and American evangelicalism.

Just how connected the Florida Bible Institute conferences really were to the Keswick movement is uncertain. Keswick conventions sprouted up all over the world in the first half of the twentieth century. Many of the speakers at the Institute's conferences were connected to the movement—men such as Vance Havner, William Evans, and J. Edwin Orr. It is likely that W. T. Watson, moved by the fervor and "Spirit-filled" teaching of Keswick, had named his conferences "Keswick" independently of the teaching and order of the movement. Whatever the exact connection between the Institute's conferences and Keswick, Watson was asked to remove *Keswick* from the name of the conferences, which he did by 1940.[10]

The effect that these movements—both the Keswick movement in particular, and the Victorious Life movement in general—had on Billy was significant during this time. He later said that while he was at the Institute, "I learned something of the crucified life. I learned what victorious living meant. I learned something of the Spirit-filled life."[11] This sums up the essence of the Victorious Life movement. And Billy carried these themes of the victorious Christian and Spirit-filled living into his early preaching ministry.

The influx of speakers at the conferences represented a who's who of American evangelicalism. And some of the phrases, mannerisms, and illustrations of these speakers were ones that could later be witnessed in Billy's own preaching.

Preachers came from all over the world, including A. B. Winchester from Toronto, whose high-pitched voice could often be heard saying, "The Bible says. . ."[12] Others included Dr. Gerald Winrod, a prophecy specialist from Kansas; H. C. Morrison, Homer

Rodeheaver, Gypsy Smith, Oswald J. Smith, Edward A. Marshall, Clinton Churchill, Albert Hughes, E. J. Pace, John McNeill, hymn writer B. D. Ackley, R. E. Neighbour, R. T. Richey, Ralph Hooper, R. R. Brown, and others.[13]

Billy's friend and fellow team member Grady Wilson later said that this slew of preachers stirred within Billy a certain "divine discontent," which ignited his own desire to preach the Gospel.[14] Billy himself said that W. B. Riley, H. H. Savage, Dr. William Evans, and Dr. Vance Havner "instilled in me a love for the Word of God, and gave me my first doctrinal anchorage."[15]

The impact of these conferences on young Billy was both profound and long lasting—in his theology as well as in his practical ministry. But they also affected the budding evangelist in another way with the visit of three unassuming conference guests in the winter of 1940.

CHAPTER 12

FACING CHALLENGES

"The time is ripe for another Luther, Wesley, Moody, _____."
VERA RESUE

By the fall of 1939, Billy's final year at the Institute, Great Britain and France had declared war on Germany, and America watched tensely as Hitler and Stalin marched their armies into Poland.

Turmoil also struck the Florida Bible Institute during Billy's final year and a half, profoundly affecting the president, W. T. Watson, who was accused of unspecified "moral indiscretions."[1] The nature of the accusations and the alleged offense remained a mystery and were only brought to light, vaguely, a half century later in Billy Graham's autobiography, *Just As I Am*. Whatever the offense, real or perceived, it was serious enough to cause "maybe a fourth" of the Institute's students to leave the small school before the fall of 1939.[2]

When Billy revealed these long-forgotten accusations in 1997, Watson's son, Bobby, who would have been under the age of ten at the time, had no recollection of the incident. The Watsons' family life and marriage did not seem to have been affected, leading Bobby to believe there was no extramarital relationship.[3] Nevertheless, W. T.

Watson had some run-ins with people over the years, and he may have made some enemies along the way who would have been less than charitable about any perceived offenses.

Billy, for his part, was adamantly convinced that Watson was completely innocent of the accusations, and he remained at the Institute, leading the students through the crisis as president of the senior class.[4]

Watson's troubles from the accusations were not limited to the school. There were also major rumblings within the St. Petersburg Tabernacle, which was keenly aware of the situation. As a result, the church struggled to make payments on its immense debt, and creditors were growing impatient.

When Watson founded the St. Petersburg Tabernacle in 1924, he was pursuing a grandiose vision that had two fundamental flaws. The first flaw was the size of the building. The St. Petersburg Tabernacle had begun in the wake of a citywide revival led by Rayman T. Richey. Watson had taken over where the Richey meetings left off, using a tent he had purchased from YMCA evangelist Reba Crawford. The meetings had continued for seven months, and a permanent building was eventually built on Fifth Avenue and Tenth Street South. It was built to house four thousand visitors, but the sanctuary was rarely filled, and most often felt empty, especially in nonwinter months. The size of the building put the church in greater debt than if Watson had built a more modest-sized one. Watson called it the greatest mistake of his ministry.[5]

The second, and perhaps more important, issue was the vision Watson had for the Tabernacle, which he founded to be "a great evangelistic center" in St. Petersburg rather than a church.[6] He brought in evangelists from around the country, including Billy Sunday, in order to reach vacationers in the winter months and the St. Petersburg community year-round. Watson himself would preach most Sunday services.

Because the Tabernacle was not a church, per se, there was no church membership, which led to an atmosphere of noncommitment. At first, this is what Watson wanted. He hoped that the Tabernacle would inject the surrounding churches with a shot of spiritual vitality. But as the years went on and financial difficulties in the 1930s strained the congregation, Watson began to reevaluate his vision. Visitors, he was finding, were not a reliable source of funding. The question of whether the Tabernacle was an evangelistic center for the lost, or a church for believers, was muddled.

Like John Minder's Tampa Gospel Tabernacle, the St. Petersburg Tabernacle was another avenue for Billy Graham to minister and preach. The Florida State Young People's Rally of the Christian and Missionary Alliance was held in Tampa on Labor Day weekend of 1939, and Billy spoke on the opening day, September 2.[7] Then, for the next week, September 3–10, Billy held a citywide Young People's Revival Campaign at the St. Petersburg Tabernacle, holding nightly services with his Florida Bible Institute classmate Ponzi Pennington.

The campaign was advertised in the St. Petersburg newspaper with the name "Billy" in quotes, highlighting the fact that his public persona was still not settled. "Hear the dynamic youthful evangelist," the advertisement blared. The ecumenical spirit of the meetings was also clear: "All denominations invited!"[8] Among other messages throughout the week, Billy preached sermons titled "Evidences of Salvation" on Sunday morning and "As in the Days of Noah" in the evening.[9]

Billy's work with W. T. Watson and the St. Petersburg Tabernacle led to yet another opportunity—this time in radio work. Before the advent of television, it was notoriously difficult for churches to get airtime on a public radio station in the 1930s. Because of this difficulty and Watson's desire to expand his ministry across the airwaves, he applied for a station license of his own from the FCC and was granted the call letters WTSP.

This gave Watson the chance to air his services and a program called *The Back Home Sacred Song Hour*, which gave students from the Institute an opportunity to get on the airwaves. When Billy got his first chance, he confided to those with him, "Please pray for me. . .my knees are knocking together. This is my first time before a radio mike."[10]

Despite Watson's innovation and cutting-edge methods, the four-thousand-seat St. Petersburg Gospel Tabernacle building was taken by creditors in February 1939.[11] It was sold under foreclosure and hosted boxing matches, rather than evangelistic meetings, before becoming an aircraft plant.

The next months would prove trying for Watson, who faced accusations, loss of his church building, loss of students, and loss of confidence from many around him. The Sunday meetings were now held in the St. Petersburg Tourist Center, which Watson rented until a new facility could be built. Watson and those around him were learning a humbling lesson.

Over the next year, the Tabernacle looked for a permanent location for their meetings. E. R. Kellog, who had wired money to the school years earlier in a miraculous answer to prayer, donated a lot to the church on Fifth Street South and Fifth Avenue. A groundbreaking ceremony was held on April 21, 1940—more than a year after the loss of the first building—led by Watson, Minder, and "assistant pastor" Billy Graham.

Dr. Watson declared at the ceremony, "All who will work on the erection of this building may feel they are on holy ground." John Minder, who was the main speaker of the event, spoke with an eye toward the events of the past year and warned those in attendance that any good work will be opposed by the devil, who works "from within as well as from without."

"God will deliver you from every thrust of Satan if you go forward with the Lord," he said. "If you are doing the will of God, you will be protected by Him always, and under any circumstances."[12]

The new building was different from the first. This time, there was no vision of filling a four-thousand-seat auditorium. And Watson was not going into debt to build the new structure, nor was it likely he would have been able to. Indeed, each block of this new building would be paid for beforehand. And if certainties were ever in Watson's visions, they were quickly dashed, as the new building was built, not where the groundbreaking ceremony had been held, but a few blocks away, on Fourth Street South and Seventh Avenue. Still, he managed to pay for the building—block by block—and began construction in the fall of 1940.[13]

Watson's counterpart in Tampa, John Minder, was trying to move his own church onto sound financial ground, and he received help from industrialist R. G. LeTourneau.

LeTourneau was an innovative designer of earth-moving equipment and also had a heart for ministry. By his own admission, he made his business a partnership with God by reversing his tithe: he gave God 90 percent of his profits and took 10 percent for himself. His business was unusually successful in the 1930s after he took this step of faith, and by the late 1930s he had gained a ministry of preaching and evangelism around the country. He flew his plane to these engagements, both to save time and to avoid the dangers of the road, where, in 1937, he had been involved in an accident with fatalities. His motto was "Not how much of my money do I give to God, but how much of God's money do I keep for myself?" Speaking at conferences and churches around the country, his favorite scripture text was "Seek ye first the kingdom of God, and his righteousness; and all these things shall be added unto you" (Matthew 6:33 KJV). Even in his generosity, he knew that he could *never* outgive God.

A leader among the Christian and Missionary Alliance, LeTourneau was no stranger to the Florida Bible Institute. He had also built a plant in the region of Toccoa, Georgia. The big draw for LeTourneau on this trip to Tampa was the Bible and Missionary Crusade of the Christian and Missionary Alliance, held at the Tampa Gospel Tabernacle from February 18 to March 3, 1940, which also drew C&MA president H. M. Shuman, R. R. Brown, S. M. Gerow, R. A. Forrest, and Thomas Moseley—virtually all of the leaders of the C&MA.[14]

The meetings included timely messages on Christian experience and prophecy and their relation to current events—a hot topic that informed and shaped Billy's own views for years to come as he sought to advise world leaders from a biblical perspective.

The highlight of the meetings came on February 29, when the Tampa Gospel Tabernacle burned $25,000 in bonds, relieving the congregation of an immense burden of debt, in part through the deep pockets and generosity of R. G. LeTourneau.[15]

As Billy's time at the Florida Bible Institute neared its end, one thing was certain: he wanted to be an evangelist.[16] When asked for his favorite verse of scripture, he declared Jude 1:3, "I exhort you that ye shall earnestly contend for the faith which was once delivered unto the saints."[17] The goal was sure; the path to get there was not.

Billy's mother was concerned that he would need more education—and from an accredited institution. Billy had gained invaluable and incalculable experience, wisdom, and insight at the Institute. But incalculable gains in a very calculating world immediately set Billy at a disadvantage. The Institute could only give him a diploma—not the college degree he might need one day.

The way forward became clear with an opportunity that seemed too good to be true for a North Carolina farm boy and Bob Jones

College dropout like Billy: an invitation to attend Wheaton College, near Chicago, Illinois.

The C&MA conferences in the winter of 1940 brought three very important people to Temple Terrace who could make this happen: Mrs. Anders Edman; her brother, Elner Edman; and Paul Fischer. During their visit, Billy caddied for the men, and they went to hear Billy preach. They were all very impressed with him and began to prod him to go to Wheaton.

Billy saw two major obstacles. First, he knew students with better grades than he had who could not get into the school. Second, Wheaton would cost more than the Florida Bible Institute and would strain him financially. Obstacles notwithstanding, Billy had impressed the right people. Mrs. Anders Edman was the mother of Wheaton's interim president, Victor Raymond Edman, and Paul Fischer's brother, Herman, was chairman of the board at the school. Getting into Wheaton was not going to be a problem.[18] In addition, Paul Fischer promised to pay Billy's first year's tuition, and Elner Edman pledged to help him with expenses.

Billy initially wrestled with the decision. Longtime friend and evangelist Jimmie Johnson came to visit during this time, and they walked and talked, Billy asking advice of his elder friend.[19] In the end, God's hand was clear. Billy would apply, be accepted, and go on to study at Wheaton.

Billy's final semester at the Institute was filled with fun, studies, ministry, and trips with the senior class. The first of these trips was through north Florida, with Melrose, the location of Lake Swan, as the home base. They traveled together on the Institute bus—a beloved, dependable vehicle that could carry the entire eleven-member graduating class, plus their sponsors.[20]

During the trip, which was taken during spring break in late March and early April, the class performed a program of music and preaching in the local churches—many of the same churches in which Billy had held revivals in previous years. Before going to Melrose, they began with services in De Leon Springs and were heard over the radio on WFOY in St. Augustine and WTMC in Ocala.[21]

The trip was not limited to ministry. They also went sightseeing at Ravine Gardens in Palatka; Green Cove Springs in Silver Springs; and the Fountain of Youth in St. Augustine. The school yearbook records one of the light moments of the trip: As the seniors gathered around, one of the students pulled out a fake sword to hold a "solemn ceremony," bestowing knighthood on Billy, who humbly bowed before his "majesty." As Billy's classmate laid the sword on the young evangelist's shoulders, he declared, "I now pronounce you—dead!"[22]

The second trip, held at the end of April, covered two hundred miles, as far south as Fort Myers. There they presented their program to the Bayshore Baptist Church and the Christian and Missionary Alliance church, as well as over the air from the Fort Myers radio station. They also held services in Sarasota and at the Baptist Church in Venice, where an Institute alumnus was now the pastor.[23]

As graduation quickly approached, the senior class presented their final two programs in the Tampa area: at Florence Villa Baptist Church on May 10 and at the Tampa Gospel Tabernacle on May 12. They also were heard over local stations WTSP and WLAK.[24]

The days of graduation festivities were a sweet culmination of what had been a precious time for the eleven graduating seniors. They had been through a lot together—trials, miraculous answers to prayer, spiritual and intellectual growth—and had watched their leaders face challenges of their own. They had lost seven members of their class over the Watson controversy, but those who remained had been knit together in love.

The flurry of graduation activities was punctuated by services of Billy's own as he visited the Tampa Tin Can Trailer Park as chaplain for the final time.[25]

Billy kept his eyes open for other preaching opportunities, as he hoped to hold evangelistic services throughout the summer before attending Wheaton. He took advantage of one such opportunity when the speaker for the baccalaureate service, Ralph Boyer, radio preacher and director of the York Gospel Center in York, Pennsylvania, came to Temple Terrace.[26] Billy asked fellow student Orpha King, who was also from York and was a member of Boyer's church, to introduce him to the preacher so he could arrange meetings in their town for the summer.[27] Arrangements were made for Billy to go to York in late July.

Boyer and Billy crisscrossed one another that Sunday. Boyer spoke at the morning service at the St. Petersburg Gospel Tabernacle and then spoke at the afternoon baccalaureate service before preaching at the Tampa Gospel Tabernacle that night, the same time at which Billy held a service at the St. Petersburg Tabernacle.[28]

The graduation ceremony, on the evening of May 13, 1940, would, in retrospect, prove to be another eerily prophetic moment in a string of such providentially ordained moments in the life of Billy Graham. The Lord had set his eyes on the young evangelist to support him through the challenges he would now face.

John Minder, the class sponsor, was also the speaker and awarded the diplomas to the graduates. But his talk was overshadowed by the addresses of the salutatorian, Henry Ellen Bush, and the valedictorian, Vera Resue. Working in tandem, Henry Ellen began with a message titled "The Challenge We Face," followed by Vera's response: "We Accept the Challenge."[29]

In a message that echoed the greatest fears and concerns of the Church in America in 1940, Henry Ellen declared, "We are living in an age of strife; everywhere we turn, we meet it. Our newspapers are full of war, crime, divorce, and financial trouble. World conditions are at the lowest." But still she offered hope: "Men always follow a leader." She proceeded to list historical leaders whom many had followed. "These are dead, but Christ marches on to victory in spite of foes, but where are the soldiers of Christ?"

Her message outlined the challenges before them: opposition to the Church, war, the atheism of Hitler and the communists, and weak churches in America. Her answer was clear: "The world is hungry for the living Christ—lived through you."[30]

Vera Resue's response contained similar fears, painting a "dark picture" of the world. Then the valedictorian proclaimed, with a glimmer of hope, "It was dark at Calvary, but the dawn of resurrection brought light to all men."

And then, as twenty-one-year-old Billy Graham sat listening, Vera shared a prophetic word of hope that echoed beyond the walls of that Florida Bible Institute building:

The early church faced darkness as Rome began to take complete control. It seemed as though the light was near extinction, but God was waiting for someone who would dare to accept the challenge. Martin Luther was that "one." He heard the Voice of God and in the face of opposition from every side, he stepped forth from the darkness bearing the True Light, "the Light that lighteth up the world." Again we see dawn; but as we delve back in [the] history of the Christian church we find that these conditions existed time and again. Each time God had a chosen *human instrument to shine forth His Light in the darkness. Men like Luther, John and Charles Wesley, Moody and others were ordinary men, but men who heard the Voice of God. Their surrounding conditions were as black as night, but they had God. "If God be with us who can be against us?" It has been said that Luther revolutionized the world. It was not he, but Christ working through him. The time is ripe for another Luther, Wesley, Moody, _____. There is room for another name in this list. There is a challenge facing us.[31]*

Unbeknownst to Vera Resue, or the others there that day, that name would be Graham.

CHAPTER 13

A YOUTH AFLAME

"Do we want a preacher that has to practice his sermons?"
ATTENDEE OF THE LEVEL GROVE REVIVAL

The Florida Bible Institute shaped Billy in profound ways. It was there that he learned the Bible, learned to preach, and surrendered himself to a call to preach; and it was where he gained the confidence to become an evangelist. Indeed, later in his life, he said, "Without a doubt, my three and a half years at the Florida Bible Institute were the happiest years of my life."[1]

The flurry of revival meetings that Billy held in north Florida during the fall of 1938 had been put on hold as his responsibilities at school and a more regular church involvement commanded his attention. Now, with school out, he once again turned his attention to revival meetings.

The summer of 1940 included three major locations for meetings, which he visited with fellow graduate and song leader Ponzi Pennington. Billy and Ponzi had worked with each other at various revival meetings throughout Florida and in their respective roles as associate pastor and song leader at the Tampa Gospel Tabernacle.

Like Billy, Ponzi had a heart for evangelism, committing himself to evangelistic work through preaching and singing.[2] Ponzi hailed from Birmingham, Alabama, where John Minder had ministered years earlier at what later became the Birmingham Gospel Tabernacle. Ponzi's heart is shown in what he picked as his favorite hymn: "He Keeps Me Singing."[3]

The first services Billy held that summer were in his hometown of Charlotte, preaching at two local churches—one in the morning and the other in the evening. Then the evangelistic duo held their first series of services in late May at the Christian and Missionary Alliance church in Lumberton, North Carolina, where W. T. Watson had been saved and where he still had strong ties.[4]

Billy's genius for self-promotion for the sake of the Gospel was further practiced here. He managed to get himself on the front page of the small local paper, with a picture and the title of *evangelist*. The article lists Billy as hailing from Tampa and promotes Ponzi as a graduate of a three-year program in voice, adding that he "has devoted his life to the presenting of the Gospel in song."[5]

In what were becoming standard evangelistic messages for Billy, he preached a sermon titled "Lost" on Wednesday night; "God's Great Judgment Day" on Thursday night; and "Belshazzar's Feast" on Friday night for a Young People's rally.[6]

Their second series of meetings was held at Level Grove Baptist Church in Cornelia, Georgia, some twenty-five miles west of where W. T. Watson had attended Bible school at Toccoa Falls Bible College, and near where he owned land in Demorest. Watson's fifty-acre property in the rolling hills on the edge of the Appalachian Mountains had once been an apple farm owned by Mr. and Mrs. J. T. Mathes, who were also on the faculty at the Florida Bible Institute. The farm had been losing money, so Watson offered to buy the land for $5,000 down and payments of $500 a year.[7]

He bought the property with a vision to help the school. He planned to have students come for the summer to work and help pay for their education. In addition, he believed the farm could help the Institute become more self-sufficient. Students could grow tomatoes, beans, or other vegetables to be canned and brought back to the Institute to use for student meals and to serve the guests at the winter conferences. In practice, it ended up being an impractical, money-losing venture, and in later years it was shut down by the Food and Drug Administration.[8]

But in the summer of 1940, the vision was operational and Billy and Ponzi picked beans and milked cows while they stayed at the Watson estate.[9] They slept in an enclosed sunroom, where visitors gathered to debate hot topics, such as whether Mussolini was the antichrist, as some preachers at the time had suggested.[10]

But Billy was in Demorest to preach, not for farmwork or debate, though he participated in both. But when he had a free moment, he slipped out back behind the barn to practice his sermons.

One day, young Bobby Watson was out front by the highway when an oil truck pulled up. The two men inside asked if the young preacher was there who was going to preach the revival. Bobby told them that he was, and that the last time he'd seen him, he was out preaching to the cows. The men headed back to town, wondering, "Do we want a preacher that has to practice his sermons?"[11]

To promote the Level Grove Baptist meetings, which began on June 13, Billy once again printed flyers to be handed out. As with his other pamphlets, he trumpeted himself as "A Young Man With A Burning Message," and goaded the community: "Your Friends Will Be There, Why Not You?"[12]

Even if some people questioned the preacher's youthfulness, the meetings were a success. Wherever Billy went to preach, people were getting saved. He exuded a sincerity not normally found in a young—or, for that matter, a more seasoned—preacher. Eventually, the crowds became too large for the Level Grove Baptist Church building.

In order to deal with the space problem, the church leaders began looking for alternate sites for the services. Their first idea was to approach the larger First Baptist Church of Cornelia. But the pastor of that church objected, saying they had just laid grass and he did not want people trampling on it. So instead they moved the services to the local high school auditorium.[13]

Though the meetings were successful, the young evangelist's zeal could also prove off-putting. On one occasion, while Billy was preaching, the noise of a crying baby broke out in the audience. When the baby's mother didn't immediately take the crying child out of the service, Billy felt that it was distracting other people from the all-important Gospel message, and from the pulpit he asked that the baby be removed.[14] Despite isolated instances of off-putting zeal such as this, the meetings, which began in mid-June, continued on into July, and overall, Billy and Ponzi were well received in Cornelia, Georgia.

Ponzi and Billy next traveled to York, Pennsylvania, about 650 miles northwest of Cornelia. The long trip by car was exacerbated by the unreliable 1931 Oldsmobile they were driving, which continually broke down. When they got to Charlotte, they borrowed Billy's father's 1937 Plymouth for the rest of the trip.[15] The week of meetings, which had been arranged during the Reverend Ralph Boyer's visit to the Florida Bible Institute for the baccalaureate address, was Billy's first preaching engagement north of the Mason-Dixon Line.

The meetings were held at the York Gospel Center on Pine and Maple Streets and started on Sunday, July 21, with services every

131

night except Monday. The local newspaper announcements included some humorous typographical errors, which perhaps served to demonstrate the cultural divide between the Southern evangelistic team and the northern town. The two local papers ran notices in their Friday editions almost a week after the services began. The *York Dispatch* announced: "Evangelist Billy Frank Graham, Charlotte, N.C., assisted by Ponci Pennington, Ala., as soloist, choir director and song leader."[16] If the *York Dispatch* missed the spelling of Ponzi's name one way, the other local paper, the *Gazette and Daily*, missed it another. It announced, "Evangelist William Frank Graham with song leader Ponel Pennington," and also failed to include his hometown of Birmingham.[17]

If there was any ribbing as a result of these misspellings, it was dispelled a week later when both papers got Ponzi's name correct and included his hometown—but the *Gazette and Daily* printed "Billie Frank."[18]

The Yankee audience also had some difficulty understanding the Southern evangelist's strong accent. In order to remedy the problem, Billy spoke louder; but several people still could not understand him. He was tempted to attribute their lack of response to "spiritual deafness," but he had to concede that his accent might be the barrier in communication. This was an important, though frustrating, lesson on the difficulties of cross-cultural communication.[19]

Despite these setbacks, the meetings were successful. Originally scheduled for one week, by Friday they had already decided to extend the meetings another week.[20]

Promotional pamphlets for the second week came with a new teaser line: "Here is youth aflame for God!"[21]

In the pamphlets, Billy announced his preaching schedule for the week, with the need to add to his preaching package because of the extended services: "Lost," "Climbing to Hell," "The Feast of

Belshazzar," "God's Program for the Future," "God Almighty's Great Judgment Day," "The Choice of Your Soul," and "As in the Days of Noah."[22] Some of these were repeat sermons with continuing refinements, but he also had to work on new ones to expand his portfolio.[23]

The trip up north also gave Billy and Ponzi the chance to go to New York City for the World's Fair, two hundred miles away. It was there that Billy first saw television and saw himself on camera as he walked by.[24] It would be the first of many television appearances for the evangelist.[25]

Back in York, Billy's peers marveled at how the Lord's hand seemed to be on him, as the church was filled nightly and decisions were being made.[26] One of these decisions reached to the heart of the pastor of the church, the Reverend Ralph Boyer. When Billy called on people to come forward one night, the pastor's wife sat playing the piano when her daughter came up to sit beside her and decided to follow Christ that night.[27]

The services were closed on Sunday, August 4, with Billy and Ponzi holding a "special testimonial service," at which the evangelistic duo shared the "stories of their lives."[28]

The summer of meetings in 1940 proved to be an important transition for Billy into a new culture. They were also his last series of meetings with Ponzi Pennington, who continued on to serve in music ministry in Baptist churches in Atlanta, Georgia.[29]

In the years after Billy moved on from the Florida Bible Institute, he occasionally visited W. T. Watson's and John Minder's churches for preaching engagements; but his ultimate path took him elsewhere. What he had gained in those three and a half years in Florida was essential to what later became a worldwide ministry.

Part 3

FANNING THE FLAME:

WHEATON COLLEGE (1940–1943)

CHAPTER 14

FIRE ON THE PRAIRIE

"Wheaton's principal impact is its spiritual impact."
V. RAYMOND EDMAN

Billy Graham was twenty-two when he stepped onto the campus of Wheaton College as a freshman in the fall of 1940, and he had already spent four years in secondary education. Initially, he was granted credits for only one semester of his earlier coursework, making him a second-semester freshman—hardly a compliment to his hard work for the previous four years. Though some more of his credits from Florida would eventually transfer to Wheaton, Billy lamented that he was not taking any Bible or homiletics courses.[1]

Wheaton was entirely different from the Florida Bible Institute. With 1,100 students enrolled, it dwarfed the tiny Florida school; and as a liberal arts college, it required a broader range of subjects. It was a discouraging start for Billy.

He reminisced often about the wonderful fellowship and opportunities he'd had at the Florida Bible Institute, and he had no significant connections or contacts in Wheaton at the time.[2] All the work he had done to establish himself as an evangelistic preacher in the South did not immediately pay dividends in Wheaton. Invitations to speak were rare, and any engagements he arranged were on his own initiative. To top things off, as in his meetings in York the previous summer, his deep Southern drawl made him stand out—not usually in a positive, sophisticated way. Billy needed to make many adjustments to be comfortable at Wheaton—and he did.

There were, however, glimmers of encouragement early on. One day as Billy was walking from the main, fortress-like academic building, Blanchard Hall, to the Student Supply Store, which students had nicknamed "the Stupe," he crossed paths with a jovial stranger.

"Hi, Bill!" the man said with a smile. "How are things in North Carolina?"

The balding, forty-year-old gentleman continued walking during the quick interchange.

Billy stopped in stunned silence, curious about the stranger who knew so much about him. Bewildered, he continued on to the Stupe and asked the other students there about the incident.

"Oh, that's Dr. Edman," one student blurted out, "interim president of the school! He knows everybody!"[3] Billy had heard of Dr. Edman when he met Edman's mother and brother in Florida the previous winter, but this was his first encounter with the man himself.

Dr. Edman, who had recently been named interim president of the school, loved the students, and the students loved him. He prayed daily for each student during his morning devotions in the early days of his presidency, and when students came to him for counsel, he often knelt with them in prayer. This intimacy and devotion had a profound impact on the student body—including Billy Graham.

Billy's first meeting with the president outside of the academic building was encouraging enough, as he was struggling to make the adjustment to Wheaton; but a second encounter encouraged him even further. It happened just a few days later, at a prayer meeting in a private home with Christian and Missionary Alliance students.

Dr. Edman approached Billy and asked, "Bill, how are things going?"

Billy replied, "Very well, sir."

Dr. Edman continued, "My mother and brother have told me quite a bit about you. I hope you will soon be able to find your way around Wheaton." And in a final touch that would endear the school's president to Billy forever, he said, "If there is anything I can do for you, please do not hesitate to call on me." Billy took this invitation to heart, seeking Dr. Edman's advice, he later said, on every major decision until Edman's death in 1967.[4]

⫝̸

In 1940, Wheaton College was growing into a leading evangelical institution. It was located twenty-five miles west of the city of Chicago, a city that had been a leader of evangelicalism for the past half century or more. Since D. L. Moody had established Chicago as a homefront for organized evangelism in the mid-1800s, the city was drawing—and creating—some of the most successful ministries in the country. It was there that Moody started what became the Moody Bible Institute, which had a worldwide impact for the kingdom of God. There were many other significant ministries as well, such as the Pacific Garden Mission, where professional baseballer-turned-preacher Billy Sunday had accepted Christ.

Perhaps just as important were the preachers who were drawn to Chicago, including Paul Rader, who experienced explosive church growth as pastor of Moody Church and the Chicago Gospel Tabernacle before ending his ministry in Fort Wayne, Indiana. Harry Ironside had a successful ministry as pastor of Moody Church in the 1930s and 40s; and influential mystic and prophet A. W. Tozer served as pastor of the Southside Gospel Tabernacle from 1928 to 1959. Chicago was thriving spiritually, and Wheaton College was catching drafts of that flame, all the while becoming an evangelical hub in its own right. Wheaton was, as one historian has noted, "a fire on the prairie."[5]

Wheaton College was founded by Jonathan Blanchard in 1860 as a devoutly Christian institution committed to the abolition of slavery, with a motto that was foundational to the vision: "For Christ and His Kingdom." Connected to abolitionists such as the family of Harriet Beecher Stowe, Wheaton became a stop in the Underground Railroad. Throughout its early history, Wheaton was committed not only to the spiritual welfare of the country, but also to its physical and material well-being. It was this holistic impulse that made the fundamentalist movement a bit nervous, while at the same time bewildering mainline liberals with its strong evangelical stance.

It would not be entirely unfair to label Wheaton a fundamentalist institution at this time in its history. Doctrinally, the school adhered to the "fundamentals of the faith" and held firmly to a policy against drinking, smoking, dancing, gambling, and secret societies, which was par for the course for fundamentalist institutions. But if Wheaton could be considered fundamentalist, it would certainly never be in the same stream of fundamentalism as Bob Jones, for example, with his increasingly separatist tendencies. Indeed, when Billy left Bob Jones College for the Florida Bible Institute, he took his first step away from the far right of fundamentalism. Wheaton was another step in that direction, as the college introduced Billy to a lively, yet more moderate, form of fundamentalism.[6]

Much like Billy had found at both Bob Jones College and the Florida Bible Institute, spiritual life at Wheaton was fueled by its daily chapel services. As did most Christian schools of the day, both semesters commenced with evangelistic services. That fall, W. H. Rogers opened the school year with a focus on Habakkuk 2:20 (KJV): "The LORD is in his holy temple: let all the earth keep silence before him."[7] The rest of the fall semester lacked some of the big names who had come to Wheaton earlier—likely because of the transition in the school's presidency. The slack was taken up by speakers from the faculty, and the beloved Dr. Edman in particular, who greatly lifted the spirits of the student body.[8] One speaker of note, however, who certainly brought joy to Billy's heart was friend and mentor Dr. W. T. Watson, who came to speak in chapel in mid-October.[9]

Dr. Edman's commitment to the spiritual life of the campus was never called into question. He firmly believed that "Wheaton's principal impact is its spiritual impact" and lived by that belief.[10] On the same day that Dr. Watson spoke in chapel—and perhaps shared the story of how the Lord had answered the Florida Bible Institute's prayers for provision of $10,000—Edman sent out a letter to the school declaring that the following Thursday, October 24, would be set aside as a day of prayer, with all classes canceled. Quoting a lengthy excerpt of E. M. Bounds's classic *Purpose in Prayer*, Edman shared, "It is true that the mightiest successes that come to God's cause are created and carried on by prayer."[11]

The interim president encouraged the students to prepare their hearts for the week leading up to the day of prayer, citing Joshua's admonition to the people of Israel: "Sanctify yourselves: for tomorrow the LORD will do wonders among you."[12] Edman encouraged the students and faculty to have "increased time and effort for personal devotions, for prayer seasons by roommates, by house groups, by spontaneous groups," and by attendance at various prayer meetings held around campus. He ended the letter, "Thus we shall be a prepared people, ready to meet our God Who is able to do exceedingly abundantly above all that we ask or even think."[13]

Another aspect of life at Wheaton that cheered the lonely newcomer's heart was that the school had a thriving athletics department. That was something that both Bob Jones College and the Florida Bible Institute lacked—Bob Jones had the resources, but not the interest; and the Florida Bible Institute could only maintain intramural sports, which Billy participated in throughout his time at the school.

Though Billy had no intention of joining any of the teams, he enjoyed the competitive atmosphere. He was known to visit the baseball team's informal practice sessions and play first base[14] or learn moves from the wrestlers at their team practice.[15]

More than anything, though, Billy went to games and matches when his schedule allowed and cheered as hard as anyone. Half a century later, he could still recall a phenomenal twenty-two-second pin by wrestler Bob Taussig. After seeing that spectacle, he said, he "never missed a match."[16]

Billy was not always involved in strictly spiritual things. He enjoyed the healthy pleasures that Wheaton had to offer.

By design, Billy scaled back his ministry opportunities to focus on the more demanding academic schedule at Wheaton. His main ministry opportunity that fall was to serve on the Gospel teams that were sent out by the school. Organized by the Christian Service Council, the ten or so teams—usually comprising one main preacher accompanied by singing trios, quartets, and sometimes soloists or song leaders—went out on Sunday afternoons and evenings to visit local churches, missions, and orphanages within Chicago and its nearby suburbs. Most often, the teams were relegated to Sunday night services held in fellowship halls, with smaller gatherings than would normally attend church in the morning.[17] Furthermore, the groups were filled with zealous, though not always greatly gifted, musicians and preachers. Year by year, the Christian Service Council tried to remedy the lack of quality. In the fall of 1940, they held auditions to increase the quality of the music.[18]

Though nobody would demean the opportunity and importance of the program, it was a bit of a step backward for the young preacher who had already preached to thousands and who'd had regular speaking engagements while in Tampa. If he was troubled by this, he certainly didn't show it, but threw himself wholeheartedly into the endeavor.

Starting the first Sunday in October and continuing until December 13, Billy went with the Gospel teams every Sunday except for two.[19] His first meetings were at the Christian Fellowship Church in Hammond, Indiana, just southeast of Chicago across the Illinois-Indiana border. Traveling with a male quartet for the afternoon and evening services, Billy preached a consistent series of messages. As he would do throughout his preaching career, he presented simple Gospel messages with an emphasis on personal decisions for Christ.[20] After a week off from the Gospel teams—perhaps spending time with Dr. Watson, who was in town—Billy preached at Des Plaines Bible Church, northeast of downtown Chicago, with a women's trio that included Wheaton student Lillian Ironside, daughter of Harry Ironside, the pastor of the Moody Church. This same trio, along with song leader Herb Anderson, also went with Billy to River Grove Church, just west of Chicago, on the first Sunday of November.

On November 8, Billy traveled with Herb Anderson to the Pacific Garden Mission in downtown Chicago. This represented a shift from the church services he had been preaching, and a return to his previous experience of preaching at trailer parks and missions in Florida. The Pacific Garden Mission was where evangelist Billy Sunday had been converted a half century earlier and where Mel Trotter, "a modern miracle of grace," was transformed from his hopeless alcoholism before he started his own rescue mission in Grand Rapids, Michigan. The Pacific Garden Mission was reaching thousands of down-and-outers for Christ through Gospel preaching and by providing food and shelter.

In the middle of November, Billy went to Portage Park Baptist Church in Chicago. Again he was accompanied by a male quartet, but this time he shared the preaching with fellow student Harwood Hess. Crammed into Billy's 1937 Plymouth, the crew prayed on their way to the services, asking the Lord to work through their singing and preaching.[21] Don Brown, a member of the quartet, recalled that the services were attended by fewer than one hundred people, of which two or three accepted Christ after hearing Billy's preaching.[22]

On Sunday evenings in early December, Billy went with the Gospel team to the Wayside Cross Mission in Aurora, about twenty miles southwest of Wheaton, with a mixed group of singers, and to South Shore Methodist Church in Chicago. At the close of one of these meetings, Billy spoke about the love of God as shown through the Crucifixion. For dramatic effect, with the lights dimmed, Billy reached out his hands as he began to describe, with his powerfully emotive voice, Jesus on the cross, dying for the sins of the human race. The preaching affected the audience as well as several of the musicians accompanying Billy—some of whom had tears rolling down their cheeks.[23]

Billy's final participation with the Gospel teams that fall was at Elmhurst Grace Church, where he preached at the Young People's service and directed the evening sing, with Walt Hoffman as song leader and a women's trio from the school.

The opportunities for him to preach with the Gospel teams were important for his development as a preacher—but perhaps it was more important for those who made decisions for Christ under his preaching.

Back at Wheaton, students began to talk to one another about this young, gifted preacher. "The Lord is going to use Billy one day," some said, though the opinion was far from unanimous.[24] Perhaps with the benefit of hindsight, one of Billy's fellow students from those days insisted that these services were "occasions to witness the power of Billy's preaching."[25]

Though Billy had begun in relative anonymity and loneliness at Wheaton, the hand of the Lord was upon him, and his charisma and preaching abilities began to show themselves in ways that would launch him to positions of leadership in the coming years. The embers that had been kindled during his time in Florida were now being fanned into flame as his budding ministry caught fire on the prairie west of Chicago.

CHAPTER 15

RESTRAINED PASSIONS

*"I gasped, 'Oh, no!' until I felt my heart
within me rise and tell me to be still."*
RUTH BELL

"If I marry," reads a poem that Ruth McCue Bell wrote in 1937 on her way across the Pacific from China to Wheaton, "he must be so tall when he is on his knees, as one has said, he reaches all the way to Heaven."[1] What follows in the poem could only be described as the counterpart to the Proverbs 31 woman.

Finding the man who could match her expectations would be a chore. By her older sister's count, Ruth dated fifty-two suitors in college.[2] But if finding the right man was hard, deciding on the man when she found him would prove an equally difficult task.

Ruth did not want to go to Wheaton College, and she did not want to date any boys when she arrived—at least in theory. In reality, her passions for love were strong, but they conflicted with her ideals, her dreams, and her commitments. Only one man could break into the heart of this young, godly, idealistic woman, and it would not be easy.

Ruth was born to medical missionaries in China in June 1920. Her father, L. Nelson Bell, was the chief surgeon and administrative superintendent of the Qingjiang General Hospital, about three hundred miles north of Shanghai. As the director, Dr. Bell made sure "the hospital existed 'primarily for the preaching of the Gospel.' "[3]

Ruth grew up surrounded by dedicated missionaries in a world where disease, death, and political instability were an ever-present reality. This environment instilled a morbid desire within Ruth. As a young girl, she would kneel beside her bed and ask God if she could die for him. Her sister, Rosa, would pray in response, "Please, God, don't listen to her."[4]

In 1927, the Bells were forced to leave China when a bloody civil war turned dangerously anti-foreign. They spent the year in the United States—first in Waynesboro, Virginia, where Dr. Bell's family lived; for a time in Holden, West Virginia; and finally in Houston, Texas—before returning to China. There they found their houses and the hospital ransacked and critical medical equipment destroyed.[5]

By age twelve, Ruth had become intrigued with Tibet, where she heard that, just as men were afraid to climb the high Himalayan Mountains, they were also afraid to preach the Gospel.[6] In response, she pledged herself to become a missionary to Tibet, the so-called roof of the globe. The dedicated young idealist was willing to sacrifice her life as a lonely, unmarried, obscure, poor, pioneering missionary for Christ's sake.

The Bells saw the need for traditional education, so in 1932, after teaching the girls at home, and later with a tutor, they sent the teenage Rosa and Ruth to school fifteen hundred miles away at the Pyeng Yang Foreign School in what would later become Pyongyang, North Korea. The school of 140 students had a strong Christian curriculum, believed in biblical authority, and had high academic standards—all three of which were significant enough for the Bells to send their daughters there instead of to the much closer Shanghai schools.

At the beginning, Ruth was dreadfully homesick, and she began writing long, morbid letters home. Her father finally intervened, suggesting to the school administrators that Ruth needed to spend more time with her peers.[7] When they came to visit, Ruth declared that God had told her that it was His will for her to return home with them, to which her father firmly responded, "Your mother and I have been praying too, and that's not the answer we got."[8]

During Ruth's junior year, the Bell family furloughed in Montreat, North Carolina, a small mountain town thirty miles east of Asheville. There, Ruth and Rosa—who had contracted tuberculosis the previous year—graduated from high school in 1936.

Ruth was only sixteen years old when she graduated, and the Bells thought she was too young to attend college. Rosa, on the other hand, had recovered from her tuberculosis and was ready to continue her education. The Bells had become interested in Wheaton College when they first heard about it from Betty Stam while resting at the China Inland Mission. Stam, who was a missionary, was later martyred with her husband, John, in 1934.

The Bells' interest was further fanned when Wheaton graduates Ken and Kay Gieser came to work at the Chinese hospital. Kay's father was vice president of the school, and the Giesers' deep spirituality made an impression.[9] So Rosa went off to Wheaton, while Ruth returned to Pyeng Yang for further study.

By the late summer of 1937, it was Ruth's turn to go to Wheaton. The plan was for her to leave by boat from Shanghai on August 19, making her way to Vancouver, British Columbia, and then traveling by train to Wheaton. But tensions that summer turned to war between China and Japan, and the bombing of the route to Shanghai made it impossible for Ruth to catch her boat. She was delighted, believing it was a sign from God.

Her parents, however, were still determined to send Ruth to America. In September, the Bells evacuated Qingjiang and made their way to Shanghai under threat of bombings and other hostilities. Ruth would later say that, under these threats, "you had a real feeling that Christ was awfully close."[10] It was in contrast to these experiences that many Wheaton students seemed dull and "provincial" to Ruth.[11]

On October 22, Ruth sailed to Seattle on the USS *Chaumont* and then took a train to Wheaton, where she arrived too late to enroll for classes.[12] Unbeknownst to her, when she left her parents, they quickly decided to return to the town where they had served for the past two decades.

Despite Ruth's initial displeasure about attending Wheaton, she decided to gain what was necessary for her to become a lifelong missionary in Tibet. She wanted training in the Bible, but she did not need a husband. She would remain an unmarried old maid, if necessary.

Billy, being older than most of his classmates, gravitated toward the more mature upperclassmen. One of these students was senior Johnny Streater, for whose company, Student Trucking Service, Billy worked moving furniture.

The two quickly became friends as they discovered they had much in common. Both, having delayed their entrance into Wheaton, were slightly older than the other students, and both had ministry experience and ministry plans for the future.

Before coming to Wheaton, Streater had served in the US Navy on the USS *Mississippi*, where he was the point man for the Navigators, a California-based discipleship ministry that was sweeping through the military in the 1930s.[13] At Wheaton, Streater was a spiritual leader and served as part of the Christian Council, a small group of students who orchestrated campus outreach such as the Gospel teams in which Billy participated.

In addition, Streater was the president of the Foreign Mission Fellowship and was vice president of the Rural Bible Crusade, which sought to reach the lost in America's often overlooked rural areas.

Beyond these ministry connections, Johnny was from Lakeland, Florida—just thirty miles from the Florida Bible Institute. He understood the culture shock that Billy faced at Wheaton.

As the two worked moving furniture, Johnny began to tell Billy about Ruth Bell. Johnny and Ruth knew each other fairly well, having served together on the Rural Bible Crusade, and they were both involved in the Foreign Mission Fellowship.

Though Billy and Ruth had never participated in the same group, she was also a part of the Gospel team ministry and served at Mooseheart Lodge, where she was heckled by the girls for being old-fashioned. To her credit, she went back to Wheaton, and instead of giving up, she redoubled her efforts by changing her hairstyle and trying to update her clothes, and then returned to working with the girls.[14]

These details probably piqued Billy's interest, but perhaps the clincher was what Streater told him about Ruth's devotional life. She was legendary around campus for her commitment to early morning devotions—starting as early as 4:00 a.m.

Billy was intrigued.

Once, while moving furniture during the first semester, Billy and Johnny were at Williston Hall, which was a women's dorm on the upper floors and housed the school dining hall on the lower level.

Johnny's eyes lit up when he saw Ruth Bell hustling from lunch on her way to class. "Ruth! Ruth!" he said. "There's someone I want you to meet."

As Billy and Ruth introduced themselves, they both realized that they had seen each other before, but hadn't known it at the time.

Ruth had been hearing from others about this dynamic young preacher, and she had passed him once as he hustled down the stairs at Blanchard Hall. She remembered thinking, *Boy, that young man is in a hurry.*

Perhaps more significantly, Ruth recalled having been impressed by Billy one Sunday as the Gospel teams prepared to go out to the local churches. As they gathered in Williston to pray for their ministry opportunities, she heard Billy's loud and earnest voice as he prayed, and she thought, *There is a man who knows to whom he is speaking.*[15] Ruth was impressed with Billy's earnestness and found him to be an inspiration with his single-minded resolve to "make Christ known in all His saving power." But though they had met together with some thirty or forty other students, they had not yet been formally introduced.

Billy had built up Ruth in his mind with the information he knew about her. He wanted a spiritual girl, and she was godly, evidenced in part by her early morning devotions. But though he had never put a face to the legend of Ruth Bell, he could recall being impressed with her beauty even before he knew who she was.[16] Now that he could make the connection, he knew that Ruth was not only godly, but she was beautiful as well.

As Ruth looked into the brilliant blue eyes of this student in work clothes, she was amused to find a young man whose Southern accent was more pronounced than her own.[17] Ruth was late for class, so after a brief introduction, she dashed off. In her time at Wheaton, she had met plenty of nice young men who had not met her high standards.

Only time would tell if Billy—or anyone, for that matter—was suitable for her.

Billy, on the other hand, was smitten from the start, but it took a few weeks before he mustered the courage to ask this lovely missionary student on a date.

⊹⇒

"Go ask her, Billy!" some students whispered. Billy's friends were goading him to ask Ruth Bell out on a date. Johnny Streater had not been the only one to think that Billy and Ruth would be perfect together. There was a growing consensus in certain circles on campus that the two should be paired up.[18] The small group of students that had gathered around Billy in the library were encouraging him to ask Ruth to the school's yearly musical rendition of Handel's *Messiah*.

Nervously, he mustered the courage to get up, walk over to Ruth's table, sit down, and ask her if she would go with him to the performance.

She turned her head and in a low voice said, "Yes."[19]

⊹⇒

The crisp December air was filled with anticipation as these two well-respected spiritual giants came together for a date in Pierce Chapel.

After enjoying the musical performance, they went to dinner at a professor's house. The two had a real interest in one another. As they made their way home, Billy reached over to grab her hand, which she quickly pulled away.[20] Billy felt rejected, and as they parted ways, he thought he had failed with her.

But he hadn't failed. The signals she sent were as confusing as her thinking. Ruth went back to her room that night, knelt down, and prayed, "God, if You let me serve You with that man, I'd consider it the greatest privilege of my life."[21]

That winter, Billy and Ruth began an undefined dating relationship. And that lack of definition would cause some problems. At the same time, Billy was restraining his own passions, determined not to get into a relationship that wasn't God's will for him, and that would leave him hurting as his breakup with Emily Cavanaugh had. His restraint came across to Ruth as a confusing form of disinterest.[22]

About two weeks after their first date, Ruth went on a date with a young man she had known before she met Billy. She saw nothing wrong with this, as her relationship status with Billy was undetermined. But Billy thought he had made his desires clear. As Ruth later said, "He got bossy, right at the start."[23] Billy pulled her aside and said, "Either you date me and nobody else, or you can date every man on this campus and you don't date me."[24] Ruth chose Billy, and they began going steady.

By February, Billy wanted her to come hear him preach at a local church where there were only about twenty people present. Ruth recalled that he got up and shouted just as loud as if he had been preaching to thousands.[25] As she sat there, half embarrassed, she wondered how she would let him know what she thought of his delivery. But then Billy gave the invitation, and three of the young people stood up to accept Christ. Ruth then realized that it wasn't *how* he preached, but *what* he preached—and his sincerity—that was effective.[26] It was the beginning of their ministry together, and a fruitful one at that.

Ruth also noticed something else. As Billy guided her by the arm toward the door, she noted his "unaffected thoughtfulness."[27] Her wall was coming down.

There was still one problem, though. Billy drove her to her house, walked her to the door, and said, "There's something I'd like you to make a matter of prayer." He explained that he had an interest in her, but there was a conflict. "I know you have been called to the mission field, and I'm not definite."[28]

Something was going to have to give.

The Foreign Mission Fellowship was a group on campus that catered to students who had grown up on the mission field and to students who planned to go to the mission field. Missionaries and missions leaders often came to speak on Monday nights to a group of fifty to seventy-five students, who would later break up into groups to pray for different parts of the world.[29]

Billy and Ruth were regular attendees of FMF during the spring of 1941, and it must have brought comfort to Ruth to gather with others to pray for the safety of her family, who had returned to the war zone in China. Her letters took two months to arrive there, as the Chinese were at war with Japan.[30]

The Wheaton yearbook for 1941 includes a picture of Billy, Johnny Streater, and future housemate Ken Hansen, with tongue-in-cheek dialogue:

"Don't you feel, Johnny, that Bill is right in looking to FMF to acquaint him with the needs and opportunities of the foreign fields?"

"I think so, Ken. I know that's especially true for someone who doesn't definitely know God's plan for his life. If a man is honestly willing to face the foreign mission field, FMF guides him to a knowledge of the possible places of service."

"You know, fellows, I honestly believe that the weekly missionary speakers we hear challenge more lives than we think. Bill, if you are thinking about missions for a life's work, you can't afford to miss any of those meetings."[31]

Humorous yearbook advertisements aside, Billy was becoming

immersed in the missions-minded elements of campus. With Ruth, he was a regular attendee of a lunch at the house of economics professor Mortimer Lane, who had been a successful businessman, worked as an economist for the US Department of Commerce and the New York Bureau of Municipal Research, and had been an editor at a business magazine. Having acquired a fortune through his other ventures, Lane taught at Wheaton for one dollar a year. He donated his time as a teacher to the school, but also privately paid tuition and housing costs for many missionary kids.[32]

Lane's home sat just west of campus and the property covered most of a city block. His house was often volunteered to accommodate traveling missionaries and speakers at the school. He also used his home as a place to invite missionary kids for Sunday lunch, after which they would pray for the concerns of missions.[33]

Billy was getting a glimpse of the enormous needs in world missions, and his heart burned for the world. But as he told Ruth, he was not sure that the Lord was calling him to be a missionary.

⊣⊨

"Bill, Ruth's one in a million."[34] That's all Dr. Edman said to Billy as they once again crossed paths on campus one day that spring. That's all he had to say to confirm what Billy was already seeing. Ruth was to be his life companion.

Ruth caught herself reluctantly falling in love as she wrote to her parents, describing Billy's "fearlessness and sometimes sternness" mixed together with thoughtfulness and gentleness. Then she wrote, "Sounds like I'm in love, doesn't it? Don't get worried. I'm not."[35]

She surely was not fooling her parents, though, even as she tried to fool herself.

On another night out with her new beau, her heart was beating wildly as Billy's hand reached for hers. This time, she did not resist as he drew her near. Shortly after, she wrote in a poem, "I gasped, 'Oh, no!' until I felt my heart within me rise and tell me to be still."[36]

Truth was, she was head-over-heels in love.

After a while, the truth began to catch up with her. She had resisted for too long. Ruth called for Billy to come by and pick her up one day, and as they drove, she told him for the first time that she loved him.[37]

Billy was exhilarated. Smiling widely, he reached for her hand, gently pulled her to himself, and said, "I would like to kiss you. . .but I think I should wait."[38]

And then he proceeded to explain his hesitation. He had been hurt a few years back by Emily Cavanaugh, and he did not want his heart to be broken again.

Needless to say, Ruth was not pleased.[39] But the truth was out. Ruth could restrain her passion no longer. She loved Billy Graham. And he had found his life partner.

CHAPTER 16

FINDING HIS FOOTING

"What did the Lord give you from His Word this morning?"
DAWSON TROTMAN

Billy's initial discomfort during his transition to Wheaton was relieved as he began to adapt to the atmosphere of the Northern school. His budding relationship with Ruth Bell helped, but circumstances in her life in the coming months would remind Billy that his life at Wheaton was about more than romance. Not that he really needed to be reminded as his ministry opportunities once again began to increase.

When Billy started school at Wheaton, he lived in the home of Dr. Fred Gerstung, a professor of German, at 741 Irving, just north of campus. Billy was a quiet, respectful boarder, who lived alone in a room he used for little more than study and sleep.[1] That first winter, Billy came down with the flu, which was of moderate concern to Mrs. Gerstung. She called Billy's mother, who told her to scrape the inside of a grapefruit for him to eat.[2]

Socially, Billy joined a literary society in which about half of the students participated.[3] Of the eight literary societies, Billy chose the

Naitermian "Knights," who were sponsored by Dr. Gerstung and Dr. Edman. As if he were writing a promotional blurb for a book, Billy is quoted in the Wheaton College yearbook as saying, "For spiritual fellowship, parliamentary drill, true congeniality, and lasting friendships, I chose [the] Naitermian Society."[4]

The societies met on Friday nights and constituted a major part of Wheaton's social life. Groups were comprised of between sixty and seventy-five students each, who gathered for music, talent shows, training, and practice in Robert's Rules of Order, and often began with a devotional.[5] Naitermian Society president Herb Anderson asked Billy to share devotions on a few occasions, and the group was impressed by his "earnest eloquence."[6]

Billy gained lasting relationships through his participation in the society. Often, after the Friday night meeting, he and some of the other students would make their way to Ken Hansen's house at 712 Howard for a time of prayer. This group often included Don Brown, Al and Lloyd Fesmire, Phil Foxwell, and Ken Hansen.[7] Not only was meeting with these spiritual leaders on campus important for Billy's social transition, but he also found new housemates for the coming years.

Chapels in the spring and fall of 1941 were gaining new momentum, with speakers both familiar and new to Billy. During the February evangelistic services led by the Reverend Howard W. Ferrin, president of Providence Bible Institute, there were stirrings of the Spirit of God as students raised their hands in worship and stood unprovoked in the pews, and several students surrendered their hearts to Christ.[8]

Other speakers of significance included Wheaton resident John R. Rice, editor of the influential fundamentalist periodical *Sword of the Lord*; evangelist Gypsy Smith, who had rebuffed Billy's autograph request at the Florida Bible Institute;[9] and Christian and Missionary Alliance pastor and mystic A. W. Tozer.[10] Not only did Tozer come to Wheaton's campus on several occasions during Billy's time there, but students often made their way to Tozer's Southside Alliance Church in Chicago to hear him speak. Billy said that he "always came away blessed in soul."[11]

That same semester, Bob Jones Jr. also came to speak. By that time, there was a rumor going around that Billy had been asked to leave Bob Jones College. It was clearly not true, but the confusion about what had really happened was never cleared up in the minds of many of his peers.[12]

The following fall brought in three speakers with budding ministries, who proved to be important in the ministry of Billy Graham: Dawson Trotman, Torrey Johnson, and Jim Rayburn.

Dawson Trotman was a California native and resident, who came to speak in September of 1941.[13] Born in 1906, Trotman had been converted in 1926 from a lifestyle of gambling, lying, and drinking. After his conversion, he developed a relentless passion for evangelism. In the early 1930s he would not go to bed without sharing "the most wonderful thing"[14] in his life—his faith. He was successful at getting "converts," but he never followed up with them, making his focus the next lost soul. When he started running into some of the same so-called converts months later and found that they were not following Christ and that nothing in their lives had changed, he began to reevaluate his methods.

Trotman's methods of evangelism, he felt, left new converts to fend for themselves and led to their own spiritual demise. So he renewed his energies in the area of discipleship. He was a no-nonsense man, whose methods were often off-putting, but never disingenuous. His approach to faith, which included disciplined and systematic Bible study, scripture memorization, prayer, and witnessing found some followers within the community at large, but really gained traction in the 1930s within the disciplined military lifestyle, especially in the US Navy, which docked many of its ships in California's San Pedro Bay.

Trotman chose the name the Navigators for his ministry, in part for its naval connection, but also to reflect one of his central teaching models—the Wheel—which helped believers navigate their lives centered on Christ. The four spokes of the wheel—prayer, Bible study, witnessing, and living the life (later changed to fellowship)—connected believers to the hub, which is Christ. The ministry's motto emphasized Trotman's passion: "To know Christ and to make Him known."

But Trotman was concerned with more than a cursory knowledge of Christ. In line with 2 Timothy 2:2 (KJV), he was trying to teach "faithful men, who shall be able to teach others also." In pursuit of such faithful men, Trotman invested time in local Christian schools that trained up leaders—such as Biola and Westmont—and also visited like-minded schools across the country, such as Dallas Theological Seminary and Columbia Bible College.[15]

Billy never became a Navigator, but he respected the organization and had Navigator friends who were impressive in their dedication to Trotman, to his principles, and most importantly to the Lord.[16] One of those friends was Johnny Streater, with whom Billy had been working and who had introduced him to Ruth.

In the early years of the Navigators, Streater had impressed Trotman—who had seen many possible disciples fall off from his demanding methods—by memorizing 105 memory verses in less than a month, becoming a devoted Bible teacher while at sea, and serving as a Gospel team leader in churches while on shore.[17] After his graduation in the spring of 1941, Streater intended to go to China as a missionary with his soon-to-be wife, Carol Lane, but the war made this an impossible option. Instead, he began working with Trotman, spreading the Navigator message and methods on military bases and in civilian settings east of the Mississippi River.[18]

Streater's connection to Trotman was strong. So when Trotman came to Wheaton, Streater arranged for him to stay with his future in-laws, the Lanes.

Excited about sharing Trotman's vision with the Wheaton campus, Streater invited Billy to come meet with this growing giant and apostle of evangelism and discipleship. If Billy had expected to meet a meek and gentle Christian leader, he was taken aback. At their first meeting, Trotman reached out to shake the young student's hand and exchanged short cordialities before asking pointedly, "What did the Lord give you from His Word this morning?"

Caught off guard by the question, Billy remained silent, wondering, what *had* God given him? Knowing that Trotman was right to ask the question, Billy could not be angry with him, and he resolved to never again be without a good answer.[19]

In chapel at Wheaton, Trotman shared about his ministry and encouraged the students by showing them that work was being done among the military, which was building up in anticipation of a possible confrontation with Germany and Italy. This was also a source of hope for those students who would be called for service during the war. He declared, "The army life is a great training place for the mission field and a mission field in itself."[20] If there was anyone who truly believed that there was a mission field in the military, it was Dawson Trotman.

In October, R. G. LeTourneau visited chapel,[21] as well as the thirty-two-year-old pastor of Midwest Bible Church, Torrey Johnson. Johnson came to hold a high school youth rally, at which "numbers were low, but spirits high."[22] These youth rallies were the seeds of what later became Youth for Christ (which Billy joined in 1945).

Johnson also started a radio program called *Chapel Hour* and another called *Songs in the Night*, which Billy listened to as a student.[23]

In November, Jim Rayburn spoke at chapel.[24] He had recently graduated from Dallas Theological Seminary and was having successful youth meetings as part of the Miracle Book Club, a Bible ministry based in Richmond, California. In the spring of 1941, he began holding "Young Life Campaigns," drawing hundreds of young people. However, differences in ministry philosophy with the Miracle Bible Club forced Rayburn to part ways. He founded a new ministry, called Young Life Clubs, whose motto was "Christ is life."[25] By November of 1941, this visionary of young people's ministry was finding support throughout the Midwest and spreading his innovative techniques around the country. Billy took notice.[26]

Both Jim Rayburn and Torrey Johnson were preoccupied with the same question: How are we going to reach this generation with the Gospel of Jesus Christ? They maintained extraordinary depth in their ministries and teaching, but they would use any scheme or gimmick possible to spread the Gospel. Rayburn, for his part, believed that he must speak "winsomely."

By contrast, Dawson Trotman was asking another question altogether: How are we going to *keep* this generation once we reach them? He had seen too many young people come to meetings and then fall off from the faith. He began calling men and women to active growth through discipleship and spiritual disciplines.

Both of these schools of thought deeply influenced Billy. God was bringing men to Wheaton who had tremendous visions to reach the lost. Billy became closely connected with all of them.

⊹

Another part of life that refreshed Billy's time at Wheaton was the group of close friends from his past who joined him there. In particular, the coming of longtime North Carolina friends Grady Wilson and Jimmie Johnson enlivened his experience.

Grady had been a successful student at Bob Jones College after Billy left—at least initially. He was president of the 280-member Ministerial Association and president of his literary society in the spring of 1940.[27] But if Billy had been singed by Dr. Bob, Grady definitely got burned.

Like Billy, Grady was raised a Presbyterian, and he became a Southern Baptist in 1938. He then was baptized in Huntersville, North Carolina, in response to pressure from his ministers, as well as to suit him for available ministry opportunities. But baptism was not enough. They wanted to ordain him into their fold.

There was a problem with this, however. Before he could be ordained, Grady needed to talk to Dr. Bob, who had formed his own Gospel Fellowship Association to "get the Gospel to as many people as possible in the shortest time possible." The association was intended to provide oversight for ministers and evangelists and cut through some of the red tape associated with churches and denominations. In short, Bob Jones believed that he could ordain students just as well as any church, and he could train them up better than any church. He was often right. Jones was gifted at raising up ministers of the Gospel, but those students had to comply with his every command.

Grady was now receiving input from the Baptist ministers that made him question Dr. Bob's proclaimed authority to do things that others believed only the Church should do. When Grady met with Dr. Bob to discuss the matter, he expressed his appreciation for what Dr. Bob had meant to his life, but said he wanted to be ordained through the Church. Dr. Bob was not pleased, and Grady was now in his sights.

Two and a half months before graduation, Dr. Bob called Grady to his office. He'd heard that Grady had been meeting with Jimmie

Johnson, his longtime friend and mentor, who, along with evangelists Fred Brown and Henry Grube, had fallen out of favor with Dr. Bob. Always aware of what his students were doing, Jones had heard that Grady and Jimmie had gone fishing together. He demanded that Grady tell him what the former student had said about him. Grady refused, saying that it would be gossip. Dr. Bob replied, "You let me decide whether it's gossip or loyalty." He then asked Grady to resign from the offices he held at the school and grounded him to the campus for the rest of the year, thus preventing him from preaching or being ordained at any other church.

These strong-arm tactics did not go over well with Grady, who was slotted to preach two meetings in Decatur, Alabama, the next weekend. Resigning from Bob Jones College was the only way he could keep that engagement. He met with Bob Jones Jr. to let him know of his decision to resign, and the younger Jones told him he would "regret this all the days of [his] life." But it was not a decision Grady would regret—even for a moment.

After preaching the services in Decatur, Grady went home to Charlotte. Uncertain of his future, he prayed one night that God would lead him to further his education, which he felt he needed. At midnight that same night, he received a call from Dr. Harold Strathearn, executive director of the R. G. LeTourneau Foundation. Vernon Patterson, a Charlotte businessman and leader of the Christian Business Men's Clubs, had told R. G. LeTourneau what had happened to Grady at Bob Jones College, and LeTourneau was moved. The business tycoon had experienced his own falling-out with Bob Jones when he was denied a request for an accounting of how his monthly donations to the school were being spent.

LeTourneau sent word to Strathearn that he wanted to pay Grady's way through any school of his choice—including Oxford, Cambridge, Yale, or Harvard.

When Strathearn got through to Grady that night, the young man began weeping, telling Dr. Strathearn about the prayer he had uttered not more than five hours earlier.

Grady shared that he had his heart set on Wheaton, but feared he would not be able to get in. Dr. Strathearn told him that R. G. LeTourneau was a good friend of Dr. Edman's and would get him in without trouble.

The next day, Grady received a call from the Wheaton president, who said he had just spoken with LeTourneau, and with Billy Graham, and that Grady would be accepted anytime he could get there.[28] He enrolled for the 1941–1942 school year, and Billy's world became more familiar.[29]

The final addition to Billy's crew at Wheaton was his childhood hero, evangelist Jimmie Johnson, who enrolled at Wheaton when he was thirty-two years old. Johnson had graduated from unaccredited Bob Jones College nearly a decade earlier but was now seeking a degree from the University of Chicago. While he was in the city, he came out to visit Billy at Wheaton and decided to transfer there to complete his studies. Johnson moved in with Billy, along with Lloyd Fesmire, in the house of Anna Hansen, whose son Ken had by then graduated.

Billy came across to many students as something less than a big man on campus.[30] He was somewhat reserved, though very polite, and had a terrific recall of names.[31] One graduate student, who later became president of Wheaton College, found him "charming but somewhat unsophisticated."[32]

Billy's reserve, at least in part, was likely a result of his determination and purposefulness. He spent his time and energy preparing for ministry opportunities, interrupted by studies. He spent most of his social life with a small coterie of friends, including Grady, Jimmie, Lloyd Fesmire, Don Brown, Ken Hansen, and Don Hoke—not to mention Ruth.[33]

This group of friends often gathered for times of prayer, and their discussions often turned to theology, with some of the others looking to Billy for his biblical insights.[34] One student recalled hearing this cohort discussing future seminary plans, and Billy blurted out, "I'm not going to *cemetery!*"[35] Seminaries were increasingly being seen as places where modernism was winning out and spiritual lives were being killed. But Billy would later regret not furthering his education.

Billy made other connections at Wheaton as well, even if indirectly. Harold Lindsell and Carl F. H. Henry were both students when Ruth first arrived on campus in 1937. Lindsell courted Ruth, and she found him a valuable friend and spiritual counselor, but she was not interested in his romantic overtures. Carl Henry was also a friend of Ruth's. He studied in the graduate program and taught some journalism courses at Wheaton until the spring of 1941. Billy later called on both Lindsell and Henry, two heavyweight thinkers on campus, to serve as editors of *Christianity Today.*

Billy's chances to hear dynamic chapel speakers and grow in old and new relationships were enhanced by his growing ministry. In the spring of 1941, he began filling in for Dr. Edman in the pulpit at the Wheaton Gospel Tabernacle and also had opportunities to hold services elsewhere.

In March, Billy spoke to the "prepsters," the high school students who met at the Academy on campus. He spoke on "The Victorious Life," with Richard Scheel as song leader, Anna Marie Eavey on the piano, and soloist Georgia Thompson, who sang "For God So Loved the World" by Howard L. Brown.[36] In the fall, Billy spoke at the Junior League, a women's charity organization, where his topic was "Victorious Living." He was accompanied by Franklin Leman, a "dramatic baritone," with Anna Marie Eavey again on piano.[37]

In addition to these isolated speaking opportunities, Billy tried to ramp up his weeklong evangelistic meetings in the spring and summer of 1941. He held the first series of meetings during spring break, April 13–20, at Moline Congregational Church in Moline, Michigan, where fellow student Chet Terpstra was a member.[38] Billy once again made promotional flyers, with "8 Great Days of REVIVAL with students of Wheaton College" emblazoned at the top. Below that, next to a picture of Billy, were teasers for all the features of the meetings: "Choruses!" "Instrumental Numbers!" "Dynamic Preaching!" "Solos!"

On the flyer, Billy describes himself as "A Young Southern Evangelist with A Burning Message You Will Never Forget!" He refers to song leader Al Smith as a "Nationally Known Composer, Song Leader, Radio Artist." About pianist and trombonist Lloyd Fesmire, he says, "Formerly with Percy Crawford's Famous Brass Quartet." The flyer also suggests that services would be broadcast on Mel Trotter's *Morning Mission* broadcast on Tuesday through Thursday mornings at 7:00 a.m., and that a youth rally would be held on the final afternoon.[39]

In May, Billy held a weekend-long gathering, with Bible teaching and evangelism, with William H. Lee Spratt, a Conservative Baptist Fellowship pastor at the Ottawa Bible Fellowship in Ottawa, Illinois, seventy-five miles southwest of Wheaton.[40]

That summer, Billy traveled south to hold meetings and reconnect with old friends and mentors during a weeklong series of services at the St. Petersburg Gospel Tabernacle, where W. T. Watson was pastor. The *St. Petersburg Times*, which regularly advertised meetings at the church, announced, "Don't miss a service—attend the YOUTH CRUSADE and evangelistic campaign." Billy was called a "Dynamic Youth Evangelist" and was accompanied by "The Melody Three" from the Florida Bible Institute, with "Stirring Messages—Special Music."[41]

Billy was finding his footing once again and hitting his stride.

CHAPTER 17

ALWAYS TOO SOON TO QUIT

"I have asked the Lord, if you were the one, to win you for me."
BILLY GRAHAM TO RUTH BELL

At Wheaton, Billy was surrounded by wonderfully spiritual people, effective and godly teachers, and gifted leaders and preachers who spoke in chapel. But none would be more influential of a teacher, speaker, or spiritual counselor than V. Raymond Edman. The Wheaton president had an inimitable ability to reach deeply into the hearts of the students—and Billy's heart was no exception. Indeed, his friendship with Dr. Edman quickly became, as he would later say, "one of the warmest, most enduring and important friendships" of his life.[1]

Victor Raymond Edman had become interim president of Wheaton in 1940 when James Oliver Buswell Jr. was forced to resign after his outspoken rebuke of the Presbyterian Church USA's growing association with modernism. Though few Wheaton students or alumni were not concerned about what was happening within the denomination, many continued to support the Presbyterian Church USA and pray and hope for its renewal. Buswell's stand with the protesting Orthodox Presbyterian movement, led by J. Gresham Machen, alienated many of the alumni, students, and faculty.

This alienation created significant division between faculty members at the school and created a crisis on campus. Dr. Edman, the head of the history department, acted as a mediator between the factions. When Buswell was asked to leave, the board asked Edman to become interim president because of his peacemaking efforts and the wise counsel he had offered during the school controversy. He accepted the position in the spring of 1940—just a semester before Billy arrived—with no intention of remaining as permanent president. Little did he know that he would become a pillar of the school for the next twenty-five years.

Born in 1900 in Chicago Heights, just south of Chicago, V. Raymond Edman had come to Christ as a high school student at an ecumenical evangelistic service held in a makeshift tabernacle. After high school, he served in the US Army in France and Germany during the First World War. Edman's patriotic view of history, which he poured into his students, was greatly colored by his experiences in the war.

When Edman returned from overseas, he enrolled temporarily at the University of Illinois, but then transferred to the Nyack Missionary Training Institute in 1921, two years after the death of its founder, A. B. Simpson. In an interesting connection, Edman's roommate at Nyack was W. T. Watson, the future founder of the Florida Bible Institute.[2]

Most Nyack students of the day served in the mission field, and Edman was no exception. He served as a missionary in Ecuador for five years before illness forced him to return to the United States. Upon his return, he served in two pastorates, one of which was the New York Gospel Tabernacle (the church that A. B. Simpson had founded), and he taught at Nyack before moving to Wheaton to teach history in 1936. Nyack asked him to return in 1939 to be president of the school, but he declined, leaving the honors to Thomas Moseley, who received his doctor of divinity degree from Wheaton College in 1940. Unbeknownst to Edman at the time, this left open the opportunity for him to become president of Wheaton in 1940.

In the fall of 1940, even though Edman was interim president, he was still teaching history to one of the largest classes on campus. Billy was one of his students, and he was impressed that Edman knew his subject "from A to Z."[3] Not only did Edman have an encyclopedic memory, but he also was able to "make maps talk"[4] and "history live."[5]

Beyond the classroom, Edman, whose inauguration to the permanent presidency came in May 1941, was fast becoming the student's favorite chapel speaker, with his short but profoundly spiritual messages. Students often were not immediately impressed by his quiet yet forceful speaking style,[6] but in the end, the impression he left would be unforgettable.[7]

In line with his view that "Wheaton's principal impact is its spiritual impact,"[8] Edman viewed chapel as the heart of the school's curriculum. He believed and taught that chapel hour was "family prayer" time.[9] As such, he not only gave it a family atmosphere in his succinct but effective prayers, but also instilled an atmosphere that suggested that chapel was a holy time and place.

As April 1 approached, he preempted April Fools' pranks by encouraging students to pull pranks in class if they must, but not in chapel. Chapel was different. "This part of the day that we spend in family worship," he told the students, "is dedicated wholly to God, and nothing inappropriate to worship should be here."[10]

His messages gave Billy and the others something to "chew on intellectually," but more than that, he spoke to their hearts.[11] Most of his messages between 1940 and 1943 were series of character studies—a seven-part series on Elijah the Tishbite; a five-part series on Balaam; [12] and a series on Hudson Taylor, the pioneering, nineteenth-century missionary to China. [13]

The impact of his messages is clear, not only from the fact that alumni from that period attest to his effectiveness, but also through a perusal of the school newspaper, the *Wheaton Record*, which, during the early 1940s, recorded "Chapel Nuggets," which were quotes from various chapel speakers and often included Edman's pithy statements. Here's a sample of how he was able to make application for his audience with an economy of words:

> *How then to have our faith increased? Only by thinking of all He is for us: His life, His death, His works, He Himself revealed to us in the Word, to be the subject of our constant thoughts, not a striving to have faith. . .but a looking off to the faithful One who seems all we need; a resting in the Loved One entirely, for time and eternity."*[14]

Perhaps such truths would be forgotten as the years passed, but Edman's witticisms would be remembered for a lifetime. For example, "Never doubt in the dark what God told you in the light,"[15] or, in reference to overcoming trials in life, "not somehow. . .but triumphantly!"[16]

Another truth that he hammered relentlessly into his students—in a talk he repeated regularly during finals and midterms to encourage the students—was this simple statement: "It's always too soon to quit." Quoting William J. Cameron, he would say, "The last dejected effort often becomes the winning stroke."[17] He might follow this with the biblical story of the Lord leading the Israelites out of Egypt and their failure to follow through on God's promises. He also taught that "quitting makes a dead end of every road—often just as it was ready to open."[18]

If Edman's messages were not sufficient to impact Billy and the other students, his open door to students was. Edman was a gifted listener, and students came to discuss issues of any kind with him.[19] Like his messages, his counsel was usually short and to the point, but insightful and encouraging. On one occasion, when Billy came to him with a question about whether or not to do a particular thing, Edman told him, "If in doubt, don't do it. When in doubt, put it out."[20]

Rarely was there a student with whom he would not begin and end a private discussion with prayer—often on his knees with an arm draped around the student's shoulder. Billy was impressed that Dr. Edman always took plenty of time with him. "I will never forget the hours of prayer" they had together, he later said.[21]

For students like Grady Wilson, who had endured a hostile encounter with Bob Jones Sr., meeting with Dr. Edman felt like a balm of healing. One time, Dr. Edman called him in and said, "Before we discuss what I'm going to discuss with you, let's kneel down and have a little prayer together."[22]

Billy hit the nail on the head when he said that Dr. Edman possessed a unique "combination of mysticism and practicality."[23]

The spring of 1941 brought challenges to Billy's relationship with Ruth. As she became more convinced of her call to the mission field, Billy's reservations about becoming a missionary grew as well. But how could Ruth renege on her commitment to the Lord?

Matters soon came to a head. In Ruth's mind, either Billy would go to the mission field with her, or she would have to end the relationship and go by herself.

At the same time, Billy was becoming intrigued by a call to American evangelism. A confrontation between the two visions was inevitable. Finally, Billy said, "I haven't tried to win you, Ruth. I haven't asked you to fall in love with me. I haven't sent you candy and flowers and lovely gifts. I have asked the Lord, if you are the one, to win you for me. If not, to keep you from falling in love with me."[24]

In March, Ruth's life took a major turn when her sister, Rosa, had an emergency appendectomy, which revealed tubercular peritonitis. Rosa was sequestered to the Zace Sanitarium, in nearby Winfield, Illinois, and Ruth dropped out of Wheaton to tend to her. Also, the girls' parents returned to the United States so that their mother, Virginia Bell, could receive treatment for malaria, which she had recently contracted.

Later, when Rosa's health had sufficiently improved, her host in Wheaton set up a bed in her sunroom, where Rosa could continue to recover, and Ruth spent the summer tending to her. The host's home was just three houses down from where Billy lived at 702 Howard.

Billy, meanwhile, left for campaigns in the South for the summer. But first he had proposed the idea of marriage. Ruth, however, was still uncertain.

As she nursed her sick sister that summer, Ruth confessed to Rosa that she indeed loved Billy, but she couldn't square it with her promise to God to return to the mission field. She felt that he had led her to Wheaton for the purpose of training for missions.

Rosa responded, "He led you to college all right, through the bombings and everything. And He helped you through some of your courses. But did you ever think He might have led you here—to meet Billy?"

Ruth tried to object, but Rosa continued, "And if He brought you two together, then He'll go right on leading you. Both of you— together. Only He'll lead you as a couple, through Billy. That's only the way it should be. Maybe God does want you over there in Tibet as an old maid missionary, but I doubt it. I think He wants you right here in this country—as Billy Graham's wife."[25]

Ruth sat in stunned silence and then returned to her room and wrote to Billy on July 6, 1941, to accept his proposal of marriage.[26]

Later that summer, Billy went to meet Ruth's parents, who had returned to Waynesboro, Virginia, on furlough from China. He was immediately put at ease by their kindness and interest in him.

Ruth also made a trip to meet Billy's parents in Charlotte, where Billy was holding services at Sharon Presbyterian Church. As they prayed together for the meetings, Ruth sensed the passion for the lost that was driving Billy—especially as he prayed for his childhood friends.

At the services, Ruth was once again apprehensive about Billy's exuberant delivery, especially given the Presbyterian audience, but once again she was silenced by the response, as several people came forward at the close of the meeting.

In September, Billy visited Ruth and gave her an engagement ring, which he was able to buy with money from a love offering taken up by Sharon Presbyterian Church and designated for that purpose.[27] Billy and Ruth were engaged, but now they would have to endure a semester apart.

As Billy began the fall semester at Wheaton, the door to the mission field was not completely closed in his mind. In fact, as late as March 1942, he was still seriously considering whether going with Ruth to serve in Tibet would be the right decision.[28] As it happened, time and circumstances would sort out their competing passions in the days ahead.

Ruth was unable to join Billy for the fall semester of 1941. Not only was she still tending to her sister, Rosa, and reconnecting with her family, but she was also showing signs of having contracted malaria. She wrote to Billy daily that semester.

In November, with Rosa's illness becoming more serious, the Bells decided it would be best to move her to the drier climate of Albuquerque, New Mexico, where treatments for her tuberculosis would be more effective. Ruth accompanied her for a few weeks in order to receive her own treatments. By December, Ruth was better, but Rosa was near death.

Ruth returned to Montreat, North Carolina, where her parents had moved, not sure whether she would ever see her sister alive again.

—

On Sunday morning, December 7, 1941, the war that the Bells had fled in China came to America with the Japanese attack on Pearl Harbor, thrusting the United States into the Second World War.

On Monday morning, when the Wheaton College community gathered for chapel, Dr. Edman stepped up to the podium and stood for a moment, unable to speak, as tears streamed down his cheeks.[29] Finally, he said, "Many times I have sat upon this platform and prayed that such a thing might not happen in this generation."[30] He knew that he would lose members of the Wheaton family to the war.

The environment on campus was soon to be changed. Dr. Edman announced, "Our patriotic duty at the present time is to perform our routine tasks to the best of our abilities," and to make sacrifices "by saving time, energy, and necessary materials."[31] Rations of sugar, tea, coffee, gasoline, toilet paper, and other supplies swept the country, and there was a scarcity of erasers, notebooks, tape, paper clips, and jewelry on campus, as resources were put toward the war effort.[32]

Billy wanted to do his part for the war. After getting approval from Dr. Edman, he announced in the *Wheaton Record* that the school bell would be rung daily at 5:00 p.m., "in order to bring about a unified effort for prayer" on behalf of those who were fighting the war. He added that "a regular remembrance of intercession for them is encouraged by this daily angelus."[33]

Still he wanted to do more. He tried to sign up to be an army chaplain, but was told he had to wait. Candidates for chaplaincy were required have a seminary degree and two full years of pastoral experience—one of which had to be full-time.[34] Billy continued to pursue this aim, adding another complicating dimension to his call.

＋═

After Ruth left her sister in Albuquerque, Rosa was given a special gift of faith. She believed she would be healed, but only if she gave God alone the glory. As things were, the medications weren't helping, and her doctors gave her little hope of recovery. With permission from her father, who was a physician, she asked her doctors to cease all medical treatment for her and to allow God alone to heal her. If she were to be healed, as she was certain she would be, she wanted no confusion as to who had done it.

After stopping treatment, she began to improve—to the astonishment of her doctors—and by late spring, X-rays showed absolutely no signs that she had ever had tuberculosis. It was a miracle.[35]

＋═

Ruth returned to Wheaton for the spring semester of 1942, and she and Billy settled once and for all the direction of their life together.

Even though Billy had continued to waver, giving Ruth hope that he would serve with her on the mission field, it was becoming increasingly clear to him that his call was to be an American evangelist.

Finally, the issue came to a head. Ruth had decided that she could not marry Billy because he did not think he was called to the mission field. When she told him that, he asked her to return the engagement ring. But she couldn't part with it.[36]

Billy pointedly asked her, "Do you believe God has brought us together?"

"Of course I do," she replied.

"Then God will lead me, and you will do the following."[37]

For Billy and Ruth, it was too soon to quit.

CHAPTER 18

THE TAB

*"Preaching and teaching God's Word, Billy Graham. . .
[stresses] the winning of souls for the Kingdom of God."*
THE *TOWER* (WHEATON COLLEGE YEARBOOK)

As V. Raymond Edman's responsibilities as college president grew, he began handing off ministry opportunities that he had previously managed himself. Billy was the recipient of the largest chunk, as Edman asked him to fill in as the preacher at the United Gospel Tabernacle in Wheaton in the spring of 1941.

The United Gospel Tabernacle, or simply "the Tab" as most people called it, had been started by Swedish students in 1926.[1] When Edman arrived at Wheaton in 1937, he began teaching a Sunday school class at the Tab, which quickly grew from five students to a class that filled the large hall where they met.[2] In the fall of 1938, Edman became the Tab's interim pastor when student pastor John Ballbach graduated. He held the position "temporarily," until he was forced to relinquish his church duties in order to attend to the responsibilities of the college presidency.[3] He turned to Billy, who preached at the Tab in both morning and evening services about two Sundays a month.

Edman told the church board, "Here is your man."[4]

Over the summer of 1941, the church board met, and at the strong advice of Dr. Edman, they called the young preacher from North Carolina to be their pastor. A front-page article in the *Wheaton Daily Journal* announced the new pastor, and a prayer meeting was held the next Sunday.[5]

Not exactly a typical church, the Tab met at the Masonic Lodge on Wesley Street, just west of Main Street in downtown Wheaton, where they rented the second-floor hall on Sunday mornings and evenings. Many Christian fundamentalists believed the Masons were a cultish sect, with secret rituals and satanic undertones. Many students who came to the services felt an initial discomfort having a service in the lodge, but once Billy began preaching in the hall, which held two or three hundred people, one began to realize "that the room had no meaning."[6] It is within these same lines that Billy would later be able to preach not only in church cathedrals or tabernacles, but also at dog tracks, coliseums, stadiums, and public squares.

The Tab was less formal than other churches as well,[7] no doubt because of its lack of a permanent building. About six families helped support the church, including a carpenter, a mail carrier, and a milkman.[8] Also in regular attendance were several professors, including Russell Mixter, Albert O'Brien,[9] and Roger Voskuyl, who was later to be called into "special service" to work on the Manhattan Project. One of the most dedicated members was Dr. Gordon H. Clark, head of the philosophy department and an Orthodox Presbyterian, who held both business and prayer meetings at his home.[10]

The most significant section of attendees, however, were the students who often visited several churches on any given Sunday, particularly College Church, Wheaton Bible Church, and the Tab.[11] The Tab was well attended by students and was a draw for groups of students looking for an activity or a free date on Sunday evening.[12]

We get an indication of Billy's pastor's heart for evangelism in his vision for the church—that through teaching and preaching God's Word, he would encourage the body toward "the winning of souls for the Kingdom of God."[13]

The student response to his preaching was generally very good. They noted his kinetic style of preaching with hand gestures, body movements, and "verve."[14] Some visitors sat near the back of the hall because of the volume at which he preached.[15] Others thought that he was not a polished expositional preacher, and still others found him "a bit pedestrian."[16]

Even though he had his critics, his classmates sensed his fire. His preaching was simple but convincing, and "full to the breaking," as one classmate noted.[17] God was using Billy to help others grow in their personal walk with the Lord,[18] and "the level of campus commitment was greatly affected by his preaching."[19]

Preaching twice each Sunday, while maintaining a full class load as well as other extracurricular activities and speaking engagements, was almost too much for Billy to bear. He had to think constantly about the messages he was preparing.

While Billy was pastor at the Tab, classmates who sat next to him in class would often see him making notes for his sermons while they were taking notes for the class.[20] At times, he came to class before a quiz and asked to see a classmate's notes, saying he had not had the time to study.[21]

Always looking for insights from others, he was known to grab a classmate and ask for help with his sermon prep. These classmates never seemed to actually assist—they just sat and listened because Billy needed to walk through his thinking with someone else.[22]

As he continued to look for messages, he also called his former classmate and friend Don Hoke, who by then was the pastor of Park Ridge Gospel Church, and the two would exchange sermons.[23] From time to time, Dr. Edman called Billy into his office to encourage him and pray with him. Now only an occasional attendee of the Tab, Edman gave Billy Gospel outlines to preach because he knew the young pastor was struggling with the load.[24]

Announcements of preachers and preaching topics in the Saturday local newspaper gives some insight into the topics of Billy's preaching, but they also show that, at times, his preaching topic was not decided in time to report it to the paper, especially during his final semester when the paper began making the church announcements on Friday instead of on Saturday.

Perhaps mimicking his predecessor in the pulpit, Billy tried his hand at character studies of Elijah and Daniel in the first few months of his pastorate. He also seemed concerned with sin, with messages entitled "Carnal or Christian, Which?"[25] and "Disobedience."[26] On the day of the Pearl Harbor attack, he preached on "A Sudden Call"[27] and finished before news of the attack broke.

In the spring of 1942, his sermons began to take on a theological nature, focusing on the Church and on the work of Christ. He also showed a concern for the devotional life—especially prayer— and gave a series of messages on Sunday evenings on "The Road to Calvary," "The Road to Emmaus," and "The Road to Rome." Though his schedule was hectic, he was finding his way and casting a vision through his messages.

＋＝

Given the frenetic nature of his college life, Billy was always looking for speakers to fill his pulpit at the Tab. Dr. Edman filled in at times, as did Dr. Gordon Clark. Sometimes Billy enlisted the help of a Wheaton alum, or even a student. Once, when Billy had a preaching engagement in Park Ridge, he invited Phil Saint, a recent graduate who was an artist and preacher, to speak at the Tab. Phil's younger brother, Nate, would become well known when he, Jim Elliot, and three others were martyred while trying to reach the Auca Indians in Ecuador. Billy also invited his friends Grady Wilson and Jimmie Johnson to fill in on occasion.

The congregation was very missions-focused, supporting multiple missionaries, so naturally the church had a steady stream of missionaries coming to speak—many from the Christian and Missionary Alliance.

During Billy's two-and-a-half-year pastorate, several guest preachers are worthy of particular note.

First, L. Nelson Bell, Ruth's father, came to speak in September 1941, just after Billy and Ruth's engagement. When the Bells left China earlier that year, the Lord's providential timing could not have been better, as war engulfed the region they had served for a quarter century soon after they left, and many of their missionary friends were imprisoned by the Japanese.

But even as the Bells escaped the war with Japan, the missionary doctor came home to a war of an entirely different nature. When Dr. Bell arrived back in the United States, he was deeply troubled to find that his denomination, the Southern Presbyterian Church, had grown increasingly liberal. Evangelicals and their teachings were being squeezed out. If he was tempted to run to a new denomination, he did not show it. Rather than flee, he chose instead to work from within the denomination.

At the time, Billy could not understand how any Christian could remain in the Southern Presbyterian Church—or really any of the mainline churches. He even went so far as to question Dr. Bell's spirituality to Ruth. She was so disturbed by his insinuation that she almost returned the engagement ring.[28]

What Billy did not know was that Dr. Bell was about to become a leader in the fight against the infiltration of modernistic liberalism within the Presbyterian movement, with the founding of the *Presbyterian Journal.* He used the new journal, which was a voice not sponsored by the denomination, to pressure the increasingly insular leadership of the denomination and "give a ringing testimony to the evangelical cause"[29] while restating and defending "the historic evangelical and reformed faith."[30]

Only in the years ahead would Billy fully recognize that his soon-to-be father-in-law was indeed a spiritual giant.

In May 1942, Billy's Florida mentor and friend, John Minder, came to Wheaton with the Florida Gospelaires, a trio of singers who had sung at some of Billy's Southern campaigns. The Florida group came to Wheaton while touring nationally with a presentation they advertised as "a vital message to a nation at war."[31] Minder spoke at the college chapel, saying, "Those men who are outstanding in our minds are those who put Christ first and decided to be obedient and to go to live for Him."[32] Minder also filled the pulpit for both Tab services one Sunday, presenting the "Story of Redemption" in picture and song at the evening meeting.

In the summer of 1942, Billy took time off from the Tab to hold evangelistic services in the South. In his absence, the pulpit was filled by Merrill Tenney, who at the time was a professor at Gordon College but who came to teach at Wheaton in 1943.[33]

Two other significant guest speakers preached at the Tab in November 1942, and both had a growing influence on the Wheaton College community, and Billy in particular: Dawson Trotman and Jim Rayburn.

Dawson Trotman of the Navigators came to Wheaton for a full week in November 1942. He spoke in chapel and at the Foreign Mission Fellowship meeting. Since his previous visit to Wheaton in the fall of 1941, his vision for the Navigators had grown from a nationwide ministry to a worldwide imperative. Particularly heavy on his heart during this trip was the fact that so many people groups around the world had no knowledge of Christ and not a single sentence of scripture in their language. At the FMF, Trotman discussed this issue, but he also shared another burden that was on his heart: the lack of men going to the mission field. Trotman felt that men in particular were abdicating their responsibility and call from God to serve overseas, even as women continued to commit their lives to the mission field. He not only challenged the young men at Wheaton, but also prayed that after the war many would take up the task of spreading the Gospel throughout the earth.[34]

Trotman was traveling across the country, casting a vision for scripture memorization, evangelism, and discipleship, and he often used his Navigator Wheel illustration. Years later, students would still remember his encouragement to them to be "prepared to always give an answer of the hope that is in you."[35]

The intense and direct founder of the Navigators was unpredictable as a speaker. He often called out those who claimed to be Navigators to quote scripture or answer questions about their faith. He despised phoniness and challenged believers to be persistent in their walk.

Billy invited Trotman to speak at the Tab and sat in the front row to listen to his message. While Trotman was preaching, he compared a Christian who was unprepared to give a scripture reference to a grocery clerk who could assure a customer that an item was in stock but didn't know where to find it on the shelf. To drive home this point in the sermon, he turned to Billy, cited a passage of scripture, and said, "Billy, where's that found?" Billy, certainly flustered and a bit embarrassed, could not answer. Dawson concluded the point saying, "If this is an important verse, you ought to know where it is."

Billy, however, was quick on his feet, and to the delight of the audience, he stumped Trotman by quoting a scripture passage to which the speaker could not offer the reference.[36] The tactic might turn most people off, but Billy's humility could tolerate such challenges, and he was perhaps delighted in Dawson's no-nonsense approach to spiritual matters.

Shortly after Trotman's visit, Jim Rayburn came to town to fill the Tab pulpit. Much like the explosive growth seen by the Navigators, Rayburn's Young Life ministry had really taken off since his previous visit to Wheaton in November 1941. He returned to Wheaton in November 1942 and began planting the seeds of a Young Life methods class he would teach in January.

Billy was rubbing elbows with some of the most important Christian leaders of the day, and he was learning the art of leading a congregation as well as how to manage his time. His leadership at the Tab and his growing responsibilities on campus were part of a great blessing that came to the college during his final semester there.

CHAPTER 19

DIGGING TRENCHES

"If we take time to dig the ditches, God will
certainly see that they are filled with Living water."
V. RAYMOND EDMAN

The school year of 1942–1943 would prove to be one of unusual spiritual blessings for the campus of Wheaton, but it would not come without the prayer, concern, and hard work of the spiritually astute in the community. As the school year drew to an end, Dr. Edman wrote to a friend, explaining the situation: "The College has always stood for the separated life, not only outwardly from certain worldly practices, but an inward separation of the heart from the world, wrought in the hearts of God's people by the indwelling of His Holy Spirit." And then the president explained the source of this vision, which included Billy. "There is a deep heart-cry on my part, as well as by many others, that true holiness may mark the life and service of the students of Wheaton."[1]

⊹⊨

Not only was the spring of 1942 busy enough for Billy with classwork, preaching at the Tab, and his rapidly developing relationship with

Ruth, who had returned to school for the semester, but the dynamic evangelist also added three evangelistic campaigns to his schedule.

The first meeting was held at Park Ridge Gospel Church in the Chicago suburbs, where friend and former classmate Don Hoke was the founding pastor. The local newspaper took note of the meetings in a short article, calling Billy "one of the most dynamic, appealing young speakers of the South," and making it clear that the meetings were interdenominational in nature, since Billy was ordained in two denominations, licensed to preach in another, and baptized in three—"in order that his sphere of ministry might not be restricted."[2]

We get a glimpse of his future plans at this time, because the article suggests that Billy planned to enroll as a chaplain of the army, and as a result, the Park Ridge meeting was the "last opportunity to hear" him in the area.[3] The January 16 meeting included a brass quartet led by Robert Lovelace and a message on "Victory or Defeat."[4]

In late March and early April, he held another series of "Pre-Easter Services" at Zion Evangelical Free Church at 4857 West Huron Street in downtown Chicago. In this instance, the young evangelist was touted by the local paper as "William Graham."[5] Finally, from April 12 to April 19, he held his Eight Great Days meetings at the College Church of Christ, a church on the edge of the Wheaton campus but independent of the college.[6]

This flurry of activity might threaten to topple most students, but Billy was compelled by an obsession to preach the Gospel of Jesus Christ wherever and whenever he could.

<hr />

In late spring of 1942, Billy decided to run for president of the Christian Council, which would put him in a key leadership position for his senior year. The council coordinated all spiritual activities and groups on campus, including the Gospel teams—which Billy had participated in during his first semester—the Boys' Brigade, Pioneer

Clubs, child evangelism, Mooseheart Sunday school, and the high school Bible clubs.[7] The president's role was intense. It involved chairing all meetings and conducting chapel programs, as well as serving as pastor and spiritual advisor to the students, all in fifteen hours a week.[8]

Each candidate was announced in the school paper before voting began, and Billy's impressive résumé and growing reputation outshone the others. The paper noted his participation in campus groups, as well as his leadership positions at the Florida Bible Institute and with the Christian and Missionary Alliance. The one thing it did not mention was his pastorate at the Tab—perhaps by then a foregone conclusion. It did, however, refer to Billy's future plans, saying that he intended "to head to the Far Eastern mission field," unless the war prevented him.[9] It is simply another glimpse into his vacillation about his future plans.

Billy won the campaign in late March and began preparing his vision for the direction of the council and the spiritual life on campus. "We want to show a spirit of evangelism next year," he told the school paper, "that will put the whole campus on a mass production basis for Christ."[10] He saw the potential for the students to be equipped for ministry, but with resources going toward the war effort and a general spiritual apathy gripping the campus, the initial results were disappointing.[11]

That spring, the upperclassmen gathered for prayer, with Billy leading the singing and others doing the speaking.[12] In May, the junior class took a trip to Jackson Park in Chicago for a picnic, and the council president-elect led a devotional around the campfire.[13]

Billy spent his summer taking classes to reduce his load for his busy senior year,[14] conducted his first wedding,[15] visited his friends in Florida, and returned to campus for the new semester to begin his new leadership responsibilities and goals.

The chapel services continued to draw important leaders of evangelicalism in the spring and fall of 1942. In January, A. W. Tozer came to speak on "The Work of the Holy Spirit in Christian Living,"[16] and Robert McQuilken called for 50 percent of the students to go to the mission field.[17] In April, Tozer returned to chapel, along with W. B. Riley, president of Northwestern Schools, with whom Billy was becoming more acquainted, and revivalist J. Edwin Orr, who declared: "Since the days of Billy Sunday at his peak in 1915, there hasn't been a nationwide revival."[18]

The fall semester in 1942 began with evangelistic services, led by Christian and Missionary Alliance pastor Colver J. Mason from New Jersey. He endeared himself to the students,[19] and his relative youth, at forty-two years of age, made them feel as if he were one of them.[20] Stirrings of the Spirit of God were evident throughout the weeklong services, which were held in the mornings and evenings. Billy reported the meetings for the *Alliance Weekly*, the periodical of the Christian and Missionary Alliance, and noted that "the windows of heaven were opened and the showers of refreshing came."[21]

The final service drew the largest attendance in the history of the Wheaton evangelistic meetings, with 1,700 gathered in the newly completed gymnasium. Many students rededicated their lives to Christ, and "burdens were lifted, hearts were surrendered, and souls born into the kingdom of God," according to the elated council president, again reporting in the *Alliance Weekly*.[22]

However, the embers that were stirred in these meetings did not become the blazing flame that Billy and others had hoped to see.

In October, Billy spoke in chapel for the Christian Council service and told his classmates that the devil was at work trying to "nullify the gains made" from the fall evangelistic services.[23] Preaching on

Acts 1:8, he focused on mobilizing the student body for service, saying that "an active participation in the Lord's work is the only way to deepen prayer life and to continue in a joyful study of God's Word."[24] He proceeded to inform the students of the needs and ministry opportunities available—between thirty and forty teachers were needed for child evangelism classes; thirty more were needed for the Boys' Brigade;[25] and the Gospel teams and high school clubs were sorely lacking for volunteers in comparison with two years earlier. The service concluded with the singing of "Where He Leads Me, I Will Follow."[26]

The service was followed up by an editorial in the *Wheaton Record*, the school newspaper, encouraging students to heed Billy's call instead of "dodging the draft of our spiritual war."[27] But the campus remained largely apathetic to Billy's exhortation.

The fall semester brought more guests of note who began to shape the spiritual life of the campus. Dawson Trotman returned for a second visit, speaking at the Foreign Mission Fellowship and in chapel for the week; and revivalist Oswald J. Smith, pastor of the People's Church in Toronto, and Jim Rayburn spoke in November.

Trotman and Rayburn, in particular, pressed the students to commit themselves to Bible study, scripture memorization, prayer, and witnessing—which was becoming the heart of both their ministries. Billy also caught the vision as a focus for the Christian Council,[28] and it became an important component for the rest of his ministry. The disciplines of Bible study, prayer, and witnessing, Billy suggested, "are the three factors which are essential to normal Christian growth."[29]

Rayburn returned in January 1943 to teach the students his Young Life methods. He arrived amid a blizzard at the Chicago airport at 2:30 in the morning on January 14, and Billy was able to reach him by 4:30 to bring him back to campus.[30] About two hundred students signed up for Rayburn's class, one of whom was the council president.[31] The previous summer, Rayburn had been inspired by Dawson Trotman and had adopted his vision for scripture memorization. This emphasis on memorizing Bible verses spread to Wheaton, where "campaigners"—as Young Life followers were now being called—could be seen all over campus with their memory verse packs.[32] Billy said that the Young Life class had two purposes: "It acquaints Christians with the methods of personal work. And it acts as a fine stimulus for the individual's spiritual life."[33]

Despite Billy's frustration about the spiritual climate on campus, there continued to be stirrings. Billy, and others, continued to hope that there would soon be more.

Not only was Billy discouraged by what he felt was a lack of student participation in ministry activities on campus, but he also was becoming concerned with sinful attitudes and actions within the student body. He confided in his house mother, Mrs. Anna Hansen, that some students were reflecting poorly on the college, and therefore on Christ, within the community at large. As they reflected silently for a few moments, Billy put his fist down in the palm of his hand and said, "Mrs. Hansen, by God's grace, I'm going to serve Him!"[34]

Billy also met with Dr. Edman to give the president an idea of the spiritual pulse of the campus.[35] Billy saw the spiritual condition in a negative light—and others did, too.

Dr. Edman later reflected that, "If we take time to dig ditches, God will certainly see that they are filled with Living water."[36] The school president primarily meant that prayer was ditch-digging— the hard but essential work of a community. He spent time with Billy in prayer and encouraged him to lead others in prayer.

The Christian Council organized weekly prayer meetings on Tuesday nights, and Billy's classmates gathered for praise, thanksgiving, and petition.[37] There were also daily prayer meetings at 7:30 in the morning, and occasional meetings for prayer in Billy's office.[38] In addition, about ten students quietly gathered on Friday nights, after the society meetings, to pray for revival in the community.[39]

On January 14, 1943, the Christian Council arranged a prayer meeting for the seniors, where "Bill Graham" spoke, and Mrs. V. Raymond Edman offered a few words. But the main purpose of the gathering was for prayer. The "particular emphasis" of the prayer meeting, according to organizers, was to pray concerning "campus problems in relation to the graduating class."[40]

At one of those prayer meetings, Billy stood up and quoted 1 Corinthians 9:27 (KJV): "But I keep under my body, and bring it into subjection: lest that by any means, when I have preached to others, I myself should be a castaway." He was concerned that the Gospel was being hindered by sinful living, and he was zealous to see that true holiness would mark his own life.[41]

The trenches that had been dug by the prayers of the faithful were about to be filled with Living water.

CHAPTER 20

THE FIRE FALLS

*"Someone came in. We did not need to ask who had come.
We knew God was in our midst."*
V. RAYMOND EDMAN

The crisp, frigid February air was about to be warmed by a movement of the Spirit of God in a profound and unexpected way during the 1943 winter evangelistic services. It was an answer to the prayers of students who had gathered in meetings, both large and small, to pray for revival.

The *Wheaton Record* reported on the upcoming meetings in early February with a short biography of the speaker, Harold P. Warren, and a summary of his intended theme.[1] Warren, an atheist-turned-Spirit-filled minister,[2] was the pastor of North Baptist Church in Flint, Michigan, and the church had doubled in size during his tenure as pastor.[3] He had preached in Wheaton's chapel in October 1941,[4] but this was his first series of meetings. He was "frightened to death."[5]

The announced emphasis on prayer and its power seems to have set low expectations for the meetings. The *Wheaton Record* suggested that Warren's "plan for soul-winning is to have a number of Christians each praying for two unregenerate persons," and praying for specific individuals.[6]

The practice of holding evangelistic services had started thirty-five years earlier, when a life-threatening illness overcame Charles Blanchard, son of the founder and second president of the school, and convinced him that Wheaton College must be, above all things, a spiritual institution.[7] The services were started to reach the spiritually lost or struggling students.

By 1943, the tone of the services had shifted from reaching the student body with the Gospel to mobilizing the students to reach others for the Gospel—both legitimate visions. God had heard the prayers of His people, and He saw fit to reach down and touch the campus community.

Warren's fears were only intensified when the Lord laid a burden on his heart to preach on sin.[8] He was not an emotional speaker,[9] but he won the "admiration and prayer-cooperation"[10] of the students by "quietly, soberly, sincerely" calling on them to have humble and broken hearts.[11]

At the opening Sunday night service, the pastor from Flint preached on "Getting the Breaks," emphasizing the necessity of being broken completely.[12] The embers gradually began to glow as several hundred students remained after the service at Warren's invitation to "lay hold of God for revival."[13]

On Monday, Warren preached at the morning chapel service on "Knowing God's Will," and in the evening on "The Lover's Greatest Question" from John 21. He impressed on the students the importance of being able to answer in the affirmative Christ's question to Peter: "Lovest thou me more than these?"[14]

Sensing an impending move of God, Dr. Edman boldly canceled all classes for Tuesday so that the students could devote themselves to prayer, "patterned after the many biblical instances where community prayer brought great blessing."[15]

It was indeed a full day of prayer. It began at 7:30 a.m., with the entire campus gathered in the chapel. At 8:30, the students broke into their respective classes. At 9:45, Pastor Warren gave the message for the chapel service. At 11:00, organizations held meetings, and the early afternoon was dedicated to house prayer.[16] At 2:30 p.m., the students reconvened for a Communion service,[17] and at 4:00, they broke up into literary societies.[18]

The flames were fanned once again at the evening service when Warren preached, followed by an invitation for students to respond for prayer and counsel in Arrow Hall behind the platform. As campus leaders, including Billy, counseled and prayed with twenty-five or thirty students,[19] one student, Leland Simcox, came to Dr. Edman and confided that he had no assurance of his salvation. Dr. Edman stood beside Simcox as the struggling student prayed for the Lord to save him. After he was finished, the wise counselor took a piece of chalk, wrote an X on the board, and said, "Now, Leland, the next time the devil tries to tell you that you haven't been saved, you just remind him of this exact time and place. X marks the spot."[20]

When they lifted up their eyes, they noticed another student, Billy Graham, who was requesting prayer with Dr. Edman. He, of course, was already assured of his salvation, but the movement of the Spirit of God in the chapel service had convinced him that he wanted more of what God had to offer. He asked the president to pray that he would have the fullness of the Spirit in his life.[21] The fire—both on campus and in the life of Billy Graham—was about to fall.

The embers were getting hot as the meetings resumed, and by Thursday they had become an all-consuming fire.

Harold Warren, the "frank" yet "humble"[22] preacher, spoke on Thursday morning about the "lack of inward searching" afflicting the human race. Taking Psalm 139 as his text,[23] he emphasized, "Search *me*, and know *me*." He called on the students to get their eyes off of the sins of others and onto their own.

After Pastor Warren was finished, Duncan Stewart, the captain of the cross country team, quietly approached Dr. Edman on the platform and asked if he could say a few words to the students.

When Stewart stepped up to the podium, he confessed that, as captain of the cross country team, he had broken college rules by leading teammates in a race in Chicago on a Sunday.[24]

Dr. Edman stepped up to assure the penitent student, as well as the other students, that Duncan was forgiven. And then, with a great deal of discernment, he added, "If there are others who have need to confess their wrongdoing, they may do so now.[25] As Dr. Edman later said about that moment, "Someone came in. We did not need to ask who had come. We knew God was in our midst."[26]

A short period of silence ensued, followed by hundreds of students "greatly moved and weeping" beginning to stand at their seats waiting for a chance to confess or give testimony.[27]

This period of spontaneous declaration included confession of criticism, cheating, theft, worldliness, spiritual pride, spiritual coldness, lack of love for souls, lack of devotional life, and other sins on which the Holy Spirit was shining his light.[28] The confessions continued for hours, as students forgot about lunch and dinner, their bodies given a supernatural "uplift and exhilaration"[29] as time seemed to stand still.

The confessions were stopped temporarily while Pastor Warren gave a message, followed by Dr. Edman's invitation for the students to come in "from the coldness and night of sin to the warmth and light of salvation."[30] The confessions resumed until midnight, when Edman closed the service in order for the students to get some rest.[31]

The confessions were not confined to chapel. The campus newspaper included a public confession by the editor, asking forgiveness for spreading a critical spirit. As a campus leader, he felt that he must make public confession.[32]

Friday's chapel continued what had started the day before. But this time, Warren felt compelled to do something bold. He turned to face the faculty and said, "I rejoice to see what is taking place among these students, *but*. . .I wonder if there is a similar spiritual need among the faculty."[33] Members of the faculty then joined the students in standing for up to five hours as they waited for their turn to speak, with as many as a hundred individuals standing at a time.[34] The morning service continued into the evening yet again.[35]

The service ended that night with a "searching invitation" by Dr. Edman, who asked those in need of prayer to meet him behind the chapel. The president reported on Saturday that "almost every known unsaved student has been won."[36]

There were critics who felt that such public confessions were inappropriate. But for the vast majority of those who were there, they sensed a real, healing touch of the Holy Spirit. As one student later reflected, it felt as if everything was "clean like when the rain comes."[37] And the students moved from confession to praise.[38]

This spontaneous work of the Spirit of God was shared by the churches in the Wheaton community when College Church, Wheaton Bible Church, and the Tab joined together in the new gym for services on Sunday night.[39] They also had a final, closing service on Monday morning.

By the end, the tone of Harold Warren's messages had changed. He had begun his series with a concern for the spiritual state of the student body, but by and large, that had been taken care of by the end of the week. Now he pushed to see the results of humble and broken hearts: "the indwelling of the Holy Spirit and a victorious life *lived for others*."[40] The fire that fell on campus that February week had to spread or it would be snuffed out.

⸝⸝

"[Wheaton's] prayerful desire," reads a note to the alumni in a report of the incident, "is that the flame shall not burn out, but that the Holy Spirit will fan it into a mighty fire that will spread from the plains of Illinois to the borders of our nation and to the world."[41] This prayer was answered in remarkable ways.

When Wheaton alumnus August Ballbach, who was serving in the war, read the report in the *Alumni News*, he was inspired and "led to direct the attention of several officers to our true 'Captain of our salvation.' "[42]

In another account, a student reported the event excitedly to her roommate, who was sick in the hospital. At first, the roommate resented it, but then the Spirit of God broke through and she became a Christian. Writing home to tell her parents caused a revival of its own in Washington DC, as the parents shared the letter with their pastor, who then read the letter aloud in the church service, after which sixty people came forward without an invitation.[43]

Furthermore, Gospel teams were sent out in unprecedented numbers to local churches to report on the campus revival— including students who had not participated all year[44]—and campus prayer services doubled in number.[45] Dr. Edman spread the message wherever he spoke, including at Nyack, where he spoke for their graduation.

The revival that Billy, his friends, and Dr. Edman had been praying for had become a reality.

During spring break, Billy went with song leader Al Smith and a quartet to visit Harold Warren's church in Flint, Michigan. On their way, they stopped at a restaurant, where they broke into song and Billy shared a word with those who were there.[46]

In Flint, they held a citywide rally, with five hundred young people present. At the close of the rally, ten people responded to Billy's invitation.[47]

On Sunday morning, the students were to lead the worship and Billy was to preach a sermon. But as he stood before a packed house, he set aside his prepared notes to share about the revival instead. Many people responded by making public confession of sin.[48]

On Sunday night, the Wheaton group led a service of special music to an even larger crowd, and Billy gave an evangelistic message.[49] The good news was also spread through another outlet: the radio. During the *Fireside Fellowship* broadcast in Flint, the quartet sang, and Billy gave a brief "résumé" of the revival.[50] On the following weekend, March 27–28, Billy held services in Rockford, Illinois, at the church of Harold Westerdahl, continuing to spread the flames from Wheaton.[51]

The fire had fallen on the campus at Wheaton, but it spread through the lives of those whose hearts had been ignited. For Billy, it was a powerful demonstration of the work of the Lord brought on by the prayers of God's people—a demonstration that would be repeated wherever he went for the rest of his ministry.

CHAPTER 21

STRIVING FOR THE GOAL

"All I want to do is save souls!"
BILLY GRAHAM

While Billy's time at the Florida Bible Institute had been the happiest years of his life, his years at Wheaton were equally formative, connecting him to people who would shape his ministry in significant ways.

One of the ways in which Billy was stretched at Wheaton was academically. Though the Florida Bible Institute had trained him ably in practical ministry and the Bible, Wheaton expanded his horizons through its liberal arts focus and its commitment to shaping students to impact all of society "for Christ and His Kingdom."

Billy initially lamented the fact that Bible classes would not be a major part of his education at Wheaton, since most of his Bible courses had transferred from the Institute. However, as time passed, he began to relish the new expansion of his knowledge—including rhetoric, literature, psychology, philosophy, and history.[1]

The most informative course he took was at the suggestion of classmates who said, "Don't leave Wheaton without a course in

Grigolia."[2] When he did, he was hooked.

Anthropology professor Alexander Grigolia, or "Griggy," as the students called him, hailed from the country of Georgia and had fled to France during the turmoil of the Russian Revolution and the Georgian declaration of independence in 1917.[3] He was a balding man in his fifties, with a pencil mustache, and he spoke in broken English, which only endeared him to his students. He was short— "five comma two," he would say[4]—but he had a towering intellect. He had earned several degrees, including an MD, before completing a PhD at the University of Pennsylvania. This one, he said, was "from the anthropological point of view."[5]

The immigrant professor was the department head and only full-time teacher in the newly formed department of anthropology. Other teachers filling in the gaps were Dr. Paul Culley, the dean of men, who was fresh from the mission field; Joseph Free of the Bible and archaeology department; and Dr. Fred Gerstung, the professor of German with whom Billy had lived during his first year at Wheaton.[6] But the main teacher and main attraction in the department was Dr. Grigolia.

Billy was interested in anthropology, which was said to be good for students interested in foreign missions,[7] or as a pre-seminary course.[8] Because he had studied Bible for three and a half years, he chose to major in anthropology. Courses included ethnology, archaeology, biological and cultural evolution of man, primitive religion, zoology, ancient history, sociology, and psychology.[9]

Dr. Grigolia, like all Wheaton professors, was a committed believer, often sharing how he had come to Christ while studying in Philadelphia;[10] and he had an ever-ready "Praise the Lord!" in response to good news.[11] The direction he took the department was in line with the Wheaton vision to shape the humanities for Christ. He was a firm creationist who decried evolutionary theory and emphasized the similarity of so-called prehistoric humans to modern humans.[12] "The missing link is still missing," he often said to his classes.[13] Teaching within the department was an attempt at a thoughtful, academic critique of evolutionary theory and the origins of man that were being disseminated by secular academicians, rather than the merely reactionary tendencies common within evangelicalism.

It would be wrong to suggest that Billy was an indifferent or incapable student. But he had no interest in competing with the academic elite in his classes. He was in class for a purpose, and he kept that purpose ever before him with the knowledge that there were more important things than making honor roll. His greatest interest was in courses that applied to his goal of spreading the Gospel;[14] but even with courses that did not readily seem to fit, he tried to make them apply.

In all, he was a fine student who was usually prepared when called upon.[15] One day in class, after Billy finished a presentation that fell short of the professor's academic standards, Dr. Grigolia articulated what the rest of the students were thinking. "Mr. Graham," he bellowed in front of Billy's peers, "you are a fine preacher, but you will never be a scientist."[16]

Still, Billy wanted to mix his evangelistic passion with his academic pursuits. This can be seen most clearly in his senior thesis, which surveyed the practice of human sacrifice around the world. It was titled "A Study of Human Sacrifice in Cultural Life of Primitives and Its Importance for Apologetics."[17] Along with their theses, senior students gave a seminar that junior and senior anthropology majors were required to attend. But Billy also used the *Wheaton Record* to invite other students who were contemplating ministry or missions to attend.[18] In the talk, he set out to "show the striking similarities and parallels [in human sacrifices] to the sacrifice of Christ, pointing out the craving in the human heart for satisfaction and removal of guilt.[19]

A 1949 sermon by Billy on the Atonement, based on Leviticus 17:11, sheds light on how he incorporated his research into his faith and preaching. In the sermon, Billy cites data from Sir James George Frazer's *The Golden Bough*, which asserts that 90 percent of the world's civilizations have practiced human sacrifice at some point in their religious history. Billy then cites "the great Christian anthropologist" Dr. Alexander Grigolia, who says that the figure is more like 95 percent, and says that "it is innate in man to believe that he had wronged or sinned against his god or gods, and that the only way of appeasement or atonement is by blood sacrifice of some sort.[20]

Billy suggested—with an argument reminiscent of C. S. Lewis's views on longing—that this general human desire points to a real human need, which is only ultimately met in the sacrificial atonement offered by Jesus Christ.[21]

Billy loved, and was proud of, his anthropological studies. He even considered pursuing graduate studies in anthropology at the University of Chicago.[22] But it was not academic prestige he desired. It was merely a piece of his passion to spread the Gospel—a goal that he pursued relentlessly.

He continued to be enriched by the daily chapel hour in Pierce Chapel with the Reverend Harris Gregg from Lookout Mountain, Tennessee. Gregg also preached at the Tab, and Billy touted him in the local paper as "the South's Foremost Teacher-Evangelist. . .a man who lives Christ, preaches Christ, wins men to Christ."[23]

Another speaker who came to Wheaton in the spring of 1943 was Mrs. Ruth Stull, a woman whom Billy would later call "a giant" in the faith.[24] Ruth Stull and her husband, Roscoe, were closely connected with Billy's Florida mentor, John Minder. They had ministered together in central Florida in the 1920s and had founded the Melrose Gospel Tabernacle, which the Stulls later left to start a ministry in Ohio, and Minder left to go to Tampa.

After serving an Ohio church for a brief period, the Stulls went as pioneering missionaries deep into the Peruvian jungles, where they worked for eight years (1927–1935) to reach the Campa Indians.

When Ruth fell ill with appendicitis, and her husband's heart showed signs of heart disease, they reluctantly returned to North America. During the 1940s, Roscoe served as a pastor in Ohio, and Ruth—with the full support of her husband—traveled the country to tell their story and call young men and women to the mission field.

Her messages gave vivid details of life on the mission field, dismantling both romantic and idealistic notions about missions while raising the views of others above the "bottom-of-the-barrel" conceptions of missionary life. As she writes in her 1951 autobiography, *Sand and Stars*, her feet were on the sand of earth, but her eyes and heart were in the stars.[25]

Stull spoke for the entire week, giving a riveting account of "modern miracles of grace" through her missionary experiences, and keeping as her theme the omnipotence, omnipresence, and faithfulness of God.[26]

If there was anyone who could refine Ruth Bell's romantic notions of missions, while at the same time elevating the importance of her vision, it was Ruth Stull. But by the spring of 1943, the circumstances of the war had put any thoughts of the mission field on hold. Perhaps this was the only thing that could keep Billy and Ruth from going to Tibet after their wedding, which was planned for that summer. But if the doors to serving overseas, or even the chaplaincy, were temporarily closed, opportunities for evangelism in the United States would soon overwhelm Ruth and Billy and shut once and for all the door to full-time overseas missions.

✠

Wherever Billy would decide to serve, he had a firm conviction of his calling as an evangelist. Classmates recall his prospective plans for an evangelistic ministry,[27] but Billy was a young man who was open to God's leading and dedicated to earnest prayer—the foundation of his ministry.

His passionate prayers have been noted by all who joined him in prayer meetings during this period. At one such meeting, in the residence where Billy lived, all the young men were seated in chairs and on beds. Billy, on the other hand, was lying prostrate on the floor, pounding the floor with a closed fist and crying out, "Lord, all I want to do is save souls!"[28]

This was the goal for which he was striving.

✠

On Good Friday, April 23, 1943, seven local churches gathered at midday at Gary Memorial Methodist Church in downtown Wheaton for a three-hour "union service," which focused on the last seven words of Christ. Each word or saying was accompanied by a hymn, a message by a local pastor, prayer, and silent meditation.[29] At the 1942 union service, Billy had spoken on the third "word" of Christ, from John 19:26–27: "Woman, behold your son; behold your mother."[30] In 1943, he spoke on the fifth word: "I thirst," from John 19:28. He also drew on John 4, Jesus' discourse with the Samaritan woman at the well.[31]

That evening, at Billy's recommendation as Christian Council president, literary society meetings were canceled for a "spontaneous" campuswide Good Friday service. Billy arranged for Dr. Edman to bring the message on "The Mark of the Cross," with various members of the student body leading musical programs.[32]

On Easter Sunday, Billy led the morning service at the Tab, preaching on "The Living among the Dead,"[33] and Dr. Edman spoke at the evening service.[34]

Billy's time in college was quickly drawing to a close, and his near future was coming more clearly into focus.

In the spring of 1943, just weeks before graduation, a deacon at Western Springs Baptist Church, southwest of Wheaton, caught wind of the gifted young preacher and came to speak with him about the pastoral vacancy at the "basement" church, which was struggling to complete its building structure.

The deacon was Robert Van Kampen, a successful businessman and president of Hitchcock Publishing Company. He asked Billy what his plans were after graduation, and the budding evangelist replied that he wanted to be a preacher of the Gospel.[35] Van Kampen was interested in calling this gifted preacher to Western Springs, but he saw two obstacles.

His first concern was whether it would be appropriate to approach the pastor of the Tab about switching churches after graduation. He decided to consult with Dr. Edman, the former Tabernacle pastor and current Wheaton College president. Edman told him that it would be a fitting time for a change, given the part-time nature of the Tab pastorate.[36]

Van Kampen was also concerned that Billy would not be interested in pastoring the small Western Springs church. So he asked pastor and radio personality Torrey Johnson, whom Billy respected, to encourage Billy to accept the position. Johnson agreed to help.[37]

The church was impressed with Billy and called him to be their pastor. Billy accepted with one condition: that he would be free to leave the church should the chaplaincy open up. But in accepting the job, he made one huge mistake. He was so excited about the offer that he accepted the position on the spot, without consulting his fiancée, Ruth. She was understandably furious about his thoughtlessness.[38]

Ruth's anger would abate, but it did raise the question of whether Billy should have accepted the position in the first place. This cloud of doubt soon grew thicker when a large church in Indiana, with a radio ministry, expressed interest in calling him as their pastor. Billy was torn. Could it be that in his haste he had missed what God really had in store for him?

That Sunday, he attended the weekly prayer meeting at Dr. Lane's house, as he and Ruth often did, and he explained the situation to the group. He asked for prayer for wisdom about the direction he should choose. He was clearly intrigued by the size and scope of ministry the Indiana church offered.[39]

During his deliberations, Billy sought the advice of Dr. Edman. Edman was never one to play God in another person's life, so he offered no direct counsel, but instead prayed with and for Billy.[40] But if Billy had learned anything from Dr. Edman and his teaching, it was this: do not question in times of darkness and doubt the Lord's guidance that he has shown in the light. In a series of messages the previous spring, the president spoke on Balaam, with a consistently repeated theme: "Be satisfied with God's first answer. Don't seek your own will in a second asking."[41]

However much Billy may have been influenced by Dr. Edman's teaching, over the next week, his heart changed. When he returned to Dr. Lane's house for the next prayer meeting, instead of seeking prayer for guidance, he came with a confession and an apology. "I had a wonderful peace deep down in my heart when I accepted the call to Western Springs Baptist Church," he told his classmates, "and I had no business entertaining thoughts about any larger church. Please forgive me. Ruth and I know that the Lord wants us at Western Springs."

After Billy left the prayer meeting, Dr. Lane turned to the remaining students and left an indelible impression on them when he said, "How many of you would do what Billy just did? If God has big things for Billy, he will bring it to pass without any embarrassment or manipulation by Billy, and He can do the same for each of you." And then Dr. Lane concluded, "Trust Him to work out His plans and purposes."[42]

Billy and Ruth graduated in June, ending two long, drawn-out college experiences for both of them. But they were experiences that made them who they were to be in the service of the King. Billy had begun as a lanky, uncertain, and fearful freshman when he first stepped onto the Bob Jones College campus in 1936. By the spring of 1943, he was a confident, purposeful, and earnest preacher of the Gospel. Ruth had come to Wheaton as an idealistic future missionary, leading the charge toward her own pursuits. She came away shaped and formed as one who would now *follow* the charge—not just Billy's, but also the charge of God.

What resulted was an on-fire ministry that would spread to the ends of the earth.

PART 4

SPREADING THE FIRE:

CONCLUSION

CHAPTER 22

UNCONTAINABLE FIRE

"Old style religion is sweeping the city of angels with
an evangelistic show overshadowing even Billy Sunday."
NEWSPAPER REPORT FROM 1949

In the six years after Billy graduated from Wheaton, and before he came to the attention of the American public as a result of national coverage of his Los Angeles Campaign in 1949, he held three positions, all of which were formative for his ministry. None of these positions was an exact fit for Billy, but they all gave him opportunities to pursue his passion: evangelistic meetings. He enriched each of the institutions he served, even while exasperating them with his relentless drive. The blaze was simply too intense to be contained.

The first post he held, beginning in August 1943, was as the pastor of Western Springs Baptist Church, a congregation of around fifty or sixty regular attendees, with an unfinished church building in the quaint suburb of Western Springs, about fifteen miles from Chicago.

Right from the get-go, the young pastor saw room for growth, but as he surveyed the community made up primarily of Congregationalists and Lutherans, he felt that the growth of the church was inhibited by its Baptist name. He recommended changing the name to the Village Church at Western Springs, which they did.

By December, the church had shown signs of growth, with more than one hundred regular attendees—twice the previous average. Billy preached on Sunday mornings and Sunday evenings, led a Young People's gathering after the Sunday night service, and taught a child evangelism class with Ruth on Wednesday afternoons.

The weekly routine of the pastorate never really suited Billy, and he regularly held meetings outside of the church. But the rhythm was broken one day when Torrey Johnson, pastor of Midwest Bible Church, approached him about having the Village Church take over one of Johnson's three radio programs. *Songs in the Night* was a program that included short devotional insights interspersed between musical numbers. After funding was met, the deacons agreed, and on January 2, 1944, Village Church aired their first program, with WMBI staff announcer George Beverly Shea, a popular radio voice, and a quartet from the Wheaton College glee club.

The program scratched the evangelist's restless itch—at least temporarily. It also helped promote the church while giving it a shot of excitement. But it also did something else: for the first time, Billy's voice was broadcast throughout the country, with insights on news items and world events, and a hopeful word from the Bible. If the church wanted their pastor for themselves, the radio ministry was not the way to do it. It had the opposite effect.

As listeners across the country began to hear Billy preach, more and more doors opened for him to hold evangelistic meetings, especially throughout the Midwest, which drew him away from his pastoral duties. In the spring of 1944, he held services at Berwyn Bible Church, Roseland Evangelical Mission Church, and Brookfield Baptist, and also spoke at the Wheaton College chapel. All of these locations were within an hour's drive, and the meetings were on days other than Sunday, but they did take Billy's time and attention. He also took a trip to Battle Creek, Michigan.

That spring, Billy got involved in another important ministry, Youth for Christ (YFC), which Torrey Johnson had founded. YFC was a movement spreading across the country with individual, independent chapters in the major cities of America. In particular, their aim was to reach young people who had gained a new sense of freedom as the Second World War came to a close. YFC's central motivation was described in their motto: "Anchored to the Rock, Geared to the Times." In Chicago, Torrey Johnson was leading the charge, doing everything he could to capture the hearts of entertainment-hungry servicemen who were in port and who were searching for meaning. As a result, he set up rallies in Chicago on Saturday nights and invited Billy to preach to nearly three thousand young people at the Orchestra Hall on Michigan Avenue on May 27. Billy was greatly encouraged when forty people came to receive Christ. Torrey Johnson knew he had found his man.

Naturally, the deacons at the Village Church were concerned that their pastor was not meeting the needs or expectations of the congregation. And Billy felt a growing tension in his soul about his role. He saw a world ripe for the Gospel, but his obligations as a pastor were preventing his full participation in the harvest.

In September 1944, a serious illness led to his eventual resignation from the Village Church. What began as a diagnosis of mumps, with a prognosis for recovery of two weeks, stretched into two months and spread to other areas of his body. A *Songs in the Night* listener sent a check for Billy to take a recovery vacation to Miami, Florida, which he and Ruth gladly accepted. The vacation was a turning point for the direction of Billy's ministry.

✢

God was superintending the spread of the fire he had placed in Billy's heart. This undeniable fact is made certain by the simultaneous, but coincidental, Miami vacation of Torrey Johnson. When Billy heard that Johnson was in Miami, he called him and the two spent a day fishing together.

Johnson's vision for Youth for Christ had grown over the past few months. He wanted to expand the independent, localized chapters of the movement into a unified organization, which would strengthen the individual ministries and extend the reach of the Gospel of Jesus Christ. The unified ministry would be called Youth for Christ International. What was perhaps most surprising was that Johnson's vision included Billy Graham—who lived less than twenty miles away from him in the Chicago area; but it took an unplanned meeting twelve hundred miles away for the plan to unfold.

Billy was on board immediately.

In January 1945, Billy became YFC International's first employee, which led to his resignation as pastor of the Village Church. Of all the positions Billy would hold during the latter half of the 1940s, his role at YFC most closely matched his skill set. In 1945, he held at least forty-five meetings—most of which were youth rallies—from the West Coast, to Canada, to the Deep South, and throughout the Midwest. During this year, he traveled more than seventeen thousand miles, most of which were by car or rail.[1]

The years of 1946 and 1947 were equally busy, and also included two trips to Western Europe and the United Kingdom, which were still reeling from the destruction wrought by the war. The second trip included Cliff Barrows as song leader when another song leader backed out shortly before the trip was to begin.

Billy's first European tour included twenty cities, most of which were locations for YFC rallies. These were held throughout the UK and in Stockholm, Copenhagen, and Brussels. The Swedish rallies were particularly successful, with ten thousand in attendance, plus overflow crowds daily.[2] Billy also held meetings with religious leaders in Amsterdam and Paris to generate support.

His second overseas tour lasted from October 1946 to March 1947, and he held rallies in more than thirty cities throughout the United Kingdom. These cities were receptive to the American evangelist and paved the way for future rallies in the years to come. Billy was pleased to see "the Holy Spirit work in these meetings."[3] Though the gatherings were geared to young people, many people brought their parents and grandparents, and there was increased interest in holding more community-wide meetings. The trip also included much-needed vacation rest in Paris and Nice, as well as Monte Carlo.

Back in the United States, Billy traveled across the country holding YFC rallies. But once again, he found that even YFC could not contain him. In November 1947, he held a two-week revival in Charlotte with the hope of reaching not only the youth, but also the entire community for Christ.

In all, between 1946 and 1947, Billy traveled more than twenty-six thousand miles in Europe and the US, not including the roughly sixteen thousand miles to and from the US and Europe, and he held meetings in more than sixty cities. His efforts were reminiscent of the driving passion of John Wesley and George Whitefield in the eighteenth century, though those two men did their traveling on horseback!

In December 1947, Billy began to wear three hats, only one of which ended up fitting. He was vice president of Youth for Christ and an independent, itinerate evangelist; and now he was an educator as well, as a result of impressing W. B. Riley, whom he had first met at the Florida Bible Institute and had crossed paths with as a student at Wheaton. Riley was the founder and president of Northwestern Bible School, and at eighty-six years of age, he was on his deathbed. In his final wishes, he asked that Billy would assume the presidency of the school. Riley died at the end of 1947, and his wish was granted when Billy and the school's board agreed to a temporary, trial presidency.

Once again, Billy found himself in a position that could not contain him, though that was not all bad. Indeed, he had observed several school presidents who had split their time with evangelistic meetings—in particular Bob Jones and W. T. Watson. But Billy pushed the envelope even further during his presidency, as both demand and opportunities for him continued to grow.

Though Billy would continue to work for Youth for Christ until late 1948, the time he spent on YFC activities began to taper off. But it did not necessarily shift to the operation of the school. Rather, Billy delegated most responsibilities to his childhood friend T. W. Wilson, who became vice president of Northwestern Schools, and to George Wilson, a brilliant administrator, to whom Billy owed much of his later organizational success. Billy continued to hold campaigns around the country, but his breakthrough was still yet to come.

As president of Northwestern Schools, Billy was gone nearly as much as he was on campus, and he missed most of the academic term. But in his four-year presidency, he instilled a vision for the students to gain "Knowledge on Fire," increased enrollment from seven hundred to twelve hundred,[4] and raised enough money to finish the construction of buildings that had been at a standstill due to a lack of funds.

By 1950 and 1951, the pace of Billy's evangelistic ministry had increased to the point where he could no longer hold positions outside of his calling as an evangelist, and he resigned from the presidency of Northwestern Schools.

As Billy's ministry grew increasingly successful, his trials also grew—both outwardly and inwardly. Outwardly, he began to see opposition to his ministry in ways that he had not seen before, and from people he never expected to oppose him. He was growing in his conviction that an evangelistic ministry must work together with community churches of all denominational types. This model contrasted with that of most fundamentalist evangelists of the previous half century, including Mordecai Ham, who had fought the local churches in the Charlotte meetings where Billy made his decision for Christ.

The advantages of churchwide cooperation were simple. Prayerfulness increased as more congregations participated, funding increased, and publicity could reach more deeply into the community. In addition, when Billy left town after a series of meetings, the churches could more readily pick up where he left off.

The budding of the new ecumenical movement hit a raw nerve among fundamentalists. The National Association of Evangelicals had begun in the early 1940s, to the dismay of fundamentalist leaders such as American Council of Christian Churches founder Carl McIntire. But the issue of ecumenism would explode with the founding of the World Council of Churches (WCC) in 1948. The WCC not only accepted liberal leaders, but also promoted them. Some people learned that Billy had attended the opening organizational meeting of the WCC, as an observer for YFC, but they didn't realize his initial opposition to it.

Billy began to use a cooperative model of evangelistic meetings for the first time in Augusta, Georgia, in October 1948, and by the summer of 1949, disgruntled fundamentalists began trying to shout him down during meetings, leaving the evangelist highly discouraged.

The internal tensions Billy felt were tremendously important for his entire ministry. The first tension was a growing conviction that he and his team must live in a manner worthy of the Gospel. In October 1948, in Modesto, California, Billy asked his team, which now included Cliff Barrows, George Beverly Shea, and Grady and

T. W. Wilson, to pray about and list the dishonorable deeds that evangelists had committed that had harmed the name of Jesus Christ.

They came together to share their lists and compiled them into what they would later call the Modesto Manifesto. Each concern raised was followed by a pledge to do all diligence to guard themselves from these deeds. Together, they resolved to (1) honestly and honorably account for and use money; (2) guard themselves against sexual immorality; (3) refrain from attacking the local church; and (4) report statistics with integrity. These resolutions bound the team together for the next half century.

The other internal struggle Billy faced during this time was even more serious and struck to the very core of his calling as an evangelist. He began to question whether he could trust the Word of God as authoritative.

This question was brought to bear by several factors. First, in the late 1940s, Billy had begun to see the ugly side of fundamentalism—from those who had nurtured his own soul. If they were wrong about church association, what else were they wrong about? Second, his YFC friend Chuck Templeton from Toronto had grown increasingly hostile to Billy's "simplistic" thinking and acceptance of traditional orthodoxy. Templeton's sharp mind and deep intellect raised questions for which Billy had no answer. And finally, Billy was reading theologians from Europe who were far less concerned with the debate over the inerrancy of scripture, which was foundational to American fundamentalists.

These issues all came to a head in the late summer of 1949 at the College Briefing Conference at Forest Home Retreat Center near Los Angeles. Templeton was on one side, accusing Billy of being fifty years behind the times in his thinking, and vivacious Bible teacher Henrietta Mears was on the other side, encouraging him to entrust himself fully to the Bible.

To Billy, everything was at stake. Go with his friend Charles, and he would need to resign as president of Northwestern Bible School and quit evangelistic preaching entirely; go with Henrietta Mears, and remain faithful to his heritage and training, and he would lose the intellectual respect he craved from Charles. He alone would have to make a choice.

He went for a late-night prayerful walk to calm his troubled soul and ponder the issue. He looked to scripture for guidance before finally laying his Bible down on a tree stump, kneeling down on the dirt, and praying a prayer of resignation: "Oh Lord," he prayed, "there are many things in this book I do not understand." He continued to raise all of his reservations, before saying, "Father, I am going to accept this as Thy Word—by *faith*!"

He got up from his knees with tears in his eyes and sensed the presence of God in a way he had not for months. The Lord honored his faith and went with him in power to his campaign in Los Angeles that September.

—╪═

The three-week Campaign for Greater Los Angeles began September 25, 1949, in an old circus tent that held five thousand people and was dubbed the Canvas Cathedral. By mid-October, the meetings were being extended, and by November, William Randolph Hearst had caught wind of the meetings and cast the story across his national network of newspapers. The tent was enlarged to accommodate the growing crowd, and by campaign's end, ten thousand per night were coming to the meetings, and thousands more were turned away for lack of space. Once again, the fire that had been rekindled through Billy's surrender at Forest Home and the sovereign work of God could not be contained. After the Los Angeles Campaign, the evangelistic ministry of Billy Graham rapidly spread across the nation and into the world.

In late 1949, people around the country were reading in news papers, magazines, and journals about an evangelist whose "evangelistic show [was] overshadowing even Billy Sunday."[5] Many had prayed for such a man to come. Some wondered, and others doubted, if such a ministry of evangelism would ever come again. Perhaps evangelism of this sort was of a bygone era.

But the Lord had been listening to the prayers of his people. He saw a group of men in 1934 on the farm of Billy Graham's father praying for such a person. He heard the call of Florida Bible Institute valedictorian Vera Resue for the next Luther, Wesley, Moody, or Sunday. He heard the cries for revival from J. Edwin Orr in the chapel of Wheaton College, and the prayers of millions of believers the world over.

The Lord found in Billy Graham a faithful servant whom he sovereignly chose to spread the fire of his Gospel throughout the earth. It was a fire never meant to be contained—a fire to engulf the entire world.

CHAPTER 23

THE SOURCE OF THE FLAME

"Today, we write the biographies of such as [Augustine, Bernard, Wesley, and Luther] and celebrate their fruit, but the tendency is to ignore the root out of which the fruit sprang."
A. W. TOZER

The years between 1936 and 1943 were immeasurably important in igniting the flame that became the worldwide evangelistic ministry of Billy Graham. God's sovereign work in sparking and fanning the fire is undeniable. From the influence of lay groups, gifted ministers, and committed educators, Billy's ministry was birthed in a purposeful evangelistic environment that intersected with the gifts of an energetic, visionary young man from a dairy farm in North Carolina.

This environment was shaped by people—people who took time for Billy. Some of these men were instrumental in igniting the fire in this young evangelist. Others walked beside him for decades as his gifts and vision came to fruition, continuing to fan the flames through their counsel, encouragement, love, and support, and by standing with him in dark days.

It is impossible to gauge one's influence over another's. When asked, Billy often spoke glowingly of his friends, using superlatives in his descriptions of their impact or Christian commitment. For example, he refers to both Dawson Trotman and V. Raymond Edman as "the most unforgettable" Christians he has ever met.

Many people invested deeply in Billy's life. His experiences, his views, and his passion were all set ablaze by men and women who gave their lives to serving others. God used these faithful servants to raise up a special laborer for His harvest.

BOB JONES SR. AND BOB JONES JR.

Even though Billy left Bob Jones College under less than favorable circumstances, he loved both Bob Jones Jr. and Bob Jones Sr. Indeed, he said that Bob Jones College was where he first learned evangelism. Whatever ill will Billy may have felt toward the Joneses, he graciously forgave, even if he never entirely forgot. And by 1944, the young pastor and evangelist was writing to Dr. Bob for advice, encouragement, and association with the seasoned evangelist.

By the mid-1940s, Billy's affection for Dr. Bob was matched by his love for very few other men in his life. He encouraged some young people with whom he came into contact to attend Bob Jones College, and as president of his own school in Minneapolis, he modeled parts of his vision after the Joneses' vision. The love was reciprocated when Bob Jones conferred an honorary doctorate on Billy in 1948, to help bolster the status of the young college president.

In 1951, Billy promoted Bob Jones College on his new, nationally broadcast radio program, *Hour of Decision*, with a visit to the new campus in Greenville, South Carolina, where the college became a university, and with an on-air interview with Bob Jones Jr.[1] The founder's son, who had by then taken over leadership of the school, had become rather close to Billy.

For Dr. Bob's part, he was delighted that a group of young men whose lives he had influenced—Billy, Grady and T. W. Wilson, Cliff Barrows, and the elder Willis Haymaker—were at the forefront of evangelistic ministry.

But things began to change by 1952. Bob Jones Jr. privately suggested that Billy's ministry was "shallow and superficial, and not having real revival."[2] This represented a tectonic shift that would affect evangelicalism for the next half century.

The breach was created by several factors, some of which were bigger than Billy and the Joneses—such as the founding of the National Association of Evangelicals and the World Council of Churches. Both Billy and the Joneses came to typify the issues involved as they became the primary leaders within their movements. The heart of the issue was whether Christians should associate with so-called compromisers, or those who rejected major tenets of the Christian faith. For the Joneses, the answer was an unequivocal *no*!

Billy's growing vision for church unity and inclusion naturally pitted him against the fighting fundamentalist movement. What pressed the issue further was Billy's statement, in 1957, to the National Association of Evangelicals: "I will go anywhere, sponsored by anybody, to preach the Gospel of Jesus Christ."[3] For Jones, accepting the invitation meant support for the sponsor; for Billy, accepting the invitation meant an opportunity to reach others for the Gospel.

The New York City Crusade that summer was a watershed moment, as the fissure turned to an all-out rupture between Billy Graham representing the evangelicals, and Bob Jones representing the fundamentalists.

Jones began prohibiting his students from participating in, or even praying for, Billy's crusades; and he publicly blasted Billy for compromise and apostasy. The rift would never be healed.

As the years passed, Billy reached out to his fundamentalist critics. Some, like John Rice, were able to reconcile with Billy. Others never could. When Bob Jones Sr. died in 1968, Billy sent a condolence letter to his erstwhile friend, Bob Jr. In return, when Billy's father-in-law, L. Nelson Bell, died in 1973, Jones sent a letter of condolence to Billy. Extending an olive branch, Billy wrote and said, "Don't you think it's time we renewed our friendship?" But for Bob Jones Jr., the issue was not a matter of friendship, but of conviction. The offer was, to say the least, rejected.[4]

By 1985, Bob Jones Jr. wrote that "Billy was doing more harm than any living man" and that he was "building the church of Antichrist." Further, he called Billy "the apostate's servant."[5]

Even though the relationship ended on such disappointing terms, the Joneses continued to have a place in Billy's heart and a role in his formation as a young evangelist. He simply was not formed to their liking.

W. T. WATSON

W. T. Watson's greatest contribution to the life of Billy Graham was the environment he created at the Florida Bible Institute, which was designed to nurture young preachers like him. At the Institute, Billy learned invaluable lessons about prayer, how to study the Bible, how to preach effectively, and how to avoid the pitfalls of ministry. In 1976, Billy told Dr. Watson, "You had a great part in my call to the ministry."[6]

After the Institute, Billy carried on a somewhat distant relationship with Watson until his death. The impact that Watson had on the evangelist came almost exclusively during Billy's days in Florida. Watson helped with crusades in the South,[7] including a crusade in St. Petersburg, but Billy relied on the counsel of others in later years.

Still, their love and respect for one another never ended. In 1981, as Watson lay in bed in a near comatose state, Billy telephoned to offer him some final words of encouragement as the phone was held to Watson's ear. As Billy spoke to Watson, those gathered around were surprised by a jolt of energy that shot into the dying leader, who grabbed for the phone and said some of the final words of his life: "Give Ruth my love."[8]

JOHN MINDER

From that spring day in 1937 when John Minder called on Billy to preach his first sermon, the young evangelist considered Minder his "father in the ministry."[9] As time carried on, Billy learned to lean on him for his "steadying influences,"[10] wise counsel, and ultimately his friendship.

On August 13, 1943, in Asheville, North Carolina, Minder performed Billy and Ruth's wedding, with assistance from Kerr Taylor, a close friend of the Bells'. The young pastor considered Minder one of his very best friends, writing that "nobody except my Dad comes first in my heart."[11] As Billy's schedule became increasingly busy in the mid-1940s, he longed for Minder's friendship and fellowship. That love never left Billy's heart, but their friendship did not remain as regular as the years passed and their paths took different directions.

Though Billy believed that Minder himself was not a great preacher, he knew preaching and helped shape Billy as a preacher.

Perhaps Minder's influence can best be summed up in his own life story. As a young man in the early 1920s, Minder walked two miles to go to church, "not so much to hear the sermon as to have the privilege of walking home with [the pastor]." Writing of this experience, Minder suggests something that was also true to Billy's evaluation of him: "The sermons that came from his lips on the way home meant more to me than the services at the church."[12]

John Minder's enduring influence on Billy Graham was that he walked with him, and along the way he counseled him, taught him, and let sermons come from his lips.

W. B. RILEY

When W. B. Riley came to the Florida Bible Institute, and again when he came to Wheaton College as a guest speaker, young Billy Graham was certainly impressed. And that respect would continue until Riley's death. Billy viewed the gifted educator as "head and shoulders" above most fundamentalist leaders of his day.[13] But even though Billy admired Riley, his respect was outdone by Riley's own exuberant praise of Billy as a result of having heard him preach on a few occasions for Youth for Christ.

In 1971, Graham was asked how Riley had influenced his evangelistic vision. Billy responded that, despite what many thought, the two were never very close, and Riley had no impact in regard to evangelism. Though Billy respected Riley's courage and personal integrity, he "learned a great deal from some of the mistakes" he thought Riley had made.[14]

Graham never listed the mistakes, but perhaps chief among them would be the appointment of a thirty-one-year-old evangelist to a school presidency. Beyond that, Billy felt that the fifty-member board that Riley had gathered and Billy inherited as president of Northwestern Schools was too big and inefficient to do the necessary work of a college. He also may have found reason to see flaws in Riley's unfinished building campaign.

More than influence, Riley shaped the direction of Billy Graham's life by giving him an otherwise impossible opportunity to lead a Bible school.

DAWSON TROTMAN

When Billy met Dawson Trotman, president of the Navigators, at Wheaton College in 1941, and then again in 1942, Trotman was philosophically opposed to mass evangelism. He believed that the role of evangelism should be personal and have as its end to make disciples, not merely converts.

But though Trotman was so adamantly opposed to the impersonal method of evangelism, by the mid- to late 1940s God had placed a half dozen of the most effective mass evangelists of the twentieth century in his path, and they were eager to listen to him. These men included Jim Rayburn of Young Life; Jack Wyrtzen of Word of Life; Bill Bright, who started Campus Crusade for Christ; and Torrey Johnson and Billy Graham of Youth for Christ.

In January 1946, the YFC International officers met in Los Angeles for strategy meetings. While they were there, they met Trotman at his home. As Graham, Johnson, Charles Templeton, Cliff Barrows, and others gathered around the Navigators leader, he impressed on them the importance of personal scripture memory and challenged them about the immense need for follow-up for new converts.[15] Some of these leaders had already been using Trotman's Topical Memory System—a scripture memory technique using pocket-sized memory cards arranged topically—and Billy, for one, took Trotman's challenge seriously.

Trotman's path crossed with Billy's yet again in August 1948 at the first YFC Congress on Evangelism in Beatenberg, Switzerland. It was at this conference that Dawson and Billy began a practice of baring their souls to one another, as they slipped away with two other leaders for prayer. They confessed their faults, weaknesses, and lack of power to one another and to God.

Billy was overwhelmed with his new responsibilities as president of a Bible school and sought the advice of those gathered. Trotman dug in. "There's not a Bible school in the country that teaches the fundamentals of leading a man to Christ and following him up to the point where he could win a man and follow him up," he explained. "That should be the *first* thing a Bible school teaches."[16] Trotman challenged Billy to get this vision on his heart, and then the students would get it onto their hearts.

The young college president took what Dawson Trotman said very seriously and invited one of the Navigators to teach a class at the Bible school. But Trotman's impact on Billy would continue beyond Billy's time as president of Northwestern.

As Billy's ministry began to take off after the 1949 Los Angeles Campaign, where Trotman helped to counsel inquirers, the evangelist saw a need for what Trotman had to offer. Billy invited him to be a part of his team in 1951, requiring six months of the year from his own worldwide ministry to develop and run a follow-up program for the crusades.

After much resistance and prayer, Trotman agreed to join Billy's team. By then, Trotman had come around from his stance in opposition to mass evangelism and had begun to see how his influence could enrich the anointed ministry of Billy Graham. At Trotman's first crusade in Shreveport, Louisiana, he kept trying "to tell Billy and the others that this is really a new field to me, but they just laughed."[17]

The system of follow-up he developed was used by and large for the next fifty years, as Trotman handed the responsibilities along to Lorne Sanny, who in turn passed them to Charlie Riggs. The system began with a six-week pre-campaign training class for personal counselors—usually made up of laypeople. These counselors were trained to determine the *real* needs of the inquirers and to answer their needs with the Word of God.

Trotman developed a method for counseling at the crusades that was both efficient and effective. When Billy gave the invitation and inquirers made their way down the aisles, counselors of the same sex, and roughly the same age, would be matched up to stand alongside them and find out why they had responded. After the discussion, a decision card was filled out, which accurately recorded whether they were inquiring, recommitting, or dedicating their lives to Christ for the first time. These cards and the inquirers were then brought to an advisor—usually a pastor—who would allow the inquirers to tell them any new commitments they made and also would answer any further questions. The inquirers were then given literature—an introductory Bible study and memory verse cards on the assurance of salvation.

Within forty-eight hours, the counselors were to contact or visit the inquirers, and within a week, the pastor of a local church from the denomination of their choice would make contact. Finally, those who made decisions were invited to a follow-up rally and sent a final letter with more literature a few weeks later.

The goal of the crusades was not simply to add converts to the rolls, but to strengthen the churches so that they would be the ultimate follow-up program.

Dawson Trotman's impact on Billy Graham's ministry was profound. But personally, Trotman instilled in Billy a love for the Word of God, especially after his 1949 crisis. Billy found in Trotman a man with whom he could bare his soul and share large visions, and a man who could offer him a "quiet rebuke."[18]

In June 1956, tragedy struck Dawson Trotman at Schroon Lake, New York, when he and a passenger who could not swim were thrown from a speedboat. The Navigator leader went to rescue the girl, and held her up; but as others from the boat reached to grab her, Trotman himself drowned. The tragedy shook the evangelical leaders he had invested in for the past decade and was broadcast throughout the world. The July 2 issue of *Time* magazine ran a nearly full-page article on his life and death, including a picture with a caption that read, "Always holding someone up." The article began, "So died Dawson Trotman."

This statement also characterizes the impact that Trotman had on

Billy—holding him and his ministry up in vision, counsel, strategy, and prayer.

V. RAYMOND EDMAN

In a 1965 letter to V. Raymond Edman, Billy Graham wrote, "Your contribution to my ministry and life cannot be properly evaluated until we stand before Christ at the Judgment Seat."[19] Billy confided to others that Edman had the greatest influence of any mortal on his life.[20] Though Billy loved and admired the Wheaton College president from the day they first met in 1940, the relationship blossomed in the mid-1950s and grew until Edman's death in 1967.

As had been the case while Billy was a student at Wheaton, Edman's ministry to the world-renowned evangelist was one of prayer, counsel, and encouragement.[21]

Of particular importance to Billy was the support Edman gave to him in the midst of the fundamentalist uprising against Billy, which peaked in the late 1950s. When friends and mentors turned against Billy, Edman came to pray with him in his darkest hour,[22] and directed the students of Wheaton to pray as well. So profound was this encouragement that in 1958, Billy and Ruth named their newborn son after Ruth's father, Nelson, and the college president—Nelson Edman, or Ned for short.

The warmth of Billy's relationship with Dr. Edman can be seen in their correspondence. "Dear Ones," Edman wrote to Billy and Ruth. Billy returned with, "My beloved Dr. Edman." "Knees down, chin up," Edman encouraged him. Billy wrote to Edman in 1965, "Your little notes of encouragement from time to time are among the most encouraging things that I receive."[23] To reciprocate, when Billy heard that Edman had suffered a detached retina, leaving him temporarily blind, Billy sent him an audio Bible to use for devotions.[24] And throughout Dr. Edman's illnesses in the last half decade of his life,

Billy's close associates, who came to be called The Team, assured Edman of their prayers.

Beyond his friendship with Billy, Edman's influence grew throughout the organization as he began to share devotions with the Billy Graham Evangelistic Association (BGEA) staff, who were encouraged by his "cheery" presence. He was called on to join Billy's closest associates for vacations to enrich them spiritually with devotions and prayer, and he won the hearts of Billy's inner circle of associates. Edman was so well respected within the organization that the BGEA board saw fit to elect him senior vice president in 1964—a largely honorary role for the ailing sixty-four-year-old college president—and made him Billy's temporary successor to the presidency, should anything happen to the evangelist.

As with Dawson Trotman, the manner of Dr. Edman's death gives insight into his impact on Billy Graham's life. On September 22, 1967, Edman stepped up to the lectern of the Wheaton College chapel to give a message titled "In the Presence of the King," in which he sought to lead the student body into the Lord's presence. Midway through the message, he collapsed to the ground and himself entered into glory, shocking and inspiring the evangelical world.

The indelible influence of V. Raymond Edman in Billy's life can be summed up in that event. Whenever Billy had contact with Dr. Edman—through letters, devotional books, or in prayer and counsel—Edman was always leading Billy sweetly and gently into the presence of the Lord Jesus Christ.

L. NELSON BELL

When Billy married Ruth McCue Bell, he not only gained an invaluable soul mate, but also gained the intimate input of her brilliant medical missionary father, L. Nelson Bell. Dr. Bell had returned from China while Billy and Ruth were students at Wheaton, and he remained in Montreat, North Carolina, for the rest of his life, serving as a successful surgeon in nearby Asheville for much of the time.

When Billy and Ruth moved to Montreat to be close to her family, Dr. Bell became an invaluable confidant and advisor to Billy. In particular, when Billy was tempted toward careers in politics or television, his father-in-law was one of the major voices persuading him to stay focused on his calling.[25]

More than that, however, Nelson Bell, the retired missionary, helped give Billy a "wider vision of world Christianity."[26] More particularly, he imparted to Billy the grand vision of the Church that became a foundation for Billy's ministry—but which also brought forward Billy's fiercest critics. Bell's own experience fighting liberalism in his Southern Presbyterian denomination shaped a firm policy that he impressed upon his evangelist son-in-law: "You take your stand, you defend the faith, but you don't retreat."[27] He was teaching Billy that the fight for the Church must be fought from within, and it is this vision that shaped Billy's cooperative evangelistic efforts. Billy said that Nelson Bell and Ruth "together did more to get my ministry church-oriented than any single factor and single influence."[28]

And when this vision came under fierce attack by the fundamentalists, Nelson Bell was Graham's most valiant defender, writing articles for journals and periodicals, and privately writing letters to Billy's critics, making Billy's case so that the evangelist could concentrate on the evangelistic task to which he was called.

Dr. Bell's final influence was an enduring one—when he and Billy had simultaneous visions in 1958 for an evangelical periodical in response to the influential, liberal *Christian Century*. The new magazine was called *Christianity Today* and is still in publication today, almost six decades later. Billy could bring his name recognition and vision to the enterprise, but Nelson Bell had three things that Billy did not: publishing experience—as editor of the *Presbyterian*

Journal—the drive to stir up support, and the determination to see it through.

The magazine was meant to reach a wider audience than Bell's *Presbyterian Journal*; it was to be a biblical and scholarly voice to combat liberalism in religious schools and churches, and for its first year it was given free to every Protestant minister. Bell wrote a regular column for the magazine called "A Layman and His Faith," which served to critique theological and practical issues within the Church.

Billy credits his father-in-law for having an incalculable influence on his thinking and methods of evangelism.[29] The imprint of L. Nelson Bell had significant ramifications for Billy's worldwide ministry, which in turn influenced Christendom and dominated the second half of the so-called Christian century.

The list could go on and on of men and women, both great and small, who ignited the fire in Billy Graham—classmates, friends, teachers, chapel speakers, prayer partners, and future associates. Many people were involved in setting this young man ablaze for the Gospel and fanning his flames when the embers seemed to smolder.

The significance of these people can hardly be overstated in answering the question of how Billy Graham became the preeminent evangelist of the twentieth century. This period in his life shows that God was sovereignly working through His people to ignite this young man's heart to reach the world with the Gospel.

Billy Graham's success happened in large part because he was close to the burning embers of these precious souls. But more than that, Billy was not content to be warmed by their embers alone. He diligently sought the Source of the flame for himself, the Lord Jesus Christ.

When Vera Resue, valedictorian of Billy's graduating class at the Florida Bible Institute, said in 1940 that "the time is ripe for another Luther, Wesley, Moody, _____," she was right. Billy Graham filled in the blank for the need of *that* hour.

Today, many long for that list of evangelists to continue to grow. But Christians first need to consider that, in this day and age, the time is ripe for groups of men and women from all walks of life to take a day off from work to pray for their cities and for the Lord to raise up laborers for his harvest, as they did on the Graham farm in 1936. The world is in need of refreshing, visionary educators to invest in the young—of mentors like John Minder and V. Raymond Edman; of mothers praying for their children, like Morrow Graham; of faithful churchmen, like L. Nelson Bell; of passionate men and women committed to evangelism and discipleship, like Dawson Trotman, Jim Rayburn, and Torrey Johnson.

As the ministry of Billy Graham draws to a close, the challenge today is for the fire of another Luther, Wesley, Moody, or Graham to be kindled. But this challenge will only be fulfilled as committed disciples of Jesus Christ give up their lives so that the true Source of the flame, the Lord Jesus Christ, might be made known. When this foundation of laborers for the harvest has been established, this nation and world will see, as it has in previous generations, the roaring flame of the spread of the Gospel of Jesus Christ.

ACKNOWLEDGMENTS

Writing this book has been a project requiring much help and support from people around the country. But first and foremost, I want to thank my wife, Charissa, for allowing me to indulge in this "obsession," which has required much sacrifice on her behalf.

I also must thank Dr. Lyle Dorsett, who as a friend, mentor, and encourager first placed within me the notion of writing a biography, and gave me resources and time with which to research and write this volume. My debt is unrepayable.

I could not possibly list the hundreds of people who have corresponded with me or granted me interviews, but I am grateful to each one. Some are mentioned in these pages. Several have gone to glory since sharing their information with me. Many have offered not only valuable information, but also friendship, prayer, and kindness; and several have opened their homes to me, for which I am eternally grateful.

Of special note, I must thank Lorene Minder, the widow of John Minder, for her kindness in sharing with me. The Reverend Bob Watson, the son of Florida Bible Institute founder W. T. Watson, shared yearbooks and pictures with me, which proved to be an invaluable resource. And I want to thank Dr. Duane Litfin, former president of Wheaton College, for allowing me to indulge in a "fishing expedition" in the files of former Wheaton president V. Raymond Edman.

I would also like to thank Keith Call, who was very helpful to me in the Wheaton College Archives, and who also connected me to Jonathan Cheek, who did invaluable research for me at Bob Jones University. Thanks also to the able staff at the Billy Graham Center Archives, especially Bob Shuster, who gave me early direction on my project; and for my friend Matt Perkins for assisting me in finding newspaper articles in Charlotte for the Ham-Ramsey Campaign.

Many have read and given helpful critique and support for the manuscript, including Chad Mize, Betsy Childs, and Dominic Zappia.

I am also grateful for the work of my agent, Gary Foster, and Paul Muckley and the staff at Barbour Publishing, Inc., who have made the publication of this work possible.

Finally, I am grateful to Billy Graham and his staff for their willingness to allow me to quote from his personal letters and resources in the Graham archives.

Many hands have helped ignite a fire in my own soul, and I am thankful for them all.

NOTES

Chapter 1: Kindling Prayer

1. The story of this prayer meeting can be found in its entirety in Vernon Patterson, "The Prayer Heard Round the World," *Decision* 16 (October 1975), 3, 12; or in part in Billy Graham, *Just As I Am* (San Francisco: HarperCollins, 1997), 24.

2. Graham, *Just As I Am*, 23.

3. Ibid.

4. Ibid., 23–24.

5. Ibid., 14.

6. See 2 Chronicles 16:9.

7. Billy Sunday's ministry had come to a relative standstill in the last decade of his life, before his death on November 6, 1935.

Chapter 2: Fire on the Sawdust Trail

1. *Charlotte Observer*, September 18, 1934.

2. *Elizabeth City Independent*, November 7, 1924, in W. O. Saunders, *The Book of Ham* (Elizabeth City, NC: The Independent, c. 1924), 3–7.

3. Ibid.

4. Saunders, *Book of Ham*, preface.

5. The text of *The Book of Ham* can be found online at http://highered411.com/Albemarle/BookOfHam.pdf.

6. Vernon W. Patterson, interview with Paul Ericksen, March 5, 1985; Billy Graham Center Archives, Collection 5, tape T4; transcript: www2.wheaton.edu/bgc/Archives/trans/005t04.htm.

7. *Charlotte Observer*, August 16, 1934.

8. Ibid.

9. Ibid.

10. *Charlotte Observer*, August 31, 1934.

11. Ibid. Emphasis added.

12. Billy Graham, *Just As I Am* (San Francisco: HarperCollins, 1997), 22.

13. Vernon Patterson interview.

14. Graham, *Just As I Am*, 26. See also Patterson interview; Grady Wilson, *Count It All Joy* (Nashville: Broadman, 1984), 14.

15. Vernon Patterson notes that these were boys acting as prostitutes, a particularly heinous sin in the 1930s.

16. Graham, *Just As I Am*, 26. See also Patterson interview; Wilson, *Count It All Joy*, 14.

17. Graham, *Just As I Am*, 26.

18. Ibid., 27.

19. Ibid., 27–28.

20. Wilson, *Count It All Joy*, 12.

Chapter 3: Unusual Fire

1. In 1947, Bob Jones College moved to Greenville, South Carolina, and became Bob Jones University.

2. Billy Graham, *Just As I Am* (San Francisco: HarperCollins, 1997), 32.

3. Ibid., 33.

4. Ibid., 34.

5. Bob Jones Jr. later wrote, through the filter of a painfully strained relationship, that the "student body was, for the most part, made up of young people too spiritual and intelligent to be taken in by [Billy's] charm." See Bob Jones, *Cornbread and Caviar: Reminiscences and Reflections* (Greenville, SC: BJU Press, 1985), 153.

6. Grady Wilson, *Count It All Joy* (Nashville: Broadman, 1984), 23.

7. R. K. Johnson, *Builder of Bridges: A Biography of Dr. Bob Jones Sr.* (Greenville, SC: BJU Press, 1982), 180–81.

8. *Fellowship News* (Bob Jones College newsletter), October 31, 1936.

9. Bob Jones College catalog, 1936–1937.

10. Johnson, *Builder of Bridges*, 196.

11. *Cleveland Daily Banner*, September 10, 1936.

12. *The Vintage* (Bob Jones College yearbook), 1936–1937.

13. Johnson, *Builder of Bridges*, 198.

14. Ibid.

15. *Cleveland Daily Banner*, September 10, 1936.

16. *Cleveland Daily Banner*, September 12, 1936.

17. *Fellowship News*, October 31, 1936.

18. Bob Jones College catalog, 1936–1937, 11.

19. *The Vintage*, 1936–1937.

20. Ibid.

21. Ibid.

22. Johnson, *Builder of Bridges*, 199.

23. In his autobiography, *Cornbread and Caviar*, Bob Jones Jr. suggests that the school faced more opposition from other fundamentalists than from anyone else, because of their Shakespeare productions.

24. *Cleveland Daily Banner*, September 12, 1936; *The Vintage* (Bob Jones College yearbook), 1936–1937.

25. *Cleveland Daily Banner*, October 17, 1936.

26. *Cleveland Daily Banner*, September 12, 1936.

27. *Cleveland Daily Banner*, October 3, 1936.

28. *The Vintage*, 1936–1937, 34.

29. Ibid.

30. *Hour of Decision*, December 1951.

Chapter 4: Singed

1. *Fellowship News* (Bob Jones College newsletter), December 12, 1936.

2. Bob Jones College catalog, 1936–1937, 11.

3. Marshall Frady, *Billy Graham: A Parable of American Righteousness* (Boston: Little Brown, 1979), 96.

4. See the 1933 Rules of Bob Jones College.

5. Ibid.

6. Billy Graham, *Just As I Am* (San Francisco: HarperCollins, 1997), 40.

7. Mrs. Pat Juby, e-mail to the author, February 6, 2005.

8. Bob Jones College catalog, 1936–1937, 15.

9. Graham, *Just As I Am*, 41.

10. Frady, *Billy Graham: A Parable*, 99.

11. Ibid., 98–99.

12. Daniel L. Turner, *Standing without Apology: The History of Bob Jones University* (Greenville, SC: BJU Press, 1997), 392. Turner, who seems to have had access to letters between Bob Jones Sr., Billy Graham, and Billy's family, notes three distinct meetings.

13. William Martin, *A Prophet with Honor: The Billy Graham Story* (New York: William Morrow, 1991), 69–70.

14. Graham, *Just As I Am*, 40. See also Daniel L. Turner, *Standing without Apology*, 392. Turner notes that Wendell Phillips, after studying for a year at the Moody Bible Institute, begged Bob Jones Sr., in 1942, to allow him to return to finish his coursework at Bob Jones College.

15. T. W. Wilson, interview with Dr. Lois Ferm, January 30, 1971; and Roy Gustafson, interview with Dr. Lois Ferm, January 8, 1976.

16. Morrow Graham, interview with Dr. Lois Ferm, June 3, 1977.

17. Martin, *Prophet with Honor*, 70.

18. Bob Jones Sr., letter to William Franklin Graham, January 11, 1937, cited in Turner, *Standing without Apology*, 392.

19. W. T. Watson, interview with Dr. Lois Ferm, February 14, 1977.

Chapter 5: The Miracle School

1. The Florida Bible Institute changed its name to Trinity College in 1947, when it moved from Temple Terrace to its current location in Dunedin, Florida.

2. W. T. Watson, Trinity Bible College alumni banquet, April 28, 1976.

3. Ibid.

4. Robert B. Ekvall, Harry M. Shuman, Alfred C. Snead, et al., *After Fifty Years: A Record of God's Working through the Christian and Missionary Alliance* (Harrisburg, PA: Christian Publications, 1939), 100–105.

5. Bob Watson (W. T. Watson's son), interview with the author, January 20, 2009.

6. Vera Resue, interview with Dr. Lois Ferm, April 18, 1980. Recording located in

the Billy Graham Center Archives, Wheaton, IL.

7. Bob Watson interview.

8. Ibid.

9. From the curriculum list located in the Vera Resue file in the Billy Graham Center Archives, Wheaton, IL.

10. Grady Wilson, *Count It All Joy* (Nashville: Broadman, 1984), 24.

11. Billy Graham, Trinity Bible College alumni banquet, April 28, 1976.

12. W. T. Watson, *The Bible School Days of Billy Graham* (Dunedin, FL: W. T. Watson, 1976), 11.

13. Vera Resue interview.

14. Ibid. During the interview, Dr. Lois Ferm comments that Graham had characterized these years as the best of his life.

Chapter 6: Into the Fire

1. Bob Watson, interview with the author, January 20, 2009.

2. 1 John 4:4 KJV. Billy Graham, Trinity Bible College alumni banquet, April 28, 1976.

3. Bob Watson interview.

4. Graham, Trinity alumni banquet.

5. Lois Ferm, "Billy Graham in Florida," *Florida Historical Quarterly*, October 1981. This article includes a picture of Billy Graham with his young students.

6. Children's Bible Ministries, www. childrensbibleministries.net/our-history.

7. W. T. Watson, Trinity Bible College alumni banquet, April 28, 1976. Also, Bob Watson, interview with the author, January 20, 2009.

8. *The Beacon* (Florida Bible Institute yearbook), 1936.

9. Emily Cavanaugh Massey, interview with Dr. Lois Ferm, 1977; Billy Graham Center Archives.

10. Ibid.

11. Lorene Minder, *John Minder: A Man Sent from God* (St. Louis: Creative Concepts, 1988), 34.

12. Ibid., 9.

13. Ibid.

14. John Minder, interview with Dr. Lois Ferm, February 14, 1977; Billy Graham Center Archives.

15. Graham, Trinity alumni banquet.

16. John Minder interview.

17. Ibid.

18. Cecil Underwood, interview with Lois Ferm, March 14, 1977.

Chapter 7: Surrender

1. Billy Graham, "I Surrender All," in *Crusade Hymn Stories*, ed. Cliff Barrows (Chicago: Hope, 1967), 117.

2. Ibid.

3. Lorene Minder, *John Minder: A Man Sent from God* (St. Louis: Creative Concepts, 1988), 26.

4. *Tampa Morning Tribune*, February 9, 1940.

5. Bob Watson, interview with the author, January 20, 2009. Watson later claimed, "Billy never got victory over that sin!"

6. *Tampa Daily Times*, July 17, 1937.

7. Billy Graham's FBI scrapbook, 1938–1940, 5, front; Billy Graham Center Archives, Collection 15, 1-1; www2. wheaton.edu/bgc/Archives/docs/ BGScrapbook1938/005a.htm.

8. Billy Graham, *Just As I Am* (San Francisco: HarperCollins, 1997), 51.

9. Ibid., 50.

10. Ibid.

11. Stanley High, *Billy Graham: The Man and His Message* (New York: McGraw-Hill, 1956), 79.

12. Minder, *John Minder*, 8.

13. 1 Corinthians 9:13–14 KJV; cited in High, *Billy Graham*, 79.

14. Billy Graham's FBI scrapbook, 1938–1940, 1, front; Billy Graham Center Archives, Collection 15, 1-1; www2. wheaton.edu/bgc/Archives/docs/ BGScrapbook1938/001a.htm.

15. *Tabernacle Tidings*, Billy Graham's FBI scrapbook, 1938–1940, 5, front; Billy Graham Center Archives, Collection 15, 1-1; www2.wheaton.edu/bgc/Archives/docs/BGScrapbook1938/005a.htm.

16. Vera Resue, interview with Dr. Lois Ferm, April 18, 1980; Billy Graham Center Archives

17. Roy Gustafson, interview with Dr. Lois Ferm, January 8, 1976; Billy Graham Center Archives.

18. Ibid.

19. Ibid.

20. Grady Wilson, *Billy Graham as a Teenager* (Grand Rapids: Zondervan, 1964), 27.

21. 2 Corinthians 1:3–4, as cited in High, *Billy Graham*, 79.

22. High, *Billy Graham*, 76.

23. Billy Graham, Trinity Bible College alumni banquet, April 28, 1976.

24. High, *Billy Graham*, 77.

25. Graham, Trinity alumni banquet.

26. High, *Billy Graham*, 76.

27. As Billy Graham later told the *Lakeland Ledger* (March 3, 1980) about his late-night walk on the golf course, "That's when I surrendered all."

Chapter 8: Fire in His Bones

1. Jeremiah 20:9.

2. Vera Resue, interview with Dr. Lois Ferm, April 18, 1980; Billy Graham Center Archives.

3. *Oak Ridger*, July 30, 2001.

4. Roy Gustafson, interview with Dr. Lois Ferm, January 8, 1976; Billy Graham Center Archives.

5. Ibid.

6. Vera Resue interview.

7. Bryam H. Glaze, quoted in W. T. Watson, *The Bible School Days of Billy Graham* (Dunedin, FL: W. T. Watson, 1976); and W. T. Watson, interview with Dr. Lois Ferm, February 14, 1977. See also Billy Graham, *Just As I Am* (San Francisco: HarperCollins, 1997), 49.

8. Stanley High, *Billy Graham: The Man and His Message* (New York: McGraw-Hill, 1956), 89. Emphasis added.

9. Bob Watson, interview with the author, January 20, 2009.

10. Ibid.

11. Ibid.

12. John MacDonald, e-mail to the author, January 13, 2005.

13. Lois Ferm, "Billy Graham in Florida," *Florida Historical Quarterly*, October 1981, 180–81.

14. Bob Watson interview.

15. Ibid.

16. Ibid.

17. Ibid.

18. W. T. Watson, *The Bible School Days of Billy Graham* (Dunedin, FL: W. T. Watson, 1976).

19. The notebook is housed in the Billy Graham Center Archives.

20. Billy Graham, *The Holy Spirit: Activating God's Power in Your Life* (Dallas: Word, 1988), 78.

21. High, *Billy Graham*, 78.

22. Ibid.

23. Ibid.

24. Lorene Minder, *John Minder: His Life and Ministry* (St. Louis: Creative Concepts, 1988), 33.

25. Billy Graham promotional flyer, in Billy Graham's FBI scrapbook, 1938–1940; Billy Graham Center Archives, Collection 15, 1-1; www2.wheaton.edu/bgc/Archives/docs/BGScrapbook1938/table.htm.

26. See William Martin, *A Prophet with Honor: The Billy Graham Story* (New York: William Morrow Co., 1991), 78. Martin cites Grady Wilson from a 1976 Billy Graham Evangelistic Association meeting. Wilson had a knack for telling stories—but also a knack for embellishing them.

27. From "This Is My Life" by Billy Graham, as told to Will Oursker, "My First Moment of Decision," quoted in

Watson, *Bible School Days*. See also Roy Gustafson, interview with Dr. Lois Ferm, January 8, 1976; Billy Graham Center Archives.

Chapter 9: A Burning Message

1. W. T. Watson, *The Bible School Days of Billy Graham* (Dunedin, FL: W. T. Watson, 1976), inside front cover.

2. Roy Gustafson, interview with Dr. Lois Ferm, January 8, 1976.

3. Watson, *Bible School Days*, 24.

4. Ibid., inside front cover.

5. Lois Ferm, "Billy Graham in Florida," *Florida Historical Quarterly*, October 1981, 181–82.

6. Ibid.

7. Cecil Underwood, interview with Dr. Lois Ferm, March 14, 1977; Billy Graham Center Archives.

8. Bob Watson, interview with the author, January 20, 2009.

9. Palatka newspaper, assorted articles, n.d., in Billy Graham's FBI scrapbook, 1938–1940; Billy Graham Center Archives, Collection 15, 1-1; www2. wheaton.edu/bgc/Archives/docs/ BGScrapbook1938/table.htm.

10. Irene McManus, interview with the author, January 25, 2004.

11. Ibid.

12. Cecil Underwood and John Minder, interview with Dr. Lois Ferm, March 14, 1977; Billy Graham Center Archives.

13. Billy Graham, *Just As I Am* (San Francisco: HarperCollins, 1997), 55.

14. Cecil Underwood and John Minder interview.

15. Ferm, "Billy Graham in Florida," 181–82. With the available resources, tracing the chronology gets a bit tricky. William Martin places this revival meeting in the summer of 1938. I base my timeline on the fact that Billy's time at Peniel preceded his time in East Palatka, and seems to have been followed soon after by the Pomona Baptist Church revival, which happened in late November 1938.

16. John Minder, interview with Dr. Lois Ferm, February 14, 1977; Billy Graham Center Archives.

17. Palatka newspaper, assorted articles.

18. Ibid.

19. Ibid.

20. Ibid.

21. Ibid.

22. John Minder interview.

23. Ibid.

24. Palatka newspaper, assorted articles.

25. Ibid.

26. Ibid.

27. John Minder interview.

28. Graham, *Just As I Am*, 55.

29. Palatka newspaper, assorted articles.

30. *History of Pomona Baptist Church*, given to the author by Gary J. Munson, pastor of First Baptist Church of Pomona Park, Florida.

31. Eva Middleton, interview with the author, January 25, 2004. Also in *History of Pomona Baptist Church*.

32. Eva Middleton interview.

33. Irene Hundley, interview with the author, February 5, 2005.

34. *History of Pomona Baptist Church*.

35. Cecil Underwood interview.

36. Billy Graham, letter to William E. Mew, December 9, 1939, published in *History of Pomona Baptist Church*. Letter is copyright © 1939 by Billy Graham, used by permission, all rights reserved.

37. Ibid.

38. *History of Pomona Baptist Church*.

39. Betty Black, interview with the author, January 25, 2004.

40. *Park Ridge Herald*, January 16, 1942.

41. *Palm Beach Post*, November 17, 1958.

42. Graham, *Just As I Am*, 55.

43. Billy Graham letter to William Mew.

44. These "two" were perhaps Grady and T. W. Wilson. In January 1939, Grady Wilson held a meeting with Ponzi Pennington at Union Mission, advertised with flyers similar to Billy's.

45. Morrow Graham, interview with Dr. Lois Ferm, June 3, 1977.

46. Ibid.

47. Ibid.

48. Cecil Underwood interview.

49. Graham, *Just As I Am*, 57.

50. Ibid.

Chapter 10: Jesus Only

1. Lorene Minder, *John Minder: His Life and Ministry* (St. Louis: Creative Concepts, 1988), 35.

2. *Tampa Daily Times*, May 28, 1938.

3. Billy Graham Center Archives, Collection 15, box 1, folder 9.

4. Ibid.

5. *Birmingham News Age Herald*, October 1, 1939. See also Minder, *John Minder*, 89, and *Alliance Weekly*, September 30, 1939.

6. Morrow Graham, interview with Dr. Lois Ferm, June 3, 1977; Billy Graham Center Archives.

7. John Minder, interview with Dr. Lois Ferm, February 14, 1977; Billy Graham Center Archives.

8. Morrow Coffey Graham, *They Call Me Mother Graham* (Old Tappan, NJ: Revell, 1977), 44.

9. Ibid.

10. Billy Graham, "A Midnight Cry," *Tabernacle Messenger*, n.d.; Billy Graham Center Archives, Collection 15. Copyright © by Billy Graham, used by permission, all rights reserved.

11. Julian Bandy became president of Toccoa Falls Bible Institute in 1957, upon the retirement of R. A. Forrest.

12. Minder, *John Minder: His Life and Ministry*, 27.

13. In an interview with Dr. Lois Ferm, John Minder said that *all* had made decisions.

14. Bob Watson, son of W. T. Watson, told the author that Billy and W. T. Watson disputed who had been holding J. W. Van DeVenter when he died. Apparently, both men claimed to have been the one holding their friend as he entered his final rest.

15. Billy Graham's FBI scrapbook, 1938–1940; Billy Graham Center Archives, Collection 15, 1-1; www2.wheaton.edu/bgc/Archives/docs/BGScrapbook1938/table.htm. There was also a biography of David Livingstone, called *Livingstone, the Pathfinder*, by Basil J. Mathews (1913).

16. In 1923, Aimee Semple McPherson founded the Foursquare Church, which holds to the same four basic elements as the Christian and Missionary Alliance. Sister Aimee claimed that she was uninfluenced by any other movement. The two movements have similarities, but also significant differences.

17. George Palmer Pardington, *Twenty-Five Wonderful Years, 1889–1914: A Popular Sketch of the Christian and Missionary Alliance* (New York: Christian Alliance, 1914), 47.

18. This view is termed *subsequentialism* by theologians, because it is an event subsequent to salvation.

19. For more discussion on the particulars of the C&MA's beliefs, see Pardington's *Twenty-Five Wonderful Years*, or a more recent analysis, Bernie A. Van De Walle, *The Heart of the Gospel: A. B. Simpson, the Fourfold Gospel, and Late Nineteenth-Century Evangelical Theology* (Eugene, OR: Pickwick, 2009).

20. Billy Graham, *The Holy Spirit* (Waco, TX: Word, 1980), 62.

21. Cliff Barrows recounts how Stephen Olford led Billy to pray for the baptism of the Holy Spirit, which he claimed to receive. Cliff Barrow, chapel message at Beeson Divinity School, February 14, 2006; Lewis A. Drummond, *The Evangelist* (Nashville: Thomas Nelson, 2009), which cites Barrows as its source.

22. Graham, *Holy Spirit*, 64. Here, Billy draws a distinction between "baptism with the Holy Spirit" and being "filled with the Holy Spirit": "As has often been said, 'One baptism, but many fillings.'"

23. Pardington, *Twenty-Five Wonderful Years*, 57.

24. See Van De Walle, *Heart of the Gospel*, 18–23.

25. See *Alliance Weekly*, October 28, 1922. From meetings at Lake Geneva with Roscoe Stull, there were reports of "a number of marked healings. One girl, fourteen years of age, who had suffered for five years from a severe case of measles and who was given no hope of any relief from physicians, was anointed and healed." The September 27, 1924, edition of the *Alliance Weekly* includes a description of John Minder's new Tampa work, where "God is putting His seal upon the preached Word in the salvation of sinners and the sanctification of believers and the healing of the sick. . . . [The Tampa Gospel Tabernacle] will be made a center of intensive evangelism and spiritual activity throughout the winter months along Full Gospel lines." Also, an article in the March 21, 1925, edition of the *Alliance Weekly* reports healings at the St. Petersburg Tabernacle, where W. T. Watson was pastor.

26. Graham, *Holy Spirit*.

27. "Billy Graham's Own Story: 'God Is My Witness': Part One," *McCall's*, April 1964, 122.

28. *Alliance Weekly*, October 17, 1942.

29. Minder, *John Minder: His Life and Ministry*, 46.

Chapter 11: At the Feet of Giants

1. Morrow Coffey Graham, *They Call Me Mother Graham* (Old Tappan, NJ: Revell, 1977), 42. Copyright © by Billy Graham, used by permission, all rights reserved.

2. Ibid., 43.

3. Billy Graham, *Just As I Am* (San Francisco: HarperCollins, 1997), 45.

4. Riley had been coming regularly to the conferences since 1926, even before the Institute was founded.

5. Morrow Coffey Graham, *They Call Me Mother Graham*, 42.

6. Bob Watson, e-mail to the author, January 24, 2009.

7. Bob Watson, interview with the author, January 20, 2009.

8. *Evening Independent*, June 29, 1940.

9. Bob Watson interview.

10. Ibid. See also the *Evening Telegraph* (St. Petersburg, FL) promotions for these years.

11. W. T. Watson, *The Bible School Days of Billy Graham* (Dunedin, FL: W. T. Watson, 1976).

12. John Minder interview with Dr. Lois Ferm, February 14, 1977; Billy Graham Center Archives.

13. This lineup of speakers comes from lists found in newspapers and pamphlets, from interviews with people associated with the Institute, and from Billy Graham's own recollections.

14. Grady Wilson, *Count It All Joy* (Nashville: Broadman, 1984), 24.

15. Billy Graham, "Trusting Jesus," in *Crusade Hymn Stories*, edited by Cliff Barrows (Chicago: Hope, 1967), 129.

Chapter 12: Facing Challenges

1. Billy Graham, *Just As I Am* (San Francisco: HarperCollins, 1997), 59. Biographer Marshall Frady, in his book *Billy Graham: A Parable of American Righteousness*, mentions charges of sexual misconduct against a man whom Graham deeply respected; but it is unclear whether the charges were against W. T. Watson or another respected Christian man.

2. Ibid.

3. Bob Watson, interview with the author, January 20, 2009.

4. Graham, *Just As I Am*, 59; also in *The Beacon* (Florida Bible Institute yearbook), 1940 edition.

5. Bob Watson interview.

6. *The Gold Book: Fiftieth Anniversary of the Founding of Gospel Tabernacle, St. Petersburg, Florida, 1924–1974* (St. Petersburg, FL: St. Petersburg Gospel Tabernacle, 1974).

7. *Alliance Weekly*, October 14, 1939.

8. *St. Petersburg (FL) Times*, September 2, 1939, and September 9, 1939.

9. Billy Graham promotional flyer, in Billy Graham's FBI scrapbook, 1938–1940; Billy Graham Center Archives, Collection 15, 1-1; www2.wheaton.edu/bgc/Archives/docs/BGScrapbook1938/table.htm.

10. *Gold Book.*

11. A Legal Notice of Master's Sale was posted in the February 9, 1940, *St. Petersburg (FL) Times*. See also the notices from February 16, 1940, and March 4, 1940.

12. *Evening Independent*, April 22, 1940, and April 23, 1940.

13. *Evening Independent*, October 26, 1940.

14. *Alliance Weekly*, April 20, 1940.

15. Ibid.

16. *The Beacon*, 1940 edition.

17. Ibid.

18. Robert B. Fischer, e-mail to the author, February 8, 2005.

19. Jimmie Johnson, interview with Dr. Lois Ferm, January 10, 1979; Billy Graham Center Archives.

20. *The Beacon*, 1940 edition.

21. Ibid.

22. Ibid.

23. Ibid.

24. *Tampa Tribune*, May 12, 1940.

25. Billy Graham's FBI scrapbook, 1938–1940, includes a full-page picture from the February 9, 1940, issue of the *Tampa Morning Tribune* of the trailer park, which perhaps served as a reminder of his affection for the people to whom he preached there; www2.wheaton.edu/bgc/Archives/docs/BGScrapbook1938/008b.htm.

26. *St. Petersburg Times*, May 12, 1940.

27. *York Daily Record*, November 15, 1997.

28. Ibid.

29. *The Beacon*, 1940 edition.

30. Ibid.

31. Ibid.

Chapter 13: A Youth Aflame

1. Dr. Lois Ferm said this during her interview with Vera Resue, April 18, 1980; Billy Graham Center Archives.

2. *The Beacon* (Florida Bible Institute yearbook), 1940 edition

3. Ibid.

4. Bob Watson, interview with the author, January 20, 2009.

5. *Robesonian*, Lumberton, North Carolina, May 29, 1940; Billy Graham's FBI scrapbook, 1938–1940; Billy Graham Center Archives, Collection 15, 1-1, 13, front; www2.wheaton.edu/bgc/Archives/docs/BGScrapbook1938/013a.htm.

6. Ibid.

7. Bob Watson interview.

8. Ibid.

9. W. T. Watson, interview with Dr. Lois Ferm, February 14, 1977. In the author's interview with Bob Watson, he told me that "nobody remembers him doing anything!"

10. Bob Watson interview.

11. Ibid. W. T. Watson also recounted this story and said, "But you know, when Billy got to preaching, we thought he didn't need practicing anyhow" (W. T. Watson interview). See also W. T. Watson, *The Bible School Days of Billy Graham* (Dunedin, FL: W. T. Watson, 1976), 24.

12. Billy Graham promotional flyer in Billy Graham's FBI scrapbook, 1938–1940; Billy Graham Center Archives Collection 15, 1-1, 6 front; www2.wheaton.edu/bgc/Archives/docs/BGScrapbook1938/006a.htm.

13. W. T. Watson interview; Watson, *Bible School Days*, 24.

14. Bob Watson interview.

15. Graham, *Just As I Am*, 60.

16. *Dispatch* (York, PA), July 26, 1940.

17. *Gazette and Daily* (York, PA), July 26, 1940.

18. *Gazette and Daily* (York, PA), August 2, 1940.

19. Graham, *Just As I Am*, 60.

20. *Dispatch* (York, PA), July 26, 1940.

21. Promotional pamphlet in Billy Graham's FBI scrapbook, 1938–1940; Billy Graham Center Archives, Collection 15, 1-1.

22. *Gazette and Daily* (York, PA), July 26, 1940, 4.

23. Graham, *Just As I Am*, 60.

24. Ibid.

25. Billy Graham also spoke at the Penn Grove Camp—a camp run by Ralph Boyer's York Gospel Center—about twenty miles away. No precise date can be determined for when this would have occurred. It may have been at a later date; Esther Hartlaub, interview with the author, February 1, 2012.

26. *Daily Record* (York, PA), November 15, 1997.

27. Ibid.

28. York (PA) *Gazette and Daily*, July 26, 1940, 4.

29. Bob Watson interview. In 1944, Pennington visited Billy's church in Western Springs as a guest.

Chapter 14: Fire on the Prairie

1. W. T. Watson, interview with Lois Ferm, February 14, 1977; Billy Graham Center Archives.

2. This can be seen in his letters to John Minder and W. T. Watson during this time.

3. This exchange and variations of it are described in Billy Graham's autobiography, *Just As I Am*; and in Billy's introduction to Earle Cairns's biography of Edman, *V. Raymond Edman: In the Presence of the King*. Dr. Edman remembers the encounter differently.

4. Billy Graham, "Introduction," in Earle Edwin Cairns, *V. Raymond Edman: In the Presence of the King* (Chicago: Moody Bible Institute, 1972), 5.

5. Warren Wyeth Willard, *Fire on the Prairie: The Story of Wheaton College* (Wheaton, IL: Van Kampen Press, 1950).

6. For two histories of the school, see Willard, *Fire on the Prairie*, and Paul M. Bechtel, *Wheaton College: A Heritage Remembered, 1860–1984* (Wheaton, IL: Harold Shaw, 1984).

7. *The Tower* (Wheaton College yearbook), 1942 edition, 161. The college yearbooks of this period covered the previous year.

8. Peter Siemens, letter to V. Raymond Edman, November 17, 1940, expressing the appreciation of many of the students for the "soul satisfying" chapel programs, especially by Dr. Edman and Dean Culley. Edman Archive, Wheaton College Archives and Special Collections.

9. *Wheaton Record*, October 11, 1940.

10. Cairns, *V. Raymond Edman*, 175–76.

11. E. M. Bounds, *Purpose in Prayer* (New York: Fleming H. Revell, 1920).

12. Joshua 3:5 KJV.

13. V. Raymond Edman, letter to the faculty and students of Wheaton College, October 15, 1940; V. Raymond Edman Collection, Wheaton College Archives and Special Collections.

14. Ted Wehling, e-mail to the author, January 18, 2005.

15. Donald R. Brown, letter to the author, March 6, 2005.

16. Bob Taussig, e-mail to the author, February 1, 2005. The event was recorded in the school newspaper, the *Wheaton Record*, March 25, 1941. As Taussig told me in his e-mail: "As far as I knew then, Billy did not know that I existed. I don't think we ever had any type of conversation. About ten-plus years ago, my wife and I were eating in a restaurant in a city I don't remember. My wife, Mary, saw Billy and said, 'Bob, there is Billy Graham. Go and greet him.' I said, 'He doesn't know me.' But I went reluctantly, and introduced myself. When Billy heard my name, his face lit up and [he] said, 'Are you Bob Taussig, the famous Wheaton wrestler? I was present when you made that 20-second pin. After that, I never missed a match.'"

17. Donald Brown letter.

18. *The Tower* (Wheaton College yearbook), 1942 edition, 160. The college yearbooks of this period covered the previous year.

19. The college newspaper, the *Wheaton Record*, detailed the trips of the Gospel teams during this period on the Friday previous to the meetings.

20. Donald Brown letter.

21. Ibid.

22. Ibid.

23. Mrs. Lois Patterson (Kunz) interview with the author, March 8, 2005.

24. Donald Brown letter. Other contemporaries of Billy's at Wheaton saw nothing of his potential and were genuinely surprised by his later success (Don Munro, e-mail to the author, January 25, 2005).

25. Donald Brown letter.

Chapter 15: Restrained Passions

1. Ruth Bell Graham, *Footprints of a Pilgrim: The Life and Loves of Ruth Bell Graham* (Nashville: W, 2001), 39. Copyright © 2001 by the Ruth Graham Literary Trust. Used by permission, all rights reserved.

2. Ibid., 57.

3. Patricia Daniels Cornwell, *A Time for Remembering: The Story of Ruth Bell Graham* (San Francisco: Harper & Row, 1983), 14.

4. Ibid., 18.

5. Ibid., 20.

6. Faith Coxe Bailey, "Meet Ruth Graham: Part I," *Moody Monthly*, November 1954.

7. Cornwell, *Time for Remembering*, 30.

8. Ibid., 30–31.

9. Bailey, "Meet Ruth Graham: Part I."

10. Ibid.

11. Ibid.

12. Ibid.

13. Betty Lee Skinner, *Daws: A Man Who Trusted God* (Colorado Springs: NavPress, 1974), 182.

14. Martha Baptista, e-mail to the author, February 4, 2005.

15. Ruth Bell Graham, *Footprints of a Pilgrim*, 62.

16. Ibid., 59.

17. Faith Coxe Bailey, "Meet Ruth Graham: Part II," *Moody Monthly*, December 1954.

18. Bob Johnson, e-mail to the author, January 27, 2005.

19. Ruth Bell Graham, *Footprints of a Pilgrim*, 59–60.

20. Ibid., 60.

21. Ibid., 54.

22. Cornwell, *Time for Remembering*, 62.

23. Bailey, "Meet Ruth Graham: Part II."

24. Ibid.

25. Ibid.

26. Ibid.

27. Ruth Bell Graham, *Footprints of a Pilgrim*, 55.

28. Ibid.

29. Helen Supplee Jongewaard, interview with the author, January 19, 2005. Also, Helen Supplee Jongewaard, interview with Robert Shuster, May 7, 1993; Billy Graham Center Archives, Collection 486, T1.

30. Ruth Bell Graham, *Footprints of a Pilgrim*, 65.

31. *The Tower* (Wheaton College yearbook), 1942 edition, 203.

32. Helen Supplee Jongewaard interview with Robert Shuster.

33. Katherine Marie Hess Feldi, interview with Robert Shuster, May 7, 1993; Billy Graham Center Archives.

34. Billy Graham, "Introduction," in Earle Edwin Cairns, *V. Raymond Edman: In the Presence of the King* (Chicago: Moody Bible Institute, 1972), 6.

35. Graham, *Footprints of a Pilgrim*, 57.

36. Ibid.

37. Ibid., 64.

38. Ibid.

39. Ruth's poetry indicates that during their ensuing argument, Billy drove his car into another car, seemingly distracted by Ruth's response.

Chapter 16: Finding His Footing

1. Roland Gerstung, interview with the author, March 29, 2005.

2. Ibid.

3. Mary Margaret Garfield Johnson, interview with Robert Shuster, May 7, 1993; Billy Graham Center Archives, Collection 485, T1.

4. *The Tower* (Wheaton College yearbook), 1942 edition, 120.

5. Garfield Johnson interview.

6. Herbert Anderson, letter to the author, April 2005.

7. N. Warren Davis, e-mail to the author, February 4, 2005.

8. *Wheaton Record*, February 18, 1941.

9. *Wheaton Record*, March 21, 1941.

10. *Wheaton Record*, April 4, 1941.

11. Billy Graham, letter to V. Raymond Edman, October 6, 1952. In the papers of V. Raymond Edman, Wheaton College Archives, © 1952 Billy Graham; used by permission, all rights reserved.

12. Through many of my correspondences and interviews, I was surprised to hear several of his peers suggest that there were unsubstantiated rumors of Billy's dismissal from Bob Jones—and even from the Florida Bible Institute.

13. *Wheaton Record*, September 26, 1941. See also Betty Lee Skinner, *Daws: A Man Who Trusted God* (Colorado Springs: NavPress, 1974), and Robert D. Foster, *The Navigator* (Colorado Springs: NavPress, 1983).

14. Skinner, *Daws*, 67.

15. See Skinner, *Daws*; and Foster, *Navigator*.

16. Skinner, *Daws*, 188.

17. Ibid., 110.

18. Ibid., 187.

19. Ibid., 182.

20. *Wheaton Record*, October 3, 1941.

21. *Wheaton Record*, October 14, 1941.

22. *Wheaton Record*, October 21, 1941.

23. Torrey Johnson was likely in and out of Wheaton during those years. He held meetings at College Church on April 12, 1943 (*Wheaton Daily Journal*, April 12, 1943).

24. *Wheaton Record*, November 11, 1941.

25. See *The Diaries of Jim Rayburn, Founder of Young Life*, selected and edited by Kit Sublett (Colorado Springs: Morning Star Press, 2008).

26. When Jim Rayburn passed away at the age of sixty-one, in 1970, Billy Graham wrote: "Jim had a profound influence on my life when I was a student at Wheaton" (Sublett, *Diaries of Jim Rayburn*).

27. Grady Wilson, interview with Dr. Lois Ferm, February 18, 1976. The rest of this story can be found in Grady Wilson, *Count It All Joy* (Nashville: Broadman, 1984), 27–30.

28. Wilson, *Count It All Joy*, 27–29.

29. *The Tower*, 1943 edition.

30. Grover C. Wilcox, e-mail to the author, February 17, 2005; Don Munro, e-mail to the author, January 25, 2005; and Chester Schneider, e-mail to the author, January 15, 2005. Also, in the November 18, 1941, issue of the *Wheaton Record*, a list of "who's who" on Wheaton's campus does not include Billy's name.

31. Grover C. Wilcox e-mail; Don Munro e-mail; and Chester Schneider e-mail.

32. Hudson T. Armerding, e-mail to the author, February 21, 2005.

33. Dr. Kenneth Hansen, interview, August 25, 1975; Billy Graham Center Archives.

34. Martha Baptista, e-mail to the author, February 4, 2005.

35. Samuel Faircloth, interview with the author, January 21, 2005.

36. *Wheaton Record*, March 4, 1941.

37. *Wheaton Record*, October 7, 1941.

38. Jim Reese, e-mail to the author, February 14, 2010. Also e-mails from Jeff Smalla and Stan and Yvonne Veldt.

39. Moline promotional flyer in Billy Graham's scrapbook; Billy Graham Center Archives, Collection 15, 1-1.

40. Billy Graham Center Archives, Collection 15, box 1, folder 6.

41. *St. Petersburg Times*, July 5, 1941, and July 12, 1941.

Chapter 17: Always Too Soon to Quit

1. Billy Graham, "Introduction," in Earle Edwin Cairns, *V. Raymond Edman: In the Presence of the King* (Chicago: Moody Bible Institute, 1972), 5–6.

2. Bob Watson, interview with the author, January 20, 2009. John Minder had already graduated from Nyack and had begun his ministry in the South.

3. Graham, "Introduction," in Cairns, *V. Raymond Edman*, 6.

4. Mary Margaret Garfield Johnson, interview with Robert Shuster, May 7, 1993; Billy Graham Center Archives.

5. Billy Graham, quoted in Cairns, *V. Raymond Edman*, 87.

6. Helen Supplee Jongewaard, interview with the author, January 19, 2005.

7. Billy recalled being impressed by Edman's "simple talks." See *In Memoriam: Dr. V. Raymond Edman, 1900–1967, Chancellor, Wheaton College, Wheaton, Illinois* (Minneapolis: Billy Graham Evangelistic Association, 1967), 11. For her part, Ruth Bell Graham enjoyed Edman's talks for their brevity. See Ruth Bell Graham, *It's My Turn* (Old Tappan, NJ: Revell, 1982).

8. Cairns, *V. Raymond Edman*, 75–76.

9. Ibid., 98–99.

10. Ibid.

11. Billy Graham, "Introduction," in Cairns, *V. Raymond Edman*, 6.

12. The Balaam talks were reprinted in the *Alliance Weekly* in the spring and summer of 1943, but "Chapel Nuggets" in the *Wheaton Record* suggest they were delivered in the fall of 1942.

13. *Wheaton Record*, September 25, 1942.

14. *Wheaton Record*, October 2, 1942.

15. V. Raymond Edman, *The Disciplines of Life: Choosing Growth in Every Circumstance* (Wheaton, IL: Scripture Press, 1948), 33.

16. See V. Raymond Edman, *Not Somehow. . . But Triumphantly!* (Grand Rapids: Zondervan, 1965).

17. Edman, *Disciplines of Life*, 139–40.

18. Ibid., 140.

19. *In Memoriam: Dr. V. Raymond Edman*, 13.

20. Billy Graham, *A Biblical Standard for Evangelists* (Minneapolis: World Wide Publications), 78.

21. Billy Graham, Wheaton College Graduate Chapel, 1985.

22. Grady Wilson, interview with Dr. Lois Ferm, February 18, 1976; Billy Graham Center Archives.

23. Cairns, *V. Raymond Edman*, 228.

24. Ruth Bell Graham, *Footprints of a Pilgrim: The Life and Loves of Ruth Bell Graham* (Nashville: W, 2001), 58. Copyright © 2001 by the Ruth Graham Literary Trust. Used by permission, all rights reserved.

25. Faith Coxe Bailey, "Meet Ruth Graham: Part II," *Moody Monthly*, December 1954.

26. Ibid.

27. Ruth Bell Graham, *Footprints of a Pilgrim*, 66.

28. *Wheaton Record*, March 24, 1942.

29. *In Memoriam: Dr. V. Raymond Edman*, 14.

30. *The Tower* (Wheaton College yearbook), 1943 edition, 18.

31. *Wheaton Record*, December 9, 1941.

32. *Wheaton Record*, May 7, 1943.

33. *Wheaton Record*, April 27, 1943.

34. *Wheaton Daily Journal*, October 16, 1942.

35. This story is recounted in several places, but the most detailed is found in John C. Pollock, *A Foreign Devil in China: The Story of L. Nelson Bell* (Minneapolis: World Wide Publications, 1988). Pollock reports that Rosa had a minor relapse in the 1960s. Despite her health issues earlier in life, Rosa lived to be ninety-five years old. She died on November 12, 2013, at her home on Orcas Island, Washington (www.islandssounder.com/news/232120291.html#).

36. Ruth Bell Graham, *Footprints of a Pilgrim*.

37. Ibid., 67. Ruth said that she almost slapped the ring back into his hand. Billy places this incident prior to their engagement. I have chosen to follow Ruth's timeline in this instance.

Chapter 18: The Tab

1. Cairns, *V. Raymond Edman*, 90.

2. Ibid., 83.

3. Ibid., 90.

4. V. Raymond Edman, "Random Recollections of Billy Graham" (unpublished manuscript, Wheaton College Archives).

5. *Wheaton Daily Journal*, September 13, 1941.

6. Katherine Marie Hess Feldi, interview with Robert Shuster, May 7, 1993; Billy Graham Center Archives.

7. Paul Dean Votaw, interview with Robert Shuster, March 4, 1980; Billy Graham Center Archives.

8. John Elson, e-mail to the author, February 2005.

9. Ibid.

10. John MacDonald, e-mail to the author, January 21, 2005. The *Wheaton Daily Journal* also lists meetings at Clark's house.

11. Helen Supplee Jongewaard interview with the author.

12. Several alumni mentioned this phenomenon of taking a date to the Tab.

13. *Wheaton Record*, August 19, 1942. See also *The Tower*, 1943 edition, 337.

14. Dale McCulley, interview with the author, March 5, 2005.

15. Bob Taussig, e-mail to the author, February 1, 2005.

16. Don Munro, e-mail to the author, January 25, 2005.

17. Helen Supplee Jongewaard, interview with Robert Shuster, May 7, 1993; Billy Graham Center Archives.

18. Alice R. Smith, e-mail to the author, February 7, 2005.

19. John Elson, e-mail to the author, February 2005.

20. Bob and Mary Johnson, letter to the author, January 27, 2005.

21. Samuel Faircloth, interview with the author, January 21, 2005.

22. John MacDonald, e-mail to the author, January 13, 2005.

23. Dr. Kenneth Hansen, interview, August 25, 1975; Billy Graham Center Archives.

24. Billy Graham, "Introduction," in Cairns, *V. Raymond Edman*, 6–7.

25. *Wheaton Daily Journal*, October 19, 1941.

26. Ibid., November 1, 1941, evening service.

27. Ibid., December 6, 1941.

28. Patricia Daniels Cornwell, *A Time for Remembering: The Story of Ruth Bell Graham* (San Francisco: Harper & Row, 1983), 73.

29. John Pollock, *A Foreign Devil in China: The Story of Dr. L. Nelson Bell, An American Surgeon in China* (Grand Rapids: Zondervan, 1971), 227.

30. Ibid., 228.

31. *Wheaton Record*, May 10, 1942.

32. *Wheaton Record*, May 22, 1942.

33. *Wheaton Daily Journal*, June 30, 1942.

34. Betty Lee Skinner, *Daws: A Man Who Trusted God* (Colorado Springs: NavPress, 1974), 224–25.

35. 1 Peter 3:15, paraphrased by Helen Supplee Jongewaard, interview with the author.

36. Skinner, *Daws*, 188–89.

Chapter 19: Digging Trenches

1. Letter from V. Raymond Edman to Joseph S. Maxwell, April 12, 1943, in Cairns, *V. Raymond Edman*, 222.

2. *Park Ridge Herald*, January 16, 1942.

3. Ibid.

4. Ibid.

5. Billy Graham Center Archives, Collection 15, box 1, folder 9.

6. Ibid.

7. *The Tower*, 1943 edition, 219.

8. *Wheaton Record*, March 27, 1942.

9. Ibid.

10. *Wheaton Record*, March 27, 1942.

11. *The Tower*, 1944 edition, 184.

12. *Wheaton Record*, March 24, 1943.

13. *Wheaton Record*, May 15, 1942.

14. *Wheaton Record*, March 24, 1942.

15. Helen Supplee Jongewaard interview with the author.

16. *Wheaton Record*, January 13, 1942.

17. *Wheaton Record*, January 16, 1942.

18. *Wheaton Record*, May 12, 1942.

19. *Alliance Weekly*, October 17, 1942.

20. *The Tower*, 1944 edition, 189.

21. *Alliance Weekly*, October 17, 1942.

22. Ibid.

23. *Wheaton Record*, October 6, 1942.

24. Ibid.

25. Ibid.

26. Ibid.

27. Ibid.

28. *The Tower*, 1944 edition, 184.

29. Ibid.

30. *The Journals of Jim Rayburn*, 116.

31. Ibid., 115.

32. *The Tower*, 1944 edition, 191.

33. *Wheaton Record*, January 12, 1942.

34. Anna Hansen, interview with Dr. Lois Ferm, August 25, 1975; Billy Graham Center Archives; http://espace.wheaton.edu/bgc/audio/annahansen.mp3.

35. Cairns, *V. Raymond Edman*, 98.

36. *Alliance Weekly*, June 26, 1943.

37. *The Tower*, 1944 edition, 190.

38. Gordon Kling, "Survey on Revival"; Billy Graham Center Archives.

39. Samuel Faircloth interview.

40. *Wheaton Record*, January 12, 1943.

41. Jean Marshall, e-mail to the author, February 23, 2005.

Chapter 20: The Fire Falls

1. *Wheaton Record*, February 5, 1943.

2. *Wheaton Record*, February 9, 1943.

3. *Wheaton Record*, February 5, 1943.

4. *Wheaton Record*, October 24, 1941.

5. Harold Warren, letter to Mary Dorsett, October 15, 1988; in Timothy K. Beougher and Lyle W. Dorsett, eds., *Accounts of a Campus Revival: Wheaton College 1995* (Wheaton, IL: Harold Shaw, 1995), 57; and Mary Dorsett, *Revival at Wheaton!* (Wheaton, IL: International Awakening, 1994), 9.

6. *Wheaton Record*, February 5, 1943.

7. *Wheaton Record*, February 16, 1943.

8. Harold Warren letter to Mary Dorsett.

9. Ibid.

10. *The Tower* (Wheaton college yearbook), 1944 edition, 189.

11. *Wheaton Record*, February 16, 1943.

12. *Wheaton Record*, February 9, 1943.

13. *Wheaton Alumni News*, January–February 1943.

14. John 21:15 KJV. Quoted in *Wheaton Record*, February 9, 1943.

15. *Wheaton Record*, February 9, 1943.

16. Ibid.

17. *Wheaton Alumni News*, January–February 1943.

18. *Wheaton Record*, February 9, 1943.

19. J. Leland Simcox, letter to Earle E. Cairns, November 18, 1968; Wheaton College Archives.

20. Ibid. This story is also found in Earle Edwin Cairns, *V. Raymond Edman: In the Presence of the King* (Chicago: Moody Bible Institute, 1972), 107–8.

21. V. Raymond Edman, "Fullness of Power," undated message given at unknown location. Available online at Discipleship Library (though misclassified under the name Raymon Edam): http://turret2. discipleshiplibrary.com/1553A.mp3.

22. Harry Shaffer, letter to Mary Dorsett, n.d.; in Beougher and L. Dorsett, *Accounts of a Campus Revival*, 58; and Mary Dorsett, *Revival at Wheaton!*, 9.

23. Ibid.

24. *Wheaton Alumni News*, January–February 1943.

25. Ibid.

26. *Alliance Weekly*, July 18, 1943.

27. Harold Warren letter to Mary Dorsett.

28. *Wheaton Alumni News*, January–February 1943.

29. Gordon Kling, *Survey on '43 Revival*, February 1995; Billy Graham Center Archives, box 514, folder 1-10.

30. *Wheaton Alumni News*, January–February 1943.

31. Mary Dorsett, "Accounts of Past Revivals" in Beougher and L. Dorsett, *Accounts of a Campus Revival*, 59; and Mary Dorsett, *Revival at Wheaton!*, 10.

32. *Wheaton Record*, February 12, 1943.

33. Harold Warren letter to Mary Dorsett.

34. *Wheaton Alumni News*, January–February 1943.

35. *Alliance Weekly*, February 27, 1943.

36. Ibid.

37. Mertis Heimbach, interview with Bob Roberts, February 1995; Billy Graham Center Archives, box 514, tape 31.

38. *Alliance Weekly*, July 10, 1943.

39. *Wheaton Record*, February 16, 1943.

40. Ibid., emphasis added.

41. *Wheaton Alumni News*, January–February 1943.

42. *Wheaton Alumni News*, May–June 1943.

43. Cairns, *V. Raymond Edman*, 108.

44. Based on a survey of the *Wheaton Record*, from fall 1940 to winter/spring 1943.

45. Helen Supplee Jongewaard, interview with Robert Shuster, May 7, 1993; Billy Graham Center Archives.

46. Laverne Rutschman, e-mail to the author, February 10, 2005.

47. *Wheaton Record*, March 23, 1943.

48. Ibid.

49. Ibid.

50. Ibid.

51. Ibid.

Chapter 21: Striving for the Goal

1. *Bulletin of Wheaton College*, 1940–1941.

2. Billy Graham, *Just As I Am* (San Francisco: HarperCollins, 1997), 65.

3. Chester Schneider, e-mail to the author, January 16, 2005.

4. Ibid.

5. *The Tower* (Wheaton College yearbook), 1943 edition, 23.

6. Ibid.

7. Ibid.

8. Chester Schneider e-mail.

9. *Bulletin of Wheaton College*, 1940–1941.

10. *Wheaton Record*, November 18, 1941. "Grigolia Speaks to Juniors," where he says he "wanted to know Christ." Also Chester Schneider e-mail.

11. *The Tower*, 1942 edition.

12. Chester Schneider e-mail.

13. Ibid.

14. Samuel Faircloth, interview with the author, January 21, 2005.

15. Helen Supplee Jongewaard, interview with the author, January 19, 2005.

16. Laverne Rutschman, e-mail to the author, February 10, 2005. A rumor was reported to the author by several sources that Dr. Grigolia had hesitated to pass Billy for his comprehensives. It's uncertain whether there is any truth to the claim, but the rumor was certainly in circulation.

17. *Wheaton Record*, December 1, 1942.

18. Ibid.

19. Ibid.

20. Billy Graham, "Atonement," in *Great Gospel Sermons*, volume 2, *Contemporary Sermons* (New York: Revell, 1949), 43.

21. Ibid. See also *Wheaton Record*, December 1, 1942.

22. Graham, *Just As I Am*, 79.

23. *Wheaton Daily Journal*, April 30, 1943.

24. Billy Graham, Trinity Bible College alumni banquet, April 28, 1976.

25. Ruth Stull, *Sand and Stars: Missionary Adventure on the Jungle Trail* (Los Angeles: Revell, 1951).

26. *Alliance Weekly*, May 1, 1943.

27. Alice R. Smith, e-mail to the author, February 12, 2005.

28. Samuel Faircloth interview.

29. *Wheaton Daily Journal*, April 22, 1943.

30. *Wheaton Daily Journal*, April 8, 1942.

31. *Wheaton Daily Journal*, April 22, 1943. Graham kept several copies of the program for his scrapbook.

32. *Wheaton Record*, April 23, 1943.

33. *Wheaton Daily Journal*, April 23, 1943.

34. Ibid.

35. Patricia Daniels Cornwell, *A Time for Remembering: The Story of Ruth Bell Graham* (San Francisco: Harper & Row, 1983), 75.

36. "Random Recollections on Billy Graham as an Undergraduate," V. Raymond Edman Collection, Wheaton College Archives and Special Collections.

37. Torrey Johnson, interview with Robert Shuster, October 23, 1984; Billy Graham Center Archives.

38. Graham, *Just As I Am*, 79.

39. Charles Chamberlain, e-mail to the author, February 2, 2005. The name of the church in question is uncertain. However, the *Alliance Weekly* from May 1, 1943, reports the death of the thirty-eight-year-old pastor of the Fort Wayne Gospel Temple, Clifford Hollifield, who died tragically in April 1943. The likelihood that this was the church that approached Billy is enhanced by the fact that he held services there in August and September of that year. (See Billy Graham's scrapbook at the Billy Graham Evangelistic Association; also the timeline offered by the Billy Graham Center Archives at Wheaton College.) Further, one year later, an unnamed church in Fort Wayne was interested in calling Billy as their pastor while he was the pastor of the Village Church. (See *Just As I Am*, 89.)

40. Billy Graham, "Introduction," in Earle Edwin Cairns, *V. Raymond Edman: In the Presence of the King* (Chicago: Moody Bible Institute, 1972), 7.

41. *Wheaton Record*, December 9, 1941. The series of messages was stenographically recorded and is available in the *Alliance Weekly* from May 16, 1943, to July 4, 1942.

42. Charles Chamberlain, e-mail to the author, February 2, 2005.

Chapter 22: Uncontainable Fire

1. This is the author's calculation, based on estimates of road travel to Billy's various meetings across the United States. One biographer suggests that Billy traveled more than 200,000 miles during this time period—an incredible, and unlikely, average of 550 miles every day of the year. 17,000 miles is a more realistic estimate.

2. Billy Graham to John Minder, September 18, 1946, in Lorene Minder, *John Minder: A Man Sent from God* (St. Louis: Creative Concepts, 1988).

3. George Beverly Shea with Fred Bauer, *Then Sings My Soul* (Old Tappan, NJ: Revell, 1968), 95.

4. Billy Graham, *Just As I Am* (San Francisco: HarperCollins, 1997), 121.

5. November 2, 1949, in newspapers across the country.

Chapter 23: The Source of the Flame

1. *Hour of Decision*, December 1951.

2. Mark Taylor Dalhouse, *Island in the Lake of Fire: Bob Jones University, Fundamentalism, and the Separatist Movement* (Athens, GA: University of Georgia Press, 1996), 81.

3. Billy Graham, National Association of Evangelicals, April 4, 1957.

4. Bob Jones, *Cornbread and Caviar: Reminiscences and Reflections* (Greenville, NC: BJU Press, 1985), 153.

5. Ibid., 100.

6. Billy Graham, Trinity Bible College alumni banquet, April 28, 1976.

7. Bob Watson, interview with the author, January 20, 2009.

8. Ibid.

9. Grady Wilson, *Count It All Joy* (Nashville: Broadman, 1984), 24.

10. Lorene Minder, *John Minder: His Life and Ministry* (St. Louis: Creative Concepts Inc, 1988), 151.

11. Letter from Billy Graham to John Minder, March 6, 1944, quoted in Minder, *John Minder: His Life and Ministry*, 146. Copyright © 1944 by Billy Graham, used by permission, all rights reserved

12. *Alliance Weekly*, February 23, 1924.

13. Billy Graham, letter to C. Allyn Russell, August 16, 1971, in C. Allyn Russell, "William Bell Riley: Architect of Fundamentalism," *Minnesota History*, spring 1972, 29–30.

14. Ibid.

15. Betty Lee Skinner, *Daws: A Man Who Trusted God* (Colorado Springs: NavPress, 1974), 279.

16. Ibid., 298.

17. Ibid., 323.

18. Ibid., 385. Graham noted this at the eulogy service for Dawson Trotman.

19. Billy Graham, letter to V. Raymond Edman, December 27, 1965; Wheaton College Archives. Copyright © 1965 by Billy Graham, used by permission, all rights reserved.

20. Earle Edwin Cairns, *V. Raymond Edman: In the Presence of the King* (Chicago: Moody Bible Institute, 1972), 214.

21. V. Raymond Edman, remarks to Dr. and Mrs. D. Szeoto, March 4, 1963.

22. Billy Graham, letter to V. Raymond Edman, November 22, 1966.

23. Billy Graham, letter to V. Raymond Edman, October 28, 1965; Wheaton College Archives. Copyright © 1965 by Billy Graham, used by permission, all rights reserved.

24. V. Raymond Edman, letter to A. S. Taylor, March 1, 1960; Wheaton College Archives.

25. John Pollock, *A Foreign Devil in China: The Story of L. Nelson Bell, An American Surgeon in China* (Grand Rapids: Zondervan, 1971), 238–39.

26. Billy Graham, "Billy Graham's Own Story: 'God Is My Witness': Part II," *McCall's*, May 1964, 119.

27. Pollock, *Foreign Devil in China*, 229.

28. Ibid.

29. Graham, "Billy Graham's Own Story," 119.

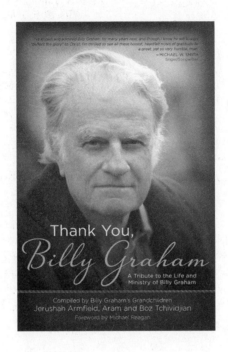